Stream Processing with Apache Flink

Fundamentals, Implementation, and Operation of Streaming Applications

Fabian Hueske and Vasiliki Kalavri

Beijing · Boston · Farnham · Sebastopol · Tokyo

Stream Processing with Apache Flink

by Fabian Hueske and Vasiliki Kalavri

Published by O'Reilly Media, Inc., 1005 Gravenstein Highway North, Sebastopol, CA 95472.

O'Reilly books may be purchased for educational, business, or sales promotional use. Online editions are also available for most titles (*http://oreilly.com*). For more information, contact our corporate/institutional sales department: 800-998-9938 or corporate@oreilly.com.

Acquisitions Editor: Rachel Roumeliotis	**Indexer:** Judith McConville
Development Editor: Alicia Young	**Interior Designer:** David Futato
Production Editor: Katherine Tozer	**Cover Designer:** Karen Montgomery
Copyeditor: Christina Edwards	**Illustrator:** Rebecca Demarest
Proofreader: Charles Roumeliotis	

April 2019:   First Edition

Revision History for the First Edition

2019-04-03:   First Release

See *http://oreilly.com/catalog/errata.csp?isbn=9781491974292* for release details.

978-1-491-97429-2

[LSI]

Table of Contents

Preface

What You Will Learn in This Book

This book will teach you everything you need to know about stream processing with Apache Flink. It consists of 11 chapters that hopefully tell a coherent story. While some chapters are descriptive and aim to introduce high-level design concepts, others are more hands-on and contain many code examples.

While we intended for the book to be read in chapter order when we were writing it, readers familiar with a chapter's content might want to skip it. Others more interested in writing Flink code right away might want to read the practical chapters first. In the following, we briefly describe the contents of each chapter, so you can directly jump to those chapters that interest you most.

- Chapter 1 gives an overview of stateful stream processing, data processing application architectures, application designs, and the benefits of stream processing over traditional approaches. It also gives you a brief look at what it is like to run your first streaming application on a local Flink instance.

- Chapter 2 discusses the fundamental concepts and challenges of stream processing, independent of Flink.

- Chapter 3 describes Flink's system architecture and internals. It discusses distributed architecture, time and state handling in streaming applications, and Flink's fault-tolerance mechanisms.

- Chapter 4 explains how to set up an environment to develop and debug Flink applications.

- Chapter 5 introduces you to the basics of the Flink's DataStream API. You will learn how to implement a DataStream application and which stream transformations, functions, and data types are supported.

- Chapter 6 discusses the time-based operators of the DataStream API. This includes window operators and time-based joins as well as process functions that provide the most flexibility when dealing with time in streaming applications.

- Chapter 7 explains how to implement stateful functions and discusses everything around this topic, such as the performance, robustness, and evolution of stateful functions. It also shows how to use Flink's queryable state.

- Chapter 8 presents Flink's most commonly used source and sink connectors. It discusses Flink's approach to end-to-end application consistency and how to implement custom connectors to ingest data from and emit data to external systems.

- Chapter 9 discusses how to set up and configure Flink clusters in various environments.

- Chapter 10 covers operation, monitoring, and maintenance of streaming applications that run 24/7.

- Finally, Chapter 11 contains resources you can use to ask questions, attend Flink-related events, and learn how Flink is currently being used.

Conventions Used in This Book

The following typographical conventions are used in this book:

Italic
Indicates new terms, URLs, email addresses, filenames, and file extensions.

`Constant width`
Used for program listings, as well as within paragraphs to refer to program elements such as variable or function names, databases, data types, environment variables, statements, and keywords. Also used for module and package names, and to show commands or other text that should be typed literally by the user and the output of commands.

`Constant width italic`
Shows text that should be replaced with user-supplied values or by values determined by context.

 This element signifies a tip or suggestion.

This element signifies a general note.

 This element signifies a warning or caution.

Using Code Examples

Supplemental material (code examples in Java and Scala) is available for download at *https://github.com/streaming-with-flink*.

This book is here to help you get your job done. In general, if example code is offered with this book, you may use it in your programs and documentation. You do not need to contact us for permission unless you're reproducing a significant portion of the code. For example, writing a program that uses several chunks of code from this book does not require permission. Selling or distributing a CD-ROM of examples from O'Reilly books does require permission. Answering a question by citing this book and quoting example code does not require permission. Incorporating a significant amount of example code from this book into your product's documentation does require permission.

We appreciate, but do not require, attribution. An attribution usually includes the title, author, publisher, and ISBN. For example: "*Stream Processing with Apache Flink* by Fabian Hueske and Vasiliki Kalavri (O'Reilly). Copyright 2019 Fabian Hueske and Vasiliki Kalavri, 978-1-491-97429-2."

If you feel your use of code examples falls outside fair use or the permission given above, feel free to contact us at *permissions@oreilly.com*.

O'Reilly Online Learning

 For almost 40 years, *O'Reilly* has provided technology and business training, knowledge, and insight to help companies succeed.

Our unique network of experts and innovators share their knowledge and expertise through books, articles, conferences, and our online learning platform. O'Reilly's online learning platform gives you on-demand access to live training courses, in-depth learning paths, interactive coding environments, and a vast collection of text and video from O'Reilly and 200+ other publishers. For more information, please visit *http://oreilly.com*.

How to Contact Us

Please address comments and questions concerning this book to the publisher:

O'Reilly Media, Inc.
1005 Gravenstein Highway North
Sebastopol, CA 95472
800-998-9938 (in the United States or Canada)
707-829-0515 (international or local)
707-829-0104 (fax)

We have a web page for this book, where we list errata, examples, and any additional information. You can access this page at *http://bit.ly/stream-proc*.

To comment or ask technical questions about this book, send email to *bookquestions@oreilly.com*.

For more information about our books, courses, conferences, and news, see our website at *http://www.oreilly.com*.

Find us on Facebook: *http://facebook.com/oreilly*

Follow us on Twitter: *http://twitter.com/oreillymedia*

Watch us on YouTube: *http://www.youtube.com/oreillymedia*

Follow the authors on Twitter: *@fhueske* and *@vkalavri*

Acknowledgments

This book couldn't have been possible without the help and support of several amazing people. We would like to thank and acknowledge some of them here.

This book summarizes knowledge obtained through years of design, development, and testing performed by the Apache Flink community at large. We are grateful to everyone who has contributed to Flink through code, documentation, reviews, bug reports, feature requests, mailing list discussions, trainings, conference talks, meetup organization, and other activities.

Special thanks go to our fellow Flink committers: Alan Gates, Aljoscha Krettek, Andra Lungu, ChengXiang Li, Chesnay Schepler, Chiwan Park, Daniel Warneke, Dawid Wysakowicz, Gary Yao, Greg Hogan, Gyula Fóra, Henry Saputra, Jamie Grier, Jark Wu, Jincheng Sun, Konstantinos Kloudas, Kostas Tzoumas, Kurt Young, Márton Balassi, Matthias J. Sax, Maximilian Michels, Nico Kruber, Paris Carbone, Robert

Metzger, Sebastian Schelter, Shaoxuan Wang, Shuyi Chen, Stefan Richter, Stephan Ewen, Theodore Vasiloudis, Thomas Weise, Till Rohrmann, Timo Walther, Tzu-Li (Gordon) Tai, Ufuk Celebi, Xiaogang Shi, Xiaowei Jiang, Xingcan Cui. With this book, we hope to reach developers, engineers, and streaming enthusiasts around the world and grow the Flink community even larger.

We've also like to thank our technical reviewers who made countless valuable suggestions helping us to improve the presentation of the content. Thank you, Adam Kawa, Aljoscha Krettek, Kenneth Knowles, Lea Giordano, Matthias J. Sax, Stephan Ewen, Ted Malaska, and Tyler Akidau.

Finally, we say a big thank you to all the people at O'Reilly who accompanied us on our two and a half year long journey and helped us to push this project over the finish line. Thank you, Alicia Young, Colleen Lobner, Christine Edwards, Katherine Tozer, Marie Beaugureau, and Tim McGovern.

## CHAPTER 1

Introduction to Stateful Stream Processing

Apache Flink is a distributed stream processor with intuitive and expressive APIs to implement stateful stream processing applications. It efficiently runs such applications at large scale in a fault-tolerant manner. Flink joined the Apache Software Foundation as an incubating project in April 2014 and became a top-level project in January 2015. Since its beginning, Flink has had a very active and continuously growing community of users and contributors. To date, more than five hundred individuals have contributed to Flink, and it has evolved into one of the most sophisticated open source stream processing engines as proven by its widespread adoption. Flink powers large-scale, business-critical applications in many companies and enterprises across different industries and around the globe.

Stream processing technology is becoming more and more popular with companies big and small because it provides superior solutions for many established use cases such as data analytics, ETL, and transactional applications, but also facilitates novel applications, software architectures, and business opportunities. In this chapter, we discuss why stateful stream processing is becoming so popular and assess its potential. We start by reviewing conventional data application architectures and point out their limitations. Next, we introduce application designs based on stateful stream processing that exhibit many interesting characteristics and benefits over traditional approaches. Finally, we briefly discuss the evolution of open source stream processors and help you run a streaming application on a local Flink instance.

Traditional Data Infrastructures

Data and data processing have been omnipresent in businesses for many decades. Over the years the collection and usage of data has grown consistently, and companies have designed and built infrastructures to manage that data. The traditional architecture that most businesses implement distinguishes two types of data processing: transactional processing and analytical processing. In this section, we discuss both types and how they manage and process data.

Transactional Processing

Companies use all kinds of applications for their day-to-day business activities, such as enterprise resource planning (ERP) systems, customer relationship management (CRM) software, and web-based applications. These systems are typically designed with separate tiers for data processing (the application itself) and data storage (a transactional database system) as shown in Figure 1-1.

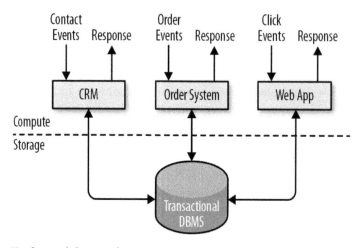

Figure 1-1. Traditional design of transactional applications that store data in a remote database system

Applications are usually connected to external services or face human users and continuously process incoming events such as orders, email, or clicks on a website. When an event is processed, an application reads its state or updates it by running transactions against the remote database system. Often, a database system serves multiple applications that sometimes access the same databases or tables.

This application design can cause problems when applications need to evolve or scale. Since multiple applications might work on the same data representation or share the same infrastructure, changing the schema of a table or scaling a database system requires careful planning and a lot of effort. A recent approach to overcoming the tight bundling of applications is the microservices design pattern. Microservices are designed as small, self-contained, and independent applications. They follow the UNIX philosophy of doing a single thing and doing it well. More complex applications are built by connecting several microservices with each other that only communicate over standardized interfaces such as RESTful HTTP connections. Because

---

microservices are strictly decoupled from each other and only communicate over well-defined interfaces, each microservice can be implemented with a different technology stack including a programming language, libraries, and datastores. Microservices and all the required software and services are typically bundled and deployed in independent containers. Figure 1-2 depicts a microservices architecture.

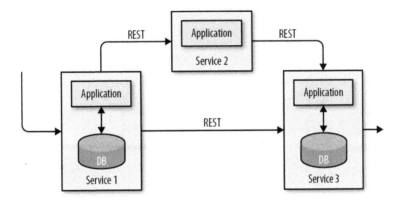

Figure 1-2. A microservices architecture

Analytical Processing

The data that is stored in the various transactional database systems of a company can provide valuable insights about a company's business operations. For example, the data of an order processing system can be analyzed to obtain sales growth over time, to identify reasons for delayed shipments, or to predict future sales in order to adjust the inventory. However, transactional data is often distributed across several disconnected database systems and is more valuable when it can be jointly analyzed. Moreover, the data often needs to be transformed into a common format.

Instead of running analytical queries directly on the transactional databases, the data is typically replicated to a data warehouse, a dedicated datastore for analytical query workloads. In order to populate a data warehouse, the data managed by the transactional database systems needs to be copied to it. The process of copying data to the data warehouse is called extract–transform–load (ETL). An ETL process extracts data from a transactional database, transforms it into a common representation that might include validation, value normalization, encoding, deduplication, and schema transformation, and finally loads it into the analytical database. ETL processes can be quite complex and often require technically sophisticated solutions to meet performance requirements. ETL processes need to run periodically to keep the data in the data warehouse synchronized.

Once the data has been imported into the data warehouse it can be queried and analyzed. Typically, there are two classes of queries executed on a data warehouse. The first type are periodic report queries that compute business-relevant statistics such as revenue, user growth, or production output. These metrics are assembled into reports that help the management to assess the business's overall health. The second type are ad-hoc queries that aim to provide answers to specific questions and support business-critical decisions, for example a query to collect revenue numbers and spending on radio commercials to evaluate the effectiveness of a marketing campaign. Both kinds of queries are executed by a data warehouse in a batch processing fashion, as shown in Figure 1-3.

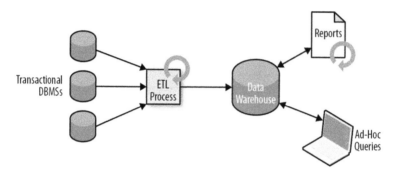

Figure 1-3. A traditional data warehouse architecture for data analytics

Today, components of the Apache Hadoop ecosystem are integral parts in the IT infrastructures of many enterprises. Instead of inserting all data into a relational database system, significant amounts of data, such as log files, social media, or web click logs, are written into Hadoop's distributed filesystem (HDFS), S3, or other bulk datastores, like Apache HBase, which provide massive storage capacity at a small cost. Data that resides in such storage systems can be queried with and processed by a SQL-on-Hadoop engine, for example Apache Hive, Apache Drill, or Apache Impala. However, the infrastructure remains basically the same as a traditional data warehouse architecture.

Stateful Stream Processing

Virtually all data is created as continuous streams of events. Think of user interactions on websites or in mobile apps, placements of orders, server logs, or sensor measurements; all of these are streams of events. In fact, it is difficult to find examples of finite, complete datasets that are generated all at once. Stateful stream processing is an application design pattern for processing unbounded streams of events and is applicable to many different use cases in the IT infrastructure of a company. Before we discuss its use cases, we briefly explain how stateful stream processing works.

Any application that processes a stream of events and does not just perform trivial record-at-a-time transformations needs to be stateful, with the ability to store and access intermediate data. When an application receives an event, it can perform arbitrary computations that involve reading data from or writing data to the state. In principle, state can be stored and accessed in many different places including program variables, local files, or embedded or external databases.

Apache Flink stores the application state locally in memory or in an embedded database. Since Flink is a distributed system, the local state needs to be protected against failures to avoid data loss in case of application or machine failure. Flink guarantees this by periodically writing a consistent checkpoint of the application state to a remote and durable storage. State, state consistency, and Flink's checkpointing mechanism will be discussed in more detail in the following chapters, but, for now, Figure 1-4 shows a stateful streaming Flink application.

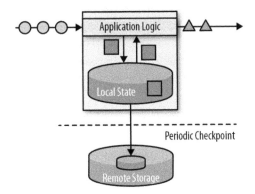

Figure 1-4. A stateful streaming application

Stateful stream processing applications often ingest their incoming events from an event log. An event log stores and distributes event streams. Events are written to a durable, append-only log, which means that the order of written events cannot be changed. A stream that is written to an event log can be read many times by the same or different consumers. Due to the append-only property of the log, events are always published to all consumers in exactly the same order. There are several event log systems available as open source software, Apache Kafka being the most popular, or as integrated services offered by cloud computing providers.

Connecting a stateful streaming application running on Flink and an event log is interesting for multiple reasons. In this architecture the event log persists the input events and can replay them in deterministic order. In case of a failure, Flink recovers a stateful streaming application by restoring its state from a previous checkpoint and resetting the read position on the event log. The application will replay (and fast forward) the input events from the event log until it reaches the tail of the stream. This technique is used to recover from failures but can also be leveraged to update an application, fix bugs and repair previously emitted results, migrate an application to a different cluster, or perform A/B tests with different application versions.

As previously stated, stateful stream processing is a versatile and flexible design architecture that can be used for many different use cases. In the following, we present three classes of applications that are commonly implemented using stateful stream processing: (1) event-driven applications, (2) data pipeline applications, and (3) data analytics applications.

Real-World Streaming Use-Cases and Deployments

If you are interested in learning more about real-world use cases and deployments, check out Apache Flink's Powered By (*http:// bit.ly/2FOxayO*) page and the talk recordings and slide decks of Flink Forward (*https://flink-forward.org/*) presentations.

We describe the classes of applications as distinct patterns to emphasize the versatility of stateful stream processing, but most real-world applications share the properties of more than one class.

Event-Driven Applications

Event-driven applications are stateful streaming applications that ingest event streams and process the events with application-specific business logic. Depending on the business logic, an event-driven application can trigger actions such as sending an alert or an email or write events to an outgoing event stream to be consumed by another event-driven application.

Typical use cases for event-driven applications include:

- Real-time recommendations (e.g., for recommending products while customers browse a retailer's website)
- Pattern detection or complex event processing (e.g., for fraud detection in credit card transactions)
- Anomaly detection (e.g., to detect attempts to intrude a computer network)

Event-driven applications are an evolution of microservices. They communicate via event logs instead of REST calls and hold application data as local state instead of writing it to and reading it from an external datastore, such as a relational database or key-value store. Figure 1-5 shows a service architecture composed of event-driven streaming applications.

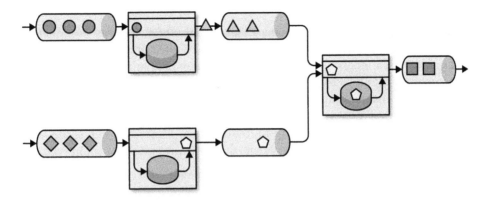

Figure 1-5. An event-driven application architecture

The applications in Figure 1-5 are connected by event logs. One application emits its output to an event log and another application consumes the events the other application emitted. The event log decouples senders and receivers and provides asynchronous, nonblocking event transfer. Each application can be stateful and can locally manage its own state without accessing external datastores. Applications can also be individually operated and scaled.

Event-driven applications offer several benefits compared to transactional applications or microservices. Local state access provides very good performance compared to reading and writing queries against remote datastores. Scaling and fault tolerance are handled by the stream processor, and by leveraging an event log as the input source the complete input of an application is reliably stored and can be deterministically replayed. Furthermore, Flink can reset the state of an application to a previous savepoint, making it possible to evolve or rescale an application without losing its state.

Event-driven applications have quite high requirements on the stream processor that runs them. Not all stream processors are equally well-suited to run event-driven applications. The expressiveness of the API and the quality of state handling and event-time support determine the business logic that can be implemented and executed. This aspect depends on the APIs of the stream processor, what kinds of state primitives it provides, and the quality of its support for event-time processing. Moreover, exactly-once state consistency and the ability to scale an application are fundamental requirements for event-driven applications. Apache Flink checks all these boxes and is a very good choice to run this class of applications.

Data Pipelines

Today's IT architectures include many different datastores, such as relational and special-purpose database systems, event logs, distributed filesystems, in-memory caches, and search indexes. All of these systems store data in different formats and data structures that provide the best performance for their specific access pattern. It is common that companies store the same data in multiple different systems to improve the performance of data accesses. For example, information for a product that is offered in a webshop can be stored in a transactional database, a web cache, and a search index. Due to this replication of data, the data stores must be kept in sync.

A traditional approach to synchronize data in different storage systems is periodic ETL jobs. However, they do not meet the latency requirements for many of today's use cases. An alternative is to use an event log to distribute updates. The updates are written to and distributed by the event log. Consumers of the log incorporate the updates into the affected data stores. Depending on the use case, the transferred data may need to be normalized, enriched with external data, or aggregated before it is ingested by the target data store.

Ingesting, transforming, and inserting data with low latency is another common use case for stateful stream processing applications. This type of application is called a data pipeline. Data pipelines must be able to process large amounts of data in a short time. A stream processor that operates a data pipeline should also feature many source and sink connectors to read data from and write data to various storage systems. Again, Flink does all of this.

Streaming Analytics

ETL jobs periodically import data into a datastore and the data is processed by ad-hoc or scheduled queries. This is batch processing regardless of whether the architecture is based on a data warehouse or components of the Hadoop ecosystem. While periodically loading data into a data analysis system has been the state of the art for many years, it adds considerable latency to the analytics pipeline.

Depending on the scheduling intervals it may take hours or days until a data point is included in a report. To some extent, the latency can be reduced by importing data into the datastore with a data pipeline application. However, even with continuous ETL there will always be a delay until an event is processed by a query. While this kind of delay may have been acceptable in the past, applications today must be able to collect data in real-time and immediately act on it (e.g., by adjusting to changing conditions in a mobile game or by personalizing user experiences for an online retailer).

Instead of waiting to be periodically triggered, a streaming analytics application continuously ingests streams of events and updates its result by incorporating the latest events with low latency. This is similar to the maintenance techniques database systems use to update materialized views. Typically, streaming applications store their result in an external data store that supports efficient updates, such as a database or key-value store. The live updated results of a streaming analytics application can be used to power dashboard applications as shown in Figure 1-6.

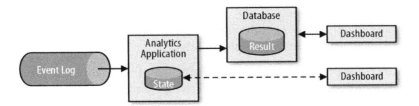

Figure 1-6. A streaming analytics application

Besides the much shorter time needed for an event to be incorporated into an analytics result, there is another, less obvious, advantage of streaming analytics applications. Traditional analytics pipelines consist of several individual components such as an ETL process, a storage system, and in the case of a Hadoop-based environment, a data processor and scheduler to trigger jobs or queries. In contrast, a stream processor that runs a stateful streaming application takes care of all these processing steps, including event ingestion, continuous computation including state maintenance, and updating the results. Moreover, the stream processor can recover from failures with exactly-once state consistency guarantees and can adjust the compute resources of an application. Stream processors like Flink also support event-time processing to produce correct and deterministic results and the ability to process large amounts of data in little time.

Streaming analytics applications are commonly used for:

- Monitoring the quality of cellphone networks
- Analyzing user behavior in mobile applications
- Ad-hoc analysis of live data in consumer technology

Although we don't cover it here, Flink also provides support for analytical SQL queries over streams.

The Evolution of Open Source Stream Processing

Data stream processing is not a novel technology. Some of the first research prototypes and commercial products date back to the late 1990s. However, the growing adoption of stream processing technology in the recent past has been driven to a large extent by the availability of mature open source stream processors. Today, distributed open source stream processors power business-critical applications in many enterprises across different industries such as (online) retail, social media, telecommunication, gaming, and banking. Open source software is a major driver of this trend, mainly due to two reasons:

1. Open source stream processing software is a commodity that everybody can evaluate and use.
2. Scalable stream processing technology is rapidly maturing and evolving due to the efforts of many open source communities.

The Apache Software Foundation alone is the home of more than a dozen projects related to stream processing. New distributed stream processing projects are continuously entering the open source stage and are challenging the state of the art with new features and capabilities. Open source communities are constantly improving the capabilities of their projects and are pushing the technical boundaries of stream processing. We will take a brief look into the past to see where open source stream processing came from and where it is today.

A Bit of History

The first generation of distributed open source stream processors (2011) focused on event processing with millisecond latencies and provided guarantees against loss of events in the case of failures. These systems had rather low-level APIs and did not provide built-in support for accurate and consistent results of streaming applications because the results depended on the timing and order of arriving events. Moreover, even though events were not lost, they could be processed more than once. In contrast to batch processors, the first open source stream processors traded result accuracy for better latency. The observation that data processing systems (at this point in time) could either provide fast or accurate results led to the design of the so-called lambda architecture, which is depicted in Figure 1-7.

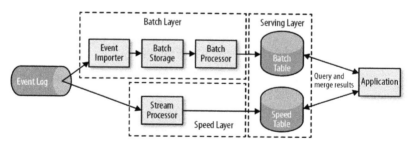

Figure 1-7. The lambda architecture

The lambda architecture augments the traditional periodic batch processing architecture with a speed layer that is powered by a low-latency stream processor. Data arriving at the lambda architecture is ingested by the stream processor and also written to batch storage. The stream processor computes approximated results in near real time and writes them into a speed table. The batch processor periodically processes the data in batch storage, writes the exact results into a batch table, and drops the corresponding inaccurate results from the speed table. Applications consume the results by merging approximated results from the speed table and the accurate results from the batch table.

The lambda architecture is no longer state of the art, but is still used in many places. The original goals of this architecture were to improve the high result latency of the original batch analytics architecture. However, it has a few notable drawbacks. First of all, it requires two semantically equivalent implementations of the application logic for two separate processing systems with different APIs. Second, the results computed by the stream processor are only approximate. Third, the lambda architecture is hard to set up and maintain.

Improving on the first generation, the next generation of distributed open source stream processors (2013) provided better failure guarantees and ensured that in case of a failure each input record affects the result exactly once. In addition, programming APIs evolved from rather low-level operator interfaces to high-level APIs with more built-in primitives. However, some improvements such as higher throughput and better failure guarantees came at the cost of increasing processing latencies from milliseconds to seconds. Moreover, results were still dependent on timing and order of arriving events.

The third generation of distributed open source stream processors (2015) addressed the dependency of results on the timing and order of arriving events. In combination with exactly-once failure semantics, systems of this generation are the first open source stream processors capable of computing consistent and accurate results. By only computing results based on actual data, these systems are also able to process historical data in the same way as "live" data. Another improvement was the dissolution of the latency/throughput tradeoff. While previous stream processors only provide either high throughput or low latency, systems of the third generation are able to serve both ends of the spectrum. Stream processors of this generation made the lambda architecture obsolete.

In addition to the system properties discussed so far, such as failure tolerance, performance, and result accuracy, stream processors have also continuously added new operational features such as highly available setups, tight integration with resource managers, such as YARN or Kubernetes, and the ability to dynamically scale streaming applications. Other features include support to upgrade application code or migrate a job to a different cluster or a new version of the stream processor without losing the current state.

A Quick Look at Flink

Apache Flink is a third-generation distributed stream processor with a competitive feature set. It provides accurate stream processing with high throughput and low latency at scale. In particular, the following features make Flink stand out:

- Event-time and processing-time semantics. Event-time semantics provide consistent and accurate results despite out-of-order events. Processing-time semantics can be used for applications with very low latency requirements.

- Exactly-once state consistency guarantees.

- Millisecond latencies while processing millions of events per second. Flink applications can be scaled to run on thousands of cores.

- Layered APIs with varying tradeoffs for expressiveness and ease of use. This book covers the DataStream API and process functions, which provide primitives for common stream processing operations, such as windowing and asynchronous operations, and interfaces to precisely control state and time. Flink's relational APIs, SQL and the LINQ-style Table API, are not discussed in this book.

- Connectors to the most commonly used storage systems such as Apache Kafka, Apache Cassandra, Elasticsearch, JDBC, Kinesis, and (distributed) filesystems such as HDFS and S3.

- Ability to run streaming applications 24/7 with very little downtime due to its highly available setup (no single point of failure), tight integration with Kubernetes, YARN, and Apache Mesos, fast recovery from failures, and the ability to dynamically scale jobs.

- Ability to update the application code of jobs and migrate jobs to different Flink clusters without losing the state of the application.

- Detailed and customizable collection of system and application metrics to identify and react to problems ahead of time.

- Last but not least, Flink is also a full-fledged batch processor.[1]

In addition to these features, Flink is a very developer-friendly framework due to its easy-to-use APIs. The embedded execution mode starts an application and the whole Flink system in a single JVM process, which can be used to run and debug Flink jobs within an IDE. This feature comes in handy when developing and testing Flink applications.

---

1 Flink's batch processing API, the DataSet API, and its operators are separate from their corresponding streaming counterparts. However, the vision of the Flink community is to treat batch processing as a special case of stream processing—the processing of bounded streams. An ongoing effort of the Flink community is to evolve Flink toward a system with a truly unified batch and streaming API and runtime.

Running Your First Flink Application

In the following, we will guide you through the process of starting a local cluster and executing a streaming application to give you a first look at Flink. The application we are going to run converts and aggregates randomly generated temperature sensor readings by time. For this example, your system needs Java 8 installed. We describe the steps for a UNIX environment, but if you are running Windows, we recommend setting up a virtual machine with Linux, Cygwin (a Linux environment for Windows), or the Windows Subsystem for Linux, introduced with Windows 10. The following steps show you how to start a local Flink cluster and submit an application for execution.

1. Go to the Apache Flink webpage (*http://flink.apache.org*) and download the Hadoop-free binary distribution of Apache Flink 1.7.1 for Scala 2.12.

2. Extract the archive file:

   ```
   $ tar xvfz flink-1.7.1-bin-scala_2.12.tgz
   ```

3. Start a local Flink cluster:

   ```
   $ cd flink-1.7.1
   $ ./bin/start-cluster.sh
   Starting cluster.
   Starting standalonesession daemon on host xxx.
   Starting taskexecutor daemon on host xxx.
   ```

4. Open Flink's Web UI by entering the URL **http://localhost:8081** in your browser. As shown in Figure 1-8, you will see some statistics about the local Flink cluster you just started. It will show that a single TaskManager (Flink's worker processes) is connected and that a single task slot (resource units provided by a TaskManager) is available.

Figure 1-8. Screenshot of Apache Flink's web dashboard showing the overview

5. Download the JAR file that includes examples in this book:

```
$ wget https://streaming-with-flink.github.io/\
examples/download/examples-scala.jar
```

You can also build the JAR file yourself by following the steps in the repository's README file.

6. Run the example on your local cluster by specifying the application's entry class and JAR file:

```
$ ./bin/flink run \
  -c io.github.streamingwithflink.chapter1.AverageSensorReadings \
  examples-scala.jar
Starting execution of program
Job has been submitted with JobID cfde9dbe315ce162444c475a08cf93d9
```

7. Inspect the web dashboard. You should see a job listed under "Running Jobs." If you click on that job, you will see the dataflow and live metrics about the operators of the running job similar to the screenshot in Figure 1-9.

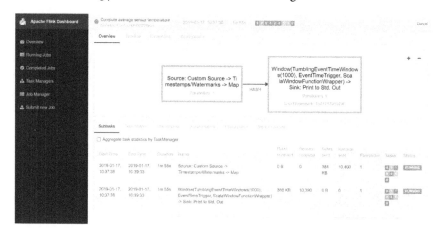

Figure 1-9. Screenshot of Apache Flink's web dashboard showing a running job

8. The output of the job is written to the standard out of Flink's worker process, which is redirected into a file in the *./log* folder by default. You can monitor the constantly produced output using the `tail` command as follows:

```
$ tail -f ./log/flink-<user>-taskexecutor-<n>-<hostname>.out
```

You should see lines like this being written to the file:

```
SensorReading(sensor_1,1547718199000,35.80018327300259)
SensorReading(sensor_6,1547718199000,15.402984393403084)
SensorReading(sensor_7,1547718199000,6.720945201171228)
SensorReading(sensor_10,1547718199000,38.101067604893444)
```

The first field of the `SensorReading` is a `sensorId`, the second field is the timestamp in milliseconds since `1970-01-01-00:00:00.000`, and the third field is an average temperature computed over 5 seconds.

9. Since you are running a streaming application, the application will continue to run until you cancel it. You can do this by selecting the job in the web dashboard and clicking the Cancel button at the top of the page.

10. Finally, you should stop the local Flink cluster:

```
$ ./bin/stop-cluster.sh
```

That's it. You just installed and started your first local Flink cluster and ran your first Flink DataStream API program! Of course, there is much more to learn about stream processing with Apache Flink and that's what this book is about.

Summary

In this chapter, we introduced stateful stream processing, discussed its use cases, and had a first look at Apache Flink. We started with a recap of traditional data infrastructures, how business applications are commonly designed, and how data is collected and analyzed in most companies today. Then we introduced the idea of stateful stream processing and explained how it addresses a wide spectrum of use cases, ranging from business applications and microservices to ETL and data analytics. We discussed how open source stream processing systems have evolved since their inception in the early 2010s and how stream processing became a viable solution for many use cases of today's businesses. Finally, we took a look at Apache Flink and the extensive features it offers and showed how to install a local Flink setup and run a first stream processing application.

## CHAPTER 2

Stream Processing Fundamentals

So far, you have seen how stream processing addresses some of the limitations of traditional batch processing and how it enables new applications and architectures. You also know a little bit about the evolution of the open source stream processing space and what a Flink streaming application looks like. In this chapter, you will enter the streaming world for good.

The goal of this chapter is to introduce the fundamental concepts of stream processing and the requirements of its frameworks. We hope that after reading this chapter, you will be able to evaluate the features of modern stream processing systems.

Introduction to Dataflow Programming

Before we delve into the fundamentals of stream processing, let's look at the background on *dataflow* programming and the terminology we will use throughout this book.

Dataflow Graphs

As the name suggests, a dataflow program describes how data flows between operations. Dataflow programs are commonly represented as directed graphs, where nodes are called operators and represent computations and edges represent data dependencies. Operators are the basic functional units of a dataflow application. They consume data from inputs, perform a computation on them, and produce data to outputs for further processing. Operators without input ports are called data sources and operators without output ports are called data sinks. A dataflow graph must have at least one data source and one data sink. Figure 2-1 shows a dataflow program that extracts and counts hashtags from an input stream of tweets.

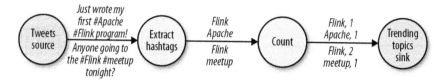

Figure 2-1. A logical dataflow graph to continuously count hashtags (nodes represent operators and edges denote data dependencies)

Dataflow graphs like the one in Figure 2-1 are called logical because they convey a high-level view of the computation logic. In order to execute a dataflow program, its logical graph is converted into a physical dataflow graph, which specifies in detail how the program is executed. For instance, if we are using a distributed processing engine, each operator might have several parallel tasks running on different physical machines. Figure 2-2 shows a physical dataflow graph for the logical graph of Figure 2-1. While in the logical dataflow graph the nodes represent operators, in the physical dataflow, the nodes are tasks. The "Extract hashtags" and "Count" operators have two parallel operator tasks, each performing a computation on a subset of the input data.

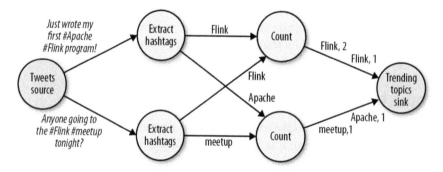

Figure 2-2. A physical dataflow plan for counting hashtags (nodes represent tasks)

Data Parallelism and Task Parallelism

You can exploit parallelism in dataflow graphs in different ways. First, you can partition your input data and have tasks of the same operation execute on the data subsets in parallel. This type of parallelism is called data parallelism. Data parallelism is useful because it allows for processing large volumes of data and spreading the computation load across several computing nodes. Second, you can have tasks from different operators performing computations on the same or different data in parallel. This type of parallelism is called task parallelism. Using task parallelism, you can better utilize the computing resources of a cluster.

Data Exchange Strategies

Data exchange strategies define how data items are assigned to tasks in a physical dataflow graph. Data exchange strategies can be automatically chosen by the execution engine depending on the semantics of the operators or explicitly imposed by the dataflow programmer. Here, we briefly review some common data exchange strategies, as shown in Figure 2-3.

- The *forward* strategy sends data from a task to a receiving task. If both tasks are located on the same physical machine (which is often ensured by task schedulers), this exchange strategy avoids network communication.

- The *broadcast* strategy sends every data item to all parallel tasks of an operator. Because this strategy replicates data and involves network communication, it is fairly expensive.

- The *key-based* strategy partitions data by a key attribute and guarantees that data items having the same key will be processed by the same task. In Figure 2-2, the output of the "Extract hashtags" operator is partitioned by the key (the hashtag), so that the count operator tasks can correctly compute the occurrences of each hashtag.

- The *random* strategy uniformly distributes data items to operator tasks in order to evenly distribute the load across computing tasks.

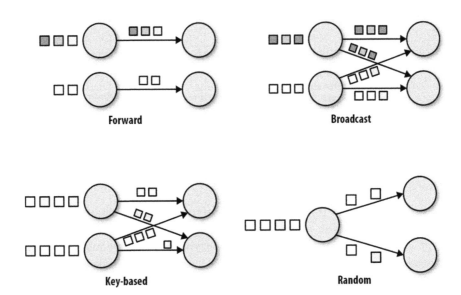

Figure 2-3. Data exchange strategies

Processing Streams in Parallel

Now that you are familiar with the basics of dataflow programming, it's time to see how these concepts apply to processing data streams in parallel. But first, let's define the term *data stream*: a data stream is a potentially unbounded sequence of events.

Events in a data stream can represent monitoring data, sensor measurements, credit card transactions, weather station observations, online user interactions, web searches, etc. In this section, you are going to learn how to process infinite streams in parallel, using the dataflow programming paradigm.

Latency and Throughput

In Chapter 1, you learned that streaming applications have different operational requirements than traditional batch programs. Requirements also differ when it comes to evaluating performance. For batch applications, we usually care about the total execution time of a job, or how long it takes for our processing engine to read the input, perform the computation, and write back the result. Since streaming applications run continuously and the input is potentially unbounded, there is no notion of total execution time in data stream processing. Instead, streaming applications must provide results for incoming data *as fast as possible* while being able to handle high *ingest rates* of events. We express these performance requirements in terms of *latency* and *throughput*.

Latency

Latency indicates how long it takes for an event to be processed. Essentially, it is the time interval between receiving an event and seeing the effect of processing this event in the output. To understand latency intuitively, consider your daily visit to your favorite coffee shop. When you enter the coffee shop, there might be other customers inside already. Thus, you wait in line and when it is your turn you place an order. The cashier receives your payment and passes your order to the barista who prepares your beverage. Once your coffee is ready, the barista calls your name and you can pick up your coffee from the counter. The service latency is the time you spend in the coffee shop, from the moment you enter until you have your first sip of coffee.

In data streaming, latency is measured in units of time, such as milliseconds. Depending on the application, you might care about *average* latency, *maximum* latency, or *percentile* latency. For example, an average latency value of 10 ms means that events are processed within 10 ms on average. Alternately, a 95th-percentile latency value of 10 ms means that 95% of events are processed within 10 ms. Average values hide the true distribution of processing delays and might make it hard to detect problems. If the barista runs out of milk right before preparing your cappuccino, you will have to wait until they bring some from the supply room. While you might get annoyed by this delay, most other customers will still be happy.

Ensuring low latency is critical for many streaming applications, such as fraud detection, system alarms, network monitoring, and offering services with strict service-level agreements. Low latency is a key characteristic of stream processing and it enables what we call *real-time* applications. Modern stream processors, like Apache Flink, can offer latencies as low as a few milliseconds. In contrast, traditional batch processing latencies typically range from a few minutes to several hours. In batch processing, you first need to gather the events in batches and only then can you process them. Thus, the latency is bounded by the arrival time of the last event in each batch and naturally depends on the batch size. True stream processing does not introduce such artificial delays and thus can achieve really low latencies. In a true streaming model, events can be processed as soon as they arrive in the system and latency more closely reflects the actual work that has to be performed on each event.

Throughput

Throughput is a measure of the system's processing capacity—its *rate* of processing. That is, throughput tells us how many events the system can process per time unit. Revisiting the coffee shop example, if the shop is open from 7 a.m. to 7 p.m. and it serves 600 customers in one day, then its average throughput would be 50 customers per hour. While you want latency to be as low as possible, you generally want throughput to be as high as possible.

Throughput is measured in events or operations per time unit. It is important to note that the rate of processing depends on the rate of arrival; low throughput does not necessarily indicate bad performance. In streaming systems you usually want to ensure that your system can handle the maximum expected rate of events. That is, you are primarily concerned with determining the *peak* throughput—the performance limit when your system is at its maximum load. To better understand the concept of peak throughput, let's consider a stream processing application that does not receive any incoming data and thus does not consume any system resources. When the first event comes in, it will be immediately processed with the minimum latency possible. For example, if you are the first customer showing up at the coffee shop right after it opened its doors in the morning, you will be served immediately. Ideally, you would like this latency to remain constant and independent of the rate of the incoming events. However, once we reach a rate of incoming events such that the system resources are fully used, we will have to start buffering events. In the coffee shop example, you will probably see this happening right after lunch. Many people show up at the same time and have to wait in line. At this point, the system has reached its peak throughput and further increasing the event rate will only result in worse latency. If the system continues to receive data at a higher rate than it can handle, buffers might become unavailable and data might get lost. This situation is commonly known as *backpressure* and there are different strategies to deal with it.

Latency Versus Throughput

At this point, it should be clear that latency and throughput are not independent metrics. If events take a long time to travel in the data processing pipeline, we cannot easily ensure high throughput. Similarly, if a system's capacity is small, events will be buffered and have to wait before they get processed.

Let's revisit the coffee shop example to clarify how latency and throughput affect each other. First, it should be clear that there is optimal latency when there is no load. That is, you will get the fastest service if you are the only customer in the coffee shop. However, during busy times, customers will have to wait in line and latency will increase. Another factor that affects latency and consequently throughput is the time it takes to process an event, or the time it takes for each customer to be served in the coffee shop. Imagine that during the Christmas holiday season, baristas have to draw a Santa Claus on the cup of each coffee they serve. This means the time needed to prepare a single beverage will increase, causing each person to spend more time in the coffees hop, thus lowering the overall throughput.

So, can you get both low latency and high throughput or is this a hopeless endeavor? You may be able to lower the latency in our coffee shop example by hiring a more skilled barista—one that prepares coffees faster. At high load, this change will also increase throughput, because more customers will be served in the same amount of time. Another way to achieve the same result is to hire a second barista and exploit parallelism. The main takeaway here is that lowering latency increases throughput. Naturally, if a system can perform operations faster, it can perform more operations in the same amount of time. In fact, that's what happens when you exploit parallelism in a stream processing pipeline. By processing several streams in parallel, you lower the latency while processing more events at the same time.

Operations on Data Streams

Stream processing engines usually provide a set of built-in operations to ingest, transform, and output streams. These operators can be combined into dataflow processing graphs to implement the logic of streaming applications. In this section, we describe the most common streaming operations.

Operations can be either *stateless* or *stateful*. Stateless operations do not maintain any internal state. That is, the processing of an event does not depend on any events seen in the past and no history is kept. Stateless operations are easy to parallelize, since events can be processed independently of each other and of their arriving order. Moreover, in the case of a failure, a stateless operator can be simply restarted and continue processing from where it left off. In contrast, stateful operators may maintain information about the events they have received before. This state can be updated by incoming events and can be used in the processing logic of future events. Stateful stream processing applications are more challenging to parallelize and operate in a fault-tolerant manner because state needs to be efficiently partitioned and reliably recovered in the case of failures. You will learn more about stateful stream processing, failure scenarios, and consistency at the end of this chapter.

Data ingestion and data egress

Data ingestion and data egress operations allow the stream processor to communicate with external systems. Data *ingestion* is the operation of fetching raw data from external sources and converting it into a format suitable for processing. Operators that implement data ingestion logic are called *data sources*. A data source can ingest data from a TCP socket, a file, a Kafka topic, or a sensor data interface. Data *egress* is the operation of producing output in a form suitable for consumption by external systems. Operators that perform data egress are called *data sinks* and examples include files, databases, message queues, and monitoring interfaces.

Transformation operations

Transformation operations are single-pass operations that process each event independently. These operations consume one event after the other and apply some transformation to the event data, producing a new output stream. The transformation logic can be either integrated in the operator or provided by a user-defined function, as shown in Figure 2-4. Functions are written by the application programmer and implement custom computation logic.

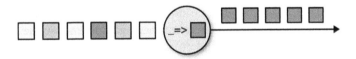

Figure 2-4. A streaming operator with a function that turns each incoming event into a darker event

Operators can accept multiple inputs and produce multiple output streams. They can also modify the structure of the dataflow graph by either splitting a stream into multiple streams or merging streams into a single flow. We discuss the semantics of all operators available in Flink in Chapter 5.

Rolling aggregations

A rolling aggregation is an aggregation, such as sum, minimum, and maximum, that is continuously updated for each input event. Aggregation operations are stateful and combine the current state with the incoming event to produce an updated aggregate value. Note that to be able to efficiently combine the current state with an event and produce a single value, the aggregation function must be associative and commutative. Otherwise, the operator would have to store the complete stream history. Figure 2-5 shows a rolling minimum aggregation. The operator keeps the current minimum value and accordingly updates it for each incoming event.

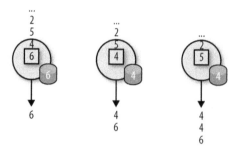

Figure 2-5. A rolling minimum aggregation operation

Window operations

Transformations and rolling aggregations process one event at a time to produce output events and potentially update state. However, some operations must collect and buffer records to compute their result. Consider, for example, a streaming join operation or a holistic aggregate, such as the median function. In order to evaluate such operations efficiently on unbounded streams, you need to limit the amount of data these operations maintain. In this section, we discuss window operations, which provide this service.

Apart from having a practical value, windows also enable semantically interesting queries on streams. You have seen how rolling aggregations encode the history of the whole stream in an aggregate value and provide us with a low-latency result for every event. This is fine for some applications, but what if you are only interested in the most recent data? Consider an application that provides real-time traffic information to drivers so that they can avoid congested routes. In this scenario, you want to know if there has been an accident in a certain location within the last few minutes. On the other hand, knowing about all accidents that have ever happened might not be so interesting in this case. What's more, by reducing the stream history to a single aggregate, you lose the information about how your data varies over time. For instance, you might want to know how many vehicles cross an intersection every 5 minutes.

Window operations continuously create finite sets of events called buckets from an unbounded event stream and let us perform computations on these finite sets. Events are usually assigned to buckets based on data properties or based on time. To properly define window operator semantics we need to determine both how events are assigned to buckets and how often the window produces a result. The behavior of windows is defined by a set of policies. Window policies decide when new buckets are created, which events are assigned to which buckets, and when the contents of a bucket get evaluated. The latter decision is based on a trigger condition. When the trigger condition is met, the bucket contents are sent to an evaluation function that applies the computation logic on the bucket elements. Evaluation functions can be aggregations like sum or minimum or custom operations applied on the bucket's collected elements. Policies can be based on time (e.g., events received in the last five seconds), on count (e.g., the last one hundred events), or on a data property. Next, we describe the semantics of common window types.

- *Tumbling* windows assign events into nonoverlapping buckets of fixed size. When the window border is passed, all the events are sent to an evaluation function for processing. Count-based tumbling windows define how many events are collected before triggering evaluation. Figure 2-6 shows a count-based tumbling window that discretizes the input stream into buckets of four elements. Time-based tumbling windows define a time interval during which events are buffered in the bucket. Figure 2-7 shows a time-based tumbling window that gathers events into buckets and triggers computation every 10 minutes.

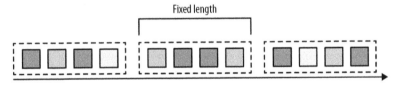

Figure 2-6. Count-based tumbling window

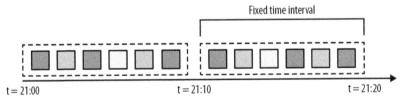

Figure 2-7. Time-based tumbling window

- *Sliding* windows assign events into overlapping buckets of fixed size. Thus, an event might belong to multiple buckets. We define sliding windows by providing their length and their *slide*. The slide value defines the interval at which a new bucket is created. The sliding count-based window of Figure 2-8 has a length of four events and slide of three events.

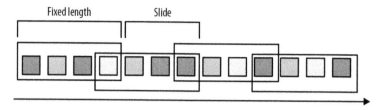

Figure 2-8. Sliding count-based window with a length of four events and a slide of three events

- *Session* windows are useful in common real-world scenarios where neither tumbling nor sliding windows can be applied. Consider an application that analyzes online user behavior. In such applications, we would like to group together events that originate from the same period of user activity or *session*. Sessions are comprised of a series of events happening in adjacent times followed by a period of inactivity. For example, user interactions with a series of news articles one after the other could be considered a session. Since the length of a session is not defined beforehand but depends on the actual data, tumbling and sliding windows cannot be applied in this scenario. Instead, we need a window operation that assigns events belonging to the same session in the same bucket. Session windows group events in sessions based on a *session gap* value that defines the time of inactivity to consider a session closed. Figure 2-9 shows a session window.

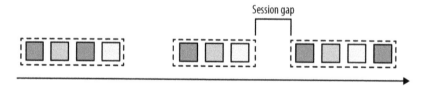

Figure 2-9. Session window

All the window types that you have seen so far are windows that operate on the full stream. But in practice you might want to partition a stream into multiple logical streams and define *parallel* windows. For instance, if you are receiving measurements from different sensors, you probably want to group the stream by sensor ID before applying a window computation. In parallel windows, each partition applies the window policies independently of other partitions. Figure 2-10 shows a parallel count-based tumbling window of length 2 that is partitioned by event color.

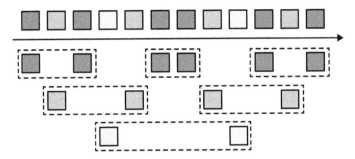

Figure 2-10. A parallel count-based tumbling window of length 2

Window operations are closely related to two dominant concepts in stream processing: time semantics and state management. Time is perhaps the most important aspect of stream processing. Even though low latency is an attractive feature of stream processing, its true value is way beyond just fast analytics. Real-world systems, networks, and communication channels are far from perfect, and streaming data can often be delayed or arrive out of order. It is crucial to understand how to deliver accurate and deterministic results under such conditions. What's more, streaming applications that process events as they are produced should also be able to process historical events in the same way, thus enabling offline analytics or even time travel analyses. Of course, none of this matters if your system cannot guard state against failures. All the window types that you have seen so far need to buffer data before producing a result. In fact, if you want to compute anything interesting in a streaming application, even a simple count, you need to maintain state. Considering that streaming applications might run for several days, months, or even years, you need to make sure that state can be reliably recovered under failures and that your system can guarantee accurate results even if things break. In the rest of this chapter, we are going to look deeper into the concepts of time and state guarantees under failures in data stream processing.

Time Semantics

In this section, we introduce time semantics and describe the different notions of time in streaming. We discuss how a stream processor can provide accurate results with out-of-order events and how you can perform historical event processing and time travel with streaming.

What Does One Minute Mean in Stream Processing?

When dealing with a potentially unbounded stream of continuously arriving events, time becomes a central aspect of applications. Let's assume you want to compute results continuously, maybe every minute. What would *one minute* really mean in the context of our streaming application?

Consider a program that analyzes events generated by users playing an online mobile game. Users are organized in teams and the application collects a team's activity and provides rewards in the game, such as extra lives and level-ups, based on how fast the team's members meet the game's goals. For example, if all users in a team pop 500 bubbles within one minute, they get a level-up. Alice is a devoted player who plays the game every morning during her commute to work. The problem is that Alice lives in Berlin and takes the subway to work. And everyone knows that the mobile internet connection in the Berlin subway is lousy. Consider the case where Alice starts popping bubbles while her phone is connected to the network and sends events to the analysis application. Then suddenly the train enters a tunnel and her phone gets disconnected. Alice keeps on playing and the game events are buffered in her phone. When the train exits the tunnel, she comes back online, and pending events are sent to the application. What should the application do? What's the meaning of one minute in this case? Does it include the time Alice was offline or not? Figure 2-11 illustrates this problem.

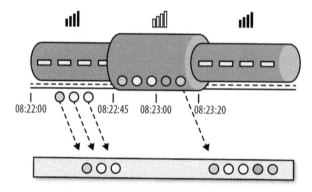

Figure 2-11. An application receiving online mobile game events played on the subway would experience a gap when the network connection is lost, but events are buffered in the player's phone and delivered when the connection is restored

Online gaming is a simple scenario showing how operator semantics should depend on the time when events actually happen and not the time when the application receives the events. In the case of a mobile game, consequences can be as bad as Alice and her team getting disappointed and never playing again. But there are much more time-critical applications whose semantics we need to guarantee. If we only consider how much data we receive within one minute, our results will vary and depend on the speed of the network connection or the speed of the processing. Instead, what really defines the amount of events in one minute is the time of the data itself.

In Alice's game example, the streaming application could operate with two different notions of time: processing time or event time. We describe both notions in the following sections.

Processing Time

Processing time is the time of the local clock on the machine where the operator processing the stream is being executed. A processing-time window includes all events that happen to have arrived at the window operator within a time period, as measured by the wall clock of its machine. As shown in Figure 2-12, in Alice's case, a processing-time window would continue counting time when her phone gets disconnected, thus not accounting for her game activity during that time.

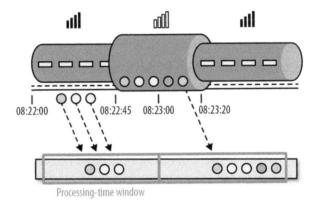

Figure 2-12. A processing-time window continues counting time even after Alice's phone gets disconnected

Event Time

Event time is the time when an event in the stream actually happened. Event time is based on a *timestamp* that is attached to the events of the stream. Timestamps usually exist inside the event data before they enter the processing pipeline (e.g., the event creation time). Figure 2-13 shows that an event-time window would correctly place events in a window, reflecting the reality of how things happened, even though some events were *delayed*.

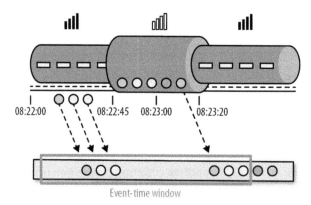

Figure 2-13. Event time correctly places events in a window, reflecting the reality of how things happened

Event time completely decouples the processing speed from the results. Operations based on event time are predictable and their results are deterministic. An event time window computation will yield the same result no matter how fast the stream is processed or when the events arrive at the operator.

Handling delayed events is only one of the challenges that you can overcome with event time. The ubiquitous problem of out-of-order data can also be solved with it. Consider Bob, another player of the online mobile game, who happens to be on the same train as Alice. Bob and Alice play the same game but have different mobile providers. While Alice's phone loses connection when inside the tunnel, Bob's phone remains connected and delivers events to the gaming application.

By relying on event time, we can guarantee result correctness even in cases of out-of-order data. What's more, when combined with replayable streams, the determinism of timestamps gives you the ability to *fast forward* the past. That is, you can replay a stream and analyze historic data as if events are happening in real time. Additionally, you can fast forward the computation to the present so that once your program catches up with the events happening now, it can continue as a real-time application using exactly the same program logic.

Watermarks

In our discussion about event-time windows so far, we have overlooked one very important aspect: *how do we decide when to trigger an event-time window?* That is, how long do we have to wait before we can be certain that we have received all events that happened before a certain point of time? And how do we even know that data will be delayed? Given the unpredictable reality of distributed systems and arbitrary delays that might be caused by external components, there are no categorically correct answers to these questions. In this section, we will see how to use *watermarks* to configure event-time window behavior.

A watermark is a global progress metric that indicates the point in time when we are confident that no more delayed events will arrive. In essence, watermarks provide a logical clock that informs the system about the current event time. When an operator receives a watermark with time T, it can assume that no further events with timestamp less than T will be received. Watermarks are essential for both event-time windows and operators handling out-of-order events. Once a watermark has been received, operators are signaled that all timestamps for a certain time interval have been observed and either trigger computation or order received events.

Watermarks provide a configurable tradeoff between results confidence and latency. *Eager* watermarks ensure low latency but provide lower confidence. In this case, late events might arrive after the watermark, and we should provide some code to handle them. On the other hand, if watermarks are too relaxed, you have high confidence but you might unnecessarily increase processing latency.

In many real-world applications, the system does not have enough knowledge to perfectly determine watermarks. In the mobile gaming example, it is practically impossible to know how long a user might remain disconnected; they could be going through a tunnel, boarding a plane, or never playing again. No matter if watermarks are user defined or automatically generated, tracking global progress in a distributed system might be problematic in the presence of straggler tasks. Hence, simply relying on watermarks might not always be a good idea. Instead, it is crucial that the stream processing system provide some mechanism to deal with events that might arrive after the watermark. Depending on the application requirements, you might want to ignore such events, log them, or use them to correct previous results.

Processing Time Versus Event Time

At this point, you might be wondering why we would even bother with processing time if event time solves all of our problems. The truth is, processing time can indeed be useful in some cases. Processing-time windows introduce the lowest latency possible. Since you do not take into consideration late events and out-of-order events, a window simply needs to buffer up events and immediately trigger computation once the specified time length is reached. Thus, for applications where speed is more important than accuracy, processing time comes in handy. Another case is when you need to periodically report results in real time, independently of their accuracy. An example application would be a real-time monitoring dashboard that displays event aggregates as they are received. Finally, processing-time windows offer a faithful representation of the streams themselves, which might be a desirable property for some use cases. For instance, you might be interested in observing the stream and counting the number of events per second to detect outages. To recap, processing time offers low latency but results depend on the speed of processing and are not deterministic. On the other hand, event time guarantees deterministic results and allows you to deal with events that are late or even out of order.

State and Consistency Models

We now turn to another extremely important aspect of stream processing—state. State is ubiquitous in data processing. It is required by any nontrivial computation. To produce a result, a function accumulates state over a period of time or number of events (e.g., to compute an aggregation or detect a pattern). Stateful operators use both incoming events and internal state to compute their output. Take, for example, a rolling aggregation operator that outputs the current sum of all the events it has seen so far. The operator keeps the current value of the sum as its internal state and updates it every time it receives a new event. Similarly, consider an operator that raises an alert when it detects a "high temperature" event followed by a "smoke" event within 10 minutes. The operator needs to store the "high temperature" event in its internal state until it sees the "smoke" event or the until 10-minute time period expires.

The importance of state becomes even more evident if we consider the case of using a batch processing system to analyze an unbounded dataset. Before the rise of modern stream processors, a common approach to process unbounded data was to repeatedly schedule jobs over small batches of incoming events on a batch processing system. When a job finishes, the result is written to persistent storage, and all operator state is lost. Once a job is scheduled for execution on the next batch, it cannot access the state of the previous job. This problem is commonly solved by delegating state management to an external system, such as a database. In contrast, in continuously running streaming jobs, state is durable across events and we can expose it as a first-class citizen in the programming model. Arguably, we could use an external system to also manage streaming state, even though this design choice might introduce additional latency.

Since streaming operators process potentially unbounded data, caution should be taken to not allow internal state to grow indefinitely. To limit the state size, operators usually maintain some kind of summary or *synopsis* of the events seen so far. Such a summary can be a count, a sum, a sample of the events seen so far, a window buffer, or a custom data structure that preserves some property of interest to the running application.

As you might imagine, supporting stateful operators comes with a few implementation challenges:

State management

> The system needs to efficiently manage the state and make sure it is protected from concurrent updates.

State partitioning

> Parallelization gets complicated, since results depend on both the state and incoming events. Fortunately, in many cases, you can partition the state by a key and manage the state of each partition independently. For example, if you are processing a stream of measurements from a set of sensors, you can use a partitioned operator state to maintain state for each sensor independently.

State recovery

> The third and biggest challenge that comes with stateful operators is ensuring that state can be recovered and results will be correct even in the presence of failures.

In the next section, we discuss task failures and result guarantees in detail.

Task Failures

Operator state in streaming jobs is very valuable and should be guarded against failures. If state gets lost during a failure, results will be incorrect after recovery. Streaming jobs run for long periods of time, and thus state might be collected over several days or even months. Reprocessing all input to reproduce lost state in the case of failures would be both very expensive and time-consuming.

In the beginning of this chapter, you saw how you can model streaming programs as dataflow graphs. Before execution, these are translated into physical dataflow graphs of connected parallel tasks, each running some operator logic, consuming input streams and producing output streams for other tasks. Typical real-world setups can easily have hundreds of such tasks running in parallel on many physical machines. In long-running, streaming jobs, each of these tasks can fail at any time. How can you ensure that such failures are handled transparently so that your streaming job can continue to run? In fact, you would like your stream processor to not only continue processing in the case of task failures, but also provide correctness guarantees about the result and operator state. We discuss all these matters in this section.

What is a task failure?

For each event in the input stream, a task is a processing step that performs the following steps: (1) receives the event, storing it in a local buffer; (2) possibly updates internal state; and (3) produces an output record. A failure can occur during any of these steps and the system has to clearly define its behavior in a failure scenario. If the task fails during the first step, will the event get lost? If it fails after it has updated its internal state, will it update it again after it recovers? And in those cases, will the output be deterministic?

 We assume reliable network connections, and that no records are dropped or duplicated and all events are eventually delivered to their destination in FIFO order. Note that Flink uses TCP connections, and thus these requirements are guaranteed. We also assume perfect failure detectors and that no task will intentionally act maliciously, meaning all nonfailed tasks follow the above steps.

In a batch processing scenario, all these questions are answered because a batch job can be simply restarted from the beginning. Hence, no events are lost and the state is completely built up from scratch. In the streaming world, however, dealing with failures is not a trivial problem. Streaming systems define their behavior in the presence of failures by offering result guarantees. Next, we review the types of guarantees offered by modern stream processors and some of the mechanisms systems implement to achieve those guarantees.

Result Guarantees

Before we describe the different types of guarantees, we need to clarify a few points that are often the source of confusion when discussing task failures in stream processors. In the rest of this chapter, when we talk about "result guarantees" we mean the consistency of the internal state of the stream processor. That is, we are concerned with what the application code sees as state value after recovering from a failure. Note that guaranteeing the consistency of an application's state is not the same a guaranteeing consistency of its output. Once data has been emitted to a sink, it is difficult to guarantee result correctness, unless the sink system supports transactions.

At-most-once

The simplest thing to do when a task fails is to do nothing to recover lost state and replay lost events. At-most-once is the trivial case that guarantees processing of each event at most once. In other words, events can be simply dropped and nothing is done to ensure result correctness. This type of guarantee is also known as "no guarantee" since even a system that drops every event can provide this guarantee. Having no guarantees whatsoever sounds like a terrible idea, but it might be fine if you can live with approximate results and all you care about is providing the lowest latency possible.

At-least-once

In most real-world applications, the expectation is that events should not get lost. This type of guarantee is called at-least-once, and it means that all events will be processed, and there is a chance that some of them are processed more than once. Duplicate processing might be acceptable if application correctness only depends on the completeness of information. For example, determining whether a specific event occurs in the input stream can be correctly realized with at-least-once guarantees. In the worst case, you will locate the event more than once. However, counting how many times a specific event occurs in the input stream might return the wrong result under at-least-once guarantees.

In order to ensure at-least-once result correctness, you need to have a way to replay events—either from the source or from some buffer. Persistent event logs write all events to durable storage, so that they can be replayed if a task fails. Another way to achieve equivalent functionality is using record acknowledgments. This method stores every event in a buffer until its processing has been acknowledged by all tasks in the pipeline, at which point the event can be discarded.

Exactly-once

Exactly-once is the strictest guarantee and hard to achieve. Exactly-once means that not only will there be no event loss, but also updates on the internal state will be applied exactly once for each event. In essence, exactly-once guarantees mean that our application will provide the correct result, as though a failure never happened.

Providing exactly-once guarantees requires at-least-once guarantees, and thus a data replay mechanism is again necessary. Additionally, the stream processor needs to ensure internal state consistency. That is, after recovery, it should know whether an event update has already been reflected on the state or not. Transactional updates are one way to achieve this result, but they can incur substantial performance overhead. Instead, Flink uses a lightweight snapshotting mechanism to achieve exactly-once result guarantees. We discuss Flink's fault-tolerance algorithm in "Checkpoints, Savepoints, and State Recovery" on page 58.

End-to-end exactly-once

The types of guarantees you have seen so far refer to the state of an application that is managed by the stream processor. In a real-world streaming application however, there will be at least one source and one sink apart from the stream processor. End-to-end guarantees refer to result correctness across the whole data processing pipeline. Each component provides its own guarantees and the end-to-end guarantee of the complete pipeline would be the weakest of each of its components. It is important to note that sometimes you can get stronger semantics with weaker guarantees. A common case is when a task performs idempotent operations, like maximum or minimum. In this case, you can achieve exactly-once semantics with at-least-once guarantees.

Summary

In this chapter, you learned the fundamentals of data stream processing. We looked at the dataflow programming model and learned how streaming applications can be expressed as distributed dataflow graphs. Next, you learned the requirements of processing infinite streams in parallel and saw the importance of latency and throughput for stream applications. We covered basic streaming operations and how to compute meaningful results on unbounded input data using windows. You learned the meaning of time in stream processing and compared the notions of event time and processing time. Finally, we learned why state is important in streaming applications and how to guard it against failures and guarantee correct results.

Up to this point, we have considered streaming concepts independently of Apache Flink. In the rest of this book, we are going to see how Flink actually implements these concepts and how you can use its DataStream API to write applications that use all of the features we have introduced so far.

## CHAPTER 3

The Architecture of Apache Flink

Chapter 2 discussed important concepts of distributed stream processing, such as parallelization, time, and state. In this chapter, we give a high-level introduction to Flink's architecture and describe how Flink addresses the aspects of stream processing we discussed earlier. In particular, we explain Flink's distributed architecture, show how it handles time and state in streaming applications, and discuss its fault-tolerance mechanisms. This chapter provides relevant background information to successfully implement and operate advanced streaming applications with Apache Flink. It will help you to understand Flink's internals and to reason about the performance and behavior of streaming applications.

System Architecture

Flink is a distributed system for stateful parallel data stream processing. A Flink setup consists of multiple processes that typically run distributed across multiple machines. Common challenges that distributed systems need to address are allocation and management of compute resources in a cluster, process coordination, durable and highly available data storage, and failure recovery.

Flink does not implement all this functionality by itself. Instead, it focuses on its core function—distributed data stream processing—and leverages existing cluster infrastructure and services. Flink is well integrated with cluster resource managers, such as Apache Mesos, YARN, and Kubernetes, but can also be configured to run as a standalone cluster. Flink does not provide durable, distributed storage. Instead, it takes advantage of distributed filesystems like HDFS or object stores such as S3. For leader election in highly available setups, Flink depends on Apache ZooKeeper.

In this section, we describe the different components of a Flink setup and how they interact with each other to execute an application. We discuss two different styles of deploying Flink applications and the way each distributes and executes tasks. Finally, we explain how Flink's highly available mode works.

Components of a Flink Setup

A Flink setup consists of four different components that work together to execute streaming applications. These components are a JobManager, a ResourceManager, a TaskManager, and a Dispatcher. Since Flink is implemented in Java and Scala, all components run on Java Virtual Machines (JVMs). Each component has the following responsibilities:

- The *JobManager* is the master process that controls the execution of a single application—each application is controlled by a different JobManager. The JobManager receives an application for execution. The application consists of a so-called JobGraph, a logical dataflow graph (see "Introduction to Dataflow Programming"), and a JAR file that bundles all the required classes, libraries, and other resources. The JobManager converts the JobGraph into a physical dataflow graph called the ExecutionGraph, which consists of tasks that can be executed in parallel. The JobManager requests the necessary resources (TaskManager slots) to execute the tasks from the ResourceManager. Once it receives enough TaskManager slots, it distributes the tasks of the ExecutionGraph to the TaskManagers that execute them. During execution, the JobManager is responsible for all actions that require a central coordination such as the coordination of checkpoints (see "Checkpoints, Savepoints, and State Recovery").

- Flink features multiple *ResourceManagers* for different environments and resource providers such as YARN, Mesos, Kubernetes, and standalone deployments. The ResourceManager is responsible for managing TaskManager slots, Flink's unit of processing resources. When a JobManager requests TaskManager slots, the ResourceManager instructs a TaskManager with idle slots to offer them to the JobManager. If the ResourceManager does not have enough slots to fulfill the JobManager's request, the ResourceManager can talk to a resource provider to provision containers in which TaskManager processes are started. The ResourceManager also takes care of terminating idle TaskManagers to free compute resources.

- *TaskManagers* are the worker processes of Flink. Typically, there are multiple TaskManagers running in a Flink setup. Each TaskManager provides a certain number of slots. The number of slots limits the number of tasks a TaskManager can execute. After it has been started, a TaskManager registers its slots to the ResourceManager. When instructed by the ResourceManager, the TaskManager offers one or more of its slots to a JobManager. The JobManager can then assign tasks to the slots to execute them. During execution, a TaskManager exchanges data with other TaskManagers that run tasks of the same application. The execution of tasks and the concept of slots is discussed in "Task Execution".

- The *Dispatcher* runs across job executions and provides a REST interface to submit applications for execution. Once an application is submitted for execution, it starts a JobManager and hands the application over. The REST interface enables the dispatcher to serve as an HTTP entry point to clusters that are behind a firewall. The dispatcher also runs a web dashboard to provide information about job executions. Depending on how an application is submitted for execution (discussed in "Application Deployment"), a dispatcher might not be required.

Figure 3-1 shows how Flink's components interact with each other when an application is submitted for execution.

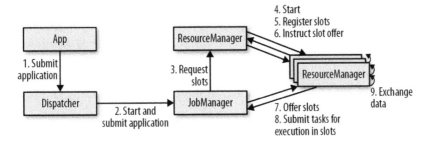

Figure 3-1. Application submission and component interactions

Figure 3-1 is a high-level sketch to visualize the responsibilities and interactions of the components of an application. Depending on the environment (YARN, Mesos, Kubernetes, standalone cluster), some steps can be omitted or components might run in the same JVM process. For instance, in a standalone setup—a setup without a resource provider—the ResourceManager can only distribute the slots of available TaskManagers and cannot start new TaskManagers on its own. In "Deployment Modes" on page 221, we will discuss how to set up and configure Flink for different environments.

Application Deployment

Flink applications can be deployed in two different styles.

Framework style
    In this mode, Flink applications are packaged into a JAR file and submitted by a client to a running service. The service can be a Flink Dispatcher, a Flink JobManager, or YARN's ResourceManager. In any case, there is a service running that accepts the Flink application and ensures it is executed. If the application was submitted to a JobManager, it immediately starts to execute the application.

If the application was submitted to a Dispatcher or YARN ResourceManager, it will spin up a JobManager and hand over the application, and the JobManager will start to execute the application.

Library style

In this mode, the Flink application is bundled in an application-specific container image, such as a Docker image. The image also includes the code to run a JobManager and ResourceManager. When a container is started from the image, it automatically launches the ResourceManager and JobManager and submits the bundled job for execution. A second, job-independent image is used to deploy TaskManager containers. A container that is started from this image automatically starts a TaskManager, which connects to the ResourceManager and registers its slots. Typically, an external resource manager such as Kubernetes takes care of starting the images and ensures that containers are restarted in case of a failure.

The framework style follows the traditional approach of submitting an application (or query) via a client to a running service. In the library style, there is no Flink service. Instead, Flink is bundled as a library together with the application in a container image. This deployment mode is common for microservices architectures. We discuss the topic of application deployment in more detail in "Running and Managing Streaming Applications" on page 245.

Task Execution

A TaskManager can execute several tasks at the same time. These tasks can be subtasks of the same operator (data parallelism), a different operator (task parallelism), or even from a different application (job parallelism). A TaskManager offers a certain number of processing slots to control the number of tasks it is able to concurrently execute. A processing slot can execute one slice of an application—one parallel task of each operator of the application. Figure 3-2 shows the relationships between TaskManagers, slots, tasks, and operators.

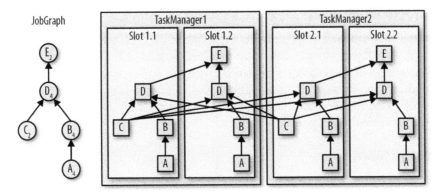

Figure 3-2. Operators, tasks, and processing slots

On the left-hand side of Figure 3-2 you see a JobGraph—the nonparallel representation of an application—consisting of five operators. Operators A and C are sources and operator E is a sink. Operators C and E have a parallelism of two. The other operators have a parallelism of four. Since the maximum operator parallelism is four, the application requires at least four available processing slots to be executed. Given two TaskManagers with two processing slots each, this requirement is fulfilled. The JobManager spans the JobGraph into an ExecutionGraph and assigns the tasks to the four available slots. The tasks of the operators with a parallelism of four are assigned to each slot. The two tasks of operators C and E are assigned to slots 1.1 and 2.1 and slots 1.2 and 2.2, respectively. Scheduling tasks as slices to slots has the advantage that many tasks are colocated on the TaskManager, which means they can efficiently exchange data within the the same process and without accessing the network. However, too many colocated tasks can also overload a TaskManager and result in bad performance. In "Controlling Task Scheduling" on page 260 we discuss how to control the scheduling of tasks.

A TaskManager executes its tasks multithreaded in the same JVM process. Threads are more lightweight than separate processes and have lower communication costs but do not strictly isolate tasks from each other. Hence, a single misbehaving task can kill a whole TaskManager process and all tasks that run on it. By configuring only a single slot per TaskManager, you can isolate applications across TaskManagers. By leveraging thread parallelism inside a TaskManager and deploying several TaskManager processes per host, Flink offers a lot of flexibility to trade off performance and resource isolation when deploying applications. We will discuss the configuration and setup of Flink clusters in detail in Chapter 9.

Highly Available Setup

Streaming applications are typically designed to run 24/7. Hence, it is important that their execution does not stop even if an involved process fails. To recover from failures, the system first needs to restart failed processes, and second, restart the application and recover its state. In this section, you will learn how Flink restarts failed processes. Restoring the state of an application is described in "Recovery from a Consistent Checkpoint" on page 60.

TaskManager failures

As discussed before, Flink requires a sufficient number of processing slots in order to execute all tasks of an application. Given a Flink setup with four TaskManagers that provide two slots each, a streaming application can be executed with a maximum parallelism of eight. If one of the TaskManagers fails, the number of available slots drops to six. In this situation, the JobManager will ask the ResourceManager to provide more processing slots. If this is not possible—for example, because the application runs in a standalone cluster—the JobManager can not restart the application until enough slots become available. The application's restart strategy determines how often the JobManager restarts the application and how long it waits between restart attempts.[1]

JobManager failures

A more challenging problem than TaskManager failures are JobManager failures. The JobManager controls the execution of a streaming application and keeps metadata about its execution, such as pointers to completed checkpoints. A streaming application cannot continue processing if the responsible JobManager process disappears. This makes the JobManager a single point of failure for applications in Flink. To overcome this problem, Flink supports a high-availability mode that migrates the responsibility and metadata for a job to another JobManager in case the original JobManager disappears.

Flink's high-availability mode is based on Apache ZooKeeper (*https:// zookeeper.apache.org/*), a system for distributed services that require coordination and consensus. Flink uses ZooKeeper for leader election and as a highly available and durable datastore. When operating in high-availability mode, the JobManager writes the JobGraph and all required metadata, such as the application's JAR file, into a remote persistent storage system. In addition, the JobManager writes a pointer to the storage location into ZooKeeper's datastore. During the execution of an application, the JobManager receives the state handles (storage locations) of the individual task

---

1 Restart strategies are discussed in more detail in Chapter 10.

checkpoints. Upon completion of a checkpoint—when all tasks have successfully written their state into the remote storage—the JobManager writes the state handles to the remote storage and a pointer to this location to ZooKeeper. Hence, all data that is required to recover from a JobManager failure is stored in the remote storage and ZooKeeper holds pointers to the storage locations. Figure 3-3 illustrates this design.

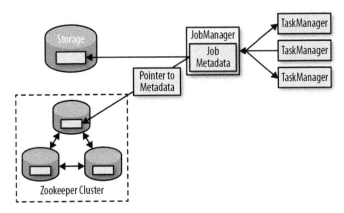

Figure 3-3. A highly available Flink setup

When a JobManager fails, all tasks that belong to its application are automatically cancelled. A new JobManager that takes over the work of the failed master performs the following steps:

1. It requests the storage locations from ZooKeeper to fetch the JobGraph, the JAR file, and the state handles of the last checkpoint of the application from the remote storage.

2. It requests processing slots from the ResourceManager to continue executing the application.

3. It restarts the application and resets the state of all its tasks to the last completed checkpoint.

When running an application as a library deployment in a container environment, such as Kubernetes, failed JobManager or TaskManager containers are usually automatically restarted by the container orchestration service. When running on YARN or on Mesos, Flink's remaining processes trigger the restart of JobManager or Task-Manager processes. Flink does not provide tooling to restart failed processes when running in a standalone cluster. Hence, it can be useful to run standby JobManagers and TaskManagers that can take over the work of failed processes. We will discuss the configuration of highly available Flink setups later in "Highly Available Setups".

Data Transfer in Flink

The tasks of a running application are continuously exchanging data. The TaskManagers take care of shipping data from sending tasks to receiving tasks. The network component of a TaskManager collects records in buffers before they are shipped, i.e., records are not shipped one by one but batched into buffers. This technique is fundamental to effectively using the networking resource and achieving high throughput. The mechanism is similar to the buffering techniques used in networking or disk I/O protocols.

Note that shipping records in buffers does imply that Flink's processing model is based on microbatches.

Each TaskManager has a pool of network buffers (by default 32 KB in size) to send and receive data. If the sender and receiver tasks run in separate TaskManager processes, they communicate via the network stack of the operating system. Streaming applications need to exchange data in a pipelined fashion—each pair of TaskManagers maintains a permanent TCP connection to exchange data.[2] With a shuffle connection pattern, each sender task needs to be able to send data to each receiving task. A TaskManager needs one dedicated network buffer for each receiving task that any of its tasks need to send data to. Figure 3-4 shows this architecture.

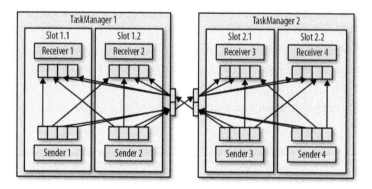

Figure 3-4. Data transfer between TaskManagers

---

2 Batch applications can—in addition to pipelined communication—exchange data by collecting outgoing data at the sender. Once the sender task completes, the data is sent as a batch over a temporary TCP connection to the receiver.

As shown in Figure 3-4, each of the four sender tasks needs at least four network buffers to send data to each of the receiver tasks and each receiver task requires at least four buffers to receive data. Buffers that need to be sent to the other TaskManager are multiplexed over the same network connection. In order to enable a smooth pipelined data exchange, a TaskManager must be able to provide enough buffers to serve all outgoing and incoming connections concurrently. With a shuffle or broadcast connection, each sending task needs a buffer for each receiving task; the number of required buffers is quadratic to the number of tasks of the involved operators. Flink's default configuration for network buffers is sufficient for small- to medium-sized setups. For larger setups, you need to tune the configuration as described in "Main Memory and Network Buffers" on page 240.

When a sender task and a receiver task run in the same TaskManager process, the sender task serializes the outgoing records into a byte buffer and puts the buffer into a queue once it is filled. The receiving task takes the buffer from the queue and deserializes the incoming records. Hence, data transfer between tasks that run on the same TaskManager does not cause network communication.

Flink features different techniques to reduce the communication costs between tasks. In the following sections, we briefly discuss credit-based flow control and task chaining.

Credit-Based Flow Control

Sending individual records over a network connection is inefficient and causes significant overhead. Buffering is needed to fully utilize the bandwidth of network connections. In the context of stream processing, one disadvantage of buffering is that it adds latency because records are collected in a buffer instead of being immediately shipped.

Flink implements a credit-based flow control mechanism that works as follows. A receiving task grants some credit to a sending task, the number of network buffers that are reserved to receive its data. Once a sender receives a credit notification, it ships as many buffers as it was granted and the size of its backlog—the number of network buffers that are filled and ready to be shipped. The receiver processes the shipped data with the reserved buffers and uses the sender's backlog size to prioritize the next credit grants for all its connected senders.

Credit-based flow control reduces latency because senders can ship data as soon as the receiver has enough resources to accept it. Moreover, it is an effective mechanism to distribute network resources in the case of skewed data distributions because credit is granted based on the size of the senders' backlog. Hence, credit-based flow control is an important building block for Flink to achieve high throughput and low latency.

Task Chaining

Flink features an optimization technique called task chaining that reduces the overhead of local communication under certain conditions. In order to satisfy the requirements for task chaining, two or more operators must be configured with the same parallelism and connected by local forward channels. The operator pipeline shown in Figure 3-5 fulfills these requirements. It consists of three operators that are all configured for a task parallelism of two and connected with local forward connections.

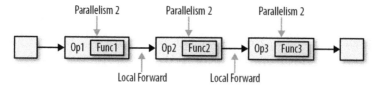

Figure 3-5. An operator pipeline that complies with the requirements of task chaining

Figure 3-6 depicts how the pipeline is executed with task chaining. The functions of the operators are fused into a single task that is executed by a single thread. Records that are produced by a function are separately handed over to the next function with a simple method call. Hence, there are basically no serialization and communication costs for passing records between functions.

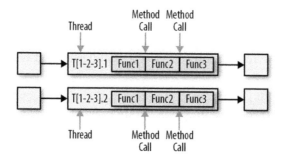

Figure 3-6. Chained task execution with fused functions in a single thread and data passing via method calls

Task chaining can significantly reduce the communication costs between local tasks, but there are also cases when it makes sense to execute a pipeline without chaining. For example, it can make sense to break a long pipeline of chained tasks or break a chain into two tasks to schedule an expensive function to different slots. Figure 3-7 shows the same pipeline executed without task chaining. All functions are evaluated by an individual task running in a dedicated thread.

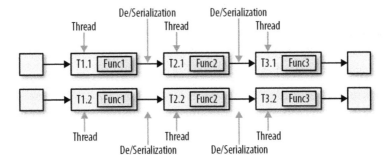

Figure 3-7. Nonchained task execution with dedicated threads and data transport via buffer channels and serialization

Task chaining is enabled by default in Flink. In "Controlling Task Chaining" on page 261, we show how to disable task chaining for an application and how to control the chaining behavior of individual operators.

Event-Time Processing

In "Time Semantics" on page 27, we highlighted the importance of time semantics for stream processing applications and explained the differences between processing time and event time. While processing time is easy to understand because it is based on the local time of the processing machine, it produces somewhat arbitrary, inconsistent, and nonreproducible results. In contrast, event-time semantics yield reproducible and consistent results, which is a hard requirement for many stream processing use cases. However, event-time applications require additional configuration compared to applications with processing-time semantics. Also, the internals of a stream processor that supports event time are more involved than the internals of a system that purely operates in processing time.

Flink provides intuitive and easy-to-use primitives for common event-time processing operations but also exposes expressive APIs to implement more advanced event-time applications with custom operators. For such advanced applications, a good understanding of Flink's internal time handling is often helpful and sometimes required. The previous chapter introduced two concepts Flink leverages to provide event-time semantics: record timestamps and watermarks. In the following, we describe how Flink internally implements and handles timestamps and watermarks to support streaming applications with event-time semantics.

Timestamps

All records that are processed by a Flink event-time streaming application must be accompanied by a timestamp. The timestamp associates a record with a specific point in time, usually the point in time at which the event that is represented by the record happened. However, applications can freely choose the meaning of the timestamps as long as the timestamps of the stream records are roughly ascending as the stream is advancing. As seen in "Time Semantics", a certain degree of timestamp out-of-orderness is given in basically all real-world use cases.

When Flink processes a data stream in event-time mode, it evaluates time-based operators based on the timestamps of records. For example, a time-window operator assigns records to windows according to their associated timestamp. Flink encodes timestamps as 16-byte Long values and attaches them as metadata to records. Its built-in operators interpret the Long value as a Unix timestamp with millisecond precision—the number of milliseconds since 1970-01-01-00:00:00.000. However, custom operators can have their own interpretation and may, for example, adjust the precision to microseconds.

Watermarks

In addition to record timestamps, a Flink event-time application must also provide watermarks. Watermarks are used to derive the current event time at each task in an event-time application. Time-based operators use this time to trigger computations and make progress. For example, a time-window task finalizes a window computation and emits the result when the task event-time passes the window's end boundary.

In Flink, watermarks are implemented as special records holding a timestamp as a Long value. Watermarks flow in a stream of regular records with annotated timestamps as Figure 3-8 shows.

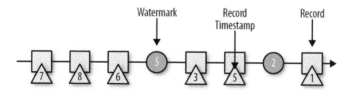

Figure 3-8. A stream with timestamped records and watermarks

Watermarks have two basic properties:

1. They must be monotonically increasing to ensure the event-time clocks of tasks are progressing and not going backward.
2. They are related to record timestamps. A watermark with a timestamp T indicates that all subsequent records should have timestamps > T.

The second property is used to handle streams with out-of-order record timestamps, such as the records with timestamps 3 and 5 in Figure 3-8. Tasks of time-based operators collect and process records with possibly unordered timestamps and finalize a computation when their event-time clock, which is advanced by the received watermarks, indicates that no more records with relevant timestamps are expected. When a task receives a record that violates the watermark property and has smaller timestamps than a previously received watermark, it may be that the computation it belongs to has already been completed. Such records are called late records. Flink provides different ways to deal with late records, which are discussed in "Handling Late Data" on page 148.

An interesting property of watermarks is that they allow an application to control result completeness and latency. Watermarks that are very tight—close to the record timestamps—result in low processing latency because a task will only briefly wait for more records to arrive before finalizing a computation. At the same time, the result completeness might suffer because relevant records might not be included in the result and would be considered as late records. Inversely, very conservative watermarks increase processing latency but improve result completeness.

Watermark Propagation and Event Time

In this section, we discuss how operators process watermarks. Flink implements watermarks as special records that are received and emitted by operator tasks. Tasks have an internal time service that maintains timers and is activated when a watermark is received. Tasks can register timers at the timer service to perform a computation at a specific point in time in the future. For example, a window operator registers a timer for every active window, which cleans up the window's state when the event time passes the window's ending time.

When a task receives a watermark, the following actions take place:

1. The task updates its internal event-time clock based on the watermark's timestamp.
2. The task's time service identifies all timers with a time smaller than the updated event time. For each expired timer, the task invokes a callback function that can perform a computation and emit records.
3. The task emits a watermark with the updated event time.

Flink restricts access to timestamps or watermarks through the DataStream API. Functions cannot read or modify record timestamps and watermarks, except for the process functions, which can read the timestamp of a currently processed record, request the current event time of the operator, and register timers.[3] None of the functions exposes an API to set the timestamps of emitted records, manipulate the event-time clock of a task, or emit watermarks. Instead, time-based DataStream operator tasks configure the timestamps of emitted records to ensure they are properly aligned with the emitted watermarks. For instance, a time-window operator task attaches the end time of a window as the timestamp to all records emitted by the window computation before it emits the watermark with the timestamp that triggered the computation of the window.

Let's now explain in more detail how a task emits watermarks and updates its event-time clock when receiving a new watermark. As you saw in "Data Parallelism and Task Parallelism" on page 18, Flink splits data streams into partitions and processes each partition in parallel by a separate operator task. Each partition is a stream of timestamped records and watermarks. Depending on how an operator is connected with its predecessor or successor operators, its tasks can receive records and watermarks from one or more input partitions and emit records and watermarks to one or more output partitions. In the following, we describe in detail how a task emits watermarks to multiple output tasks and how it advances its event-time clock from the watermarks it receives from its input tasks.

A task maintains a partition watermark for each input partition. When it receives a watermark from a partition, it updates the respective partition watermark to be the maximum of the received value and the current value. Subsequently, the task updates its event-time clock to be the minimum of all partition watermarks. If the event-time clock advances, the task processes all triggered timers and finally broadcasts its new event time to all downstream tasks by emitting a corresponding watermark to all connected output partitions.

Figure 3-9 shows how a task with four input partitions and three output partitions receives watermarks, updates its partition watermarks and event-time clock, and emits watermarks.

---

3 Process functions are discussed in more detail in Chapter 6.

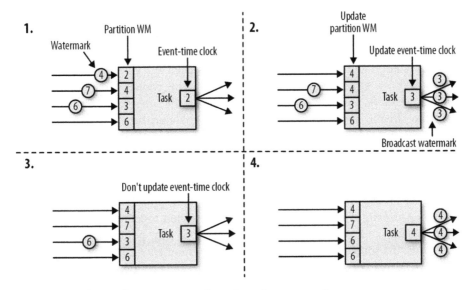

Figure 3-9. Updating the event time of a task with watermarks

The tasks of operators with two or more input streams such as Union or CoFlatMap (see "Multistream Transformations") also compute their event-time clock as the minimum of all partition watermarks—they do not distinguish between partition watermarks of different input streams. Consequently, records of both inputs are processed based on the same event-time clock. This behavior can cause problems if the event times of the individual input streams of an application are not aligned.

Flink's watermark-handling and propagation algorithm ensures operator tasks emit properly aligned timestamped records and watermarks. However, it relies on the fact that all partitions continuously provide increasing watermarks. As soon as one partition does not advance its watermarks or becomes completely idle and does not ship any records or watermarks, the event-time clock of a task will not advance and the timers of the task will not trigger. This situation can be problematic for time-based operators that rely on an advancing clock to perform computations and clean up their state. Consequently, the processing latencies and state size of time-based operators can significantly increase if a task does not receive new watermarks from all input tasks at regular intervals.

A similar effect appears for operators with two input streams whose watermarks significantly diverge. The event-time clocks of a task with two input streams will correspond to the watermarks of the slower stream and usually the records or intermediate results of the faster stream are buffered in state until the event-time clock allows processing them.

Timestamp Assignment and Watermark Generation

So far we have explained what timestamps and watermarks are and how they are internally handled by Flink. However, we have not yet discussed where they originate from. Timestamps and watermarks are usually assigned and generated when a stream is ingested by a streaming application. Because the choice of the timestamp is application-specific and the watermarks depend on the timestamps and characteristics of the stream, applications have to explicitly assign timestamps and generate watermarks. A Flink DataStream application can assign timestamps and generate watermarks to a stream in three ways:

1. At the source: Timestamps and watermarks can be assigned and generated by a `SourceFunction` when a stream is ingested into an application. A source function emits a stream of records. Records can be emitted together with an associated timestamp, and watermarks can be emitted at any point in time as special records. If a source function (temporarily) does not emit anymore watermarks, it can declare itself idle. Flink will exclude stream partitions produced by idle source functions from the watermark computation of subsequent operators. The idle mechanism of sources can be used to address the problem of not advancing watermarks as discussed earlier. Source functions are discussed in more detail in "Implementing a Custom Source Function" on page 202.

2. Periodic assigner: The DataStream API provides a user-defined function called `AssignerWithPeriodicWatermarks` that extracts a timestamp from each record and is periodically queried for the current watermark. The extracted timestamps are assigned to the respective record and the queried watermarks are ingested into the stream. This function will be discussed in "Assigning Timestamps and Generating Watermarks" on page 111.

3. Punctuated assigner: `AssignerWithPunctuatedWatermarks` is another user-defined function that extracts a timestamp from each record. It can be used to generate watermarks that are encoded in special input records. In contrast to the `AssignerWithPeriodicWatermarks` function, this function can—but does not need to—extract a watermark from each record. We discuss this function in detail in "Assigning Timestamps and Generating Watermarks" as well.

User-defined timestamp assignment functions are usually applied as close to a source operator as possible because it can be very difficult to reason about the order of records and their timestamps after they have been processed by an operator. This is also the reason it is not a good idea to override existing timestamps and watermarks in the middle of a streaming application, although this is possible with user-defined functions.

State Management

In Chapter 2 we pointed out that most streaming applications are stateful. Many operators continuously read and update some kind of state such as records collected in a window, reading positions of an input source, or custom, application-specific operator states like machine learning models. Flink treats all states—regardless of built-in or user-defined operators—the same. In this section, we discuss the different types of states Flink supports. We explain how state is stored and maintained by state backends and how stateful applications can be scaled by redistributing state.

In general, all data maintained by a task and used to compute the results of a function belong to the state of the task. You can think of state as a local or instance variable that is accessed by a task's business logic. Figure 3-10 shows the typical interaction between a task and its state.

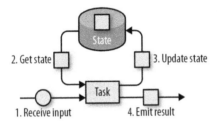

Figure 3-10. A stateful stream processing task

A task receives some input data. While processing the data, the task can read and update its state and compute its result based on its input data and state. A simple example is a task that continuously counts how many records it receives. When the task receives a new record, it accesses the state to get the current count, increments the count, updates the state, and emits the new count.

The application logic to read from and write to state is often straightforward. However, efficient and reliable management of state is more challenging. This includes handling of very large states, possibly exceeding memory, and ensuring that no state is lost in case of failures. All issues related to state consistency, failure handling, and efficient storage and access are taken care of by Flink so that developers can focus on the logic of their applications.

In Flink, state is always associated with a specific operator. In order to make Flink's runtime aware of the state of an operator, the operator needs to register its state. There are two types of state, *operator state* and *keyed state*, that are accessible from different scopes and discussed in the following sections.

Operator State

Operator state is scoped to an operator task. This means that all records processed by the same parallel task have access to the same state. Operator state cannot be accessed by another task of the same or a different operator. Figure 3-11 shows how tasks access operator state.

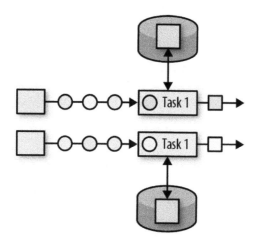

Figure 3-11. Tasks with operator state

Flink offers three primitives for operator state:

List state
> Represents state as a list of entries.

Union list state
> Represents state as a list of entries as well. But it differs from regular list state in how it is restored in the case of a failure or when an application is started from a savepoint. We discuss this difference later in this chapter.

Broadcast state
> Designed for the special case where the state of each task of an operator is identical. This property can be leveraged during checkpoints and when rescaling an operator. Both aspects are discussed in later sections of this chapter.

Keyed State

Keyed state is maintained and accessed with respect to a key defined in the records of an operator's input stream. Flink maintains one state instance per key value and partitions all records with the same key to the operator task that maintains the state for this key. When a task processes a record, it automatically scopes the state access to the key of the current record. Consequently, all records with the same key access the same state. Figure 3-12 shows how tasks interact with keyed state.

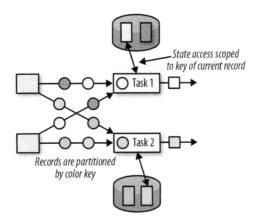

Figure 3-12. Tasks with keyed state

You can think of keyed state as a key-value map that is partitioned (or sharded) on the key across all parallel tasks of an operator. Flink provides different primitives for keyed state that determine the type of the value stored for each key in this distributed key-value map. We will briefly discuss the most common keyed state primitives.

Value state
> Stores a single value of arbitrary type per key. Complex data structures can also be stored as value state.

List state
> Stores a list of values per key. The list entries can be of arbitrary type.

Map state
> Stores a key-value map per key. The key and value of the map can be of arbitrary type.

State primitives expose the structure of the state to Flink and enable more efficient state accesses. They are discussed further in "Declaring Keyed State at RuntimeContext" on page 154.

State Backends

A task of a stateful operator typically reads and updates its state for each incoming record. Because efficient state access is crucial to processing records with low latency, each parallel task locally maintains its state to ensure fast state accesses. How exactly the state is stored, accessed, and maintained is determined by a pluggable component that is called a state backend. A state backend is responsible for two things: local state management and checkpointing state to a remote location.

For local state management, a state backend stores all keyed states and ensures that all accesses are correctly scoped to the current key. Flink provides state backends that manage keyed state as objects stored in in-memory data structures on the JVM heap. Another state backend serializes state objects and puts them into RocksDB, which writes them to local hard disks. While the first option gives very fast state access, it is limited by the size of the memory. Accessing state stored by the RocksDB state backend is slower but its state may grow very large.

State checkpointing is important because Flink is a distributed system and state is only locally maintained. A TaskManager process (and with it, all tasks running on it) may fail at any point in time. Hence, its storage must be considered volatile. A state backend takes care of checkpointing the state of a task to a remote and persistent storage. The remote storage for checkpointing could be a distributed filesystem or a database system. State backends differ in how state is checkpointed. For instance, the RocksDB state backend supports incremental checkpoints, which can significantly reduce the checkpointing overhead for very large state sizes.

We will discuss the different state backends and their advantages and disadvantages in more detail in "Choosing a State Backend" on page 169.

Scaling Stateful Operators

A common requirement for streaming applications is to adjust the parallelism of operators due to increasing or decreasing input rates. While scaling stateless operators is trivial, changing the parallelism of stateful operators is much more challenging because their state needs to be repartitioned and assigned to more or fewer parallel tasks. Flink supports four patterns for scaling different types of state.

Operators with keyed state are scaled by repartitioning keys to fewer or more tasks. However, to improve the efficiency of the necessary state transfer between tasks, Flink does not redistribute individual keys. Instead, Flink organizes keys in so-called key groups. A key group is a partition of keys and Flink's way of assigning keys to tasks. Figure 3-13 shows how keyed state is repartitioned in key groups.

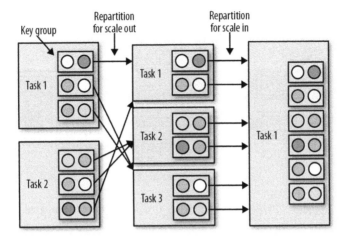

Figure 3-13. Scaling an operator with keyed state out and in

Operators with operator list state are scaled by redistributing the list entries. Conceptually, the list entries of all parallel operator tasks are collected and evenly redistributed to a smaller or larger number of tasks. If there are fewer list entries than the new parallelism of an operator, some tasks will start with empty state. Figure 3-14 shows the redistribution of operator list state.

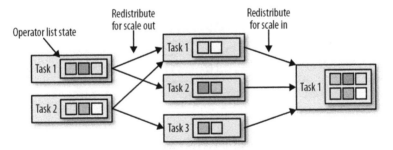

Figure 3-14. Scaling an operator with operator list state out and in

Operators with operator union list state are scaled by broadcasting the full list of state entries to each task. The task can then choose which entries to use and which to discard. Figure 3-15 shows how operator union list state is redistributed.

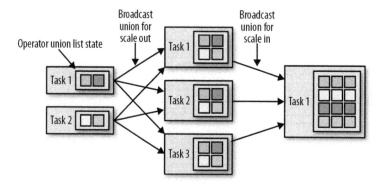

Figure 3-15. Scaling an operator with operator union list state out and in

Operators with operator broadcast state are scaled up by copying the state to new tasks. This works because broadcasting state ensures that all tasks have the same state. In the case of downscaling, the surplus tasks are simply canceled since state is already replicated and will not be lost. Figure 3-16 shows the redistribution of operator broadcast state.

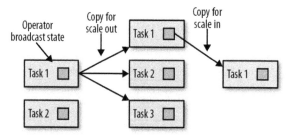

Figure 3-16. Scaling an operator with operator broadcast state out and in

Checkpoints, Savepoints, and State Recovery

Flink is a distributed data processing system, and as such, has to deal with failures such as killed processes, failing machines, and interrupted network connections. Since tasks maintain their state locally, Flink has to ensure that this state is not lost and remains consistent in case of a failure.

In this section, we present Flink's checkpointing and recovery mechanism to guarantee exactly-once state consistency. We also discuss Flink's unique savepoint feature, a "Swiss Army knife"-like tool that addresses many challenges of operating streaming applications.

Consistent Checkpoints

Flink's recovery mechanism is based on consistent checkpoints of application state. A consistent checkpoint of a stateful streaming application is a copy of the state of each of its tasks at a point when all tasks have processed exactly the same input. This can be explained by looking at the steps of a naive algorithm that takes a consistent checkpoint of an application. The steps of this naive algorithm would be:

1. Pause the ingestion of all input streams.

2. Wait for all in-flight data to be completely processed, meaning all tasks have processed all their input data.

3. Take a checkpoint by copying the state of each task to a remote, persistent storage. The checkpoint is complete when all tasks have finished their copies.

4. Resume the ingestion of all streams.

Note that Flink does not implement this naive mechanism. We will present Flink's more sophisticated checkpointing algorithm later in this section.

Figure 3-17 shows a consistent checkpoint of a simple application.

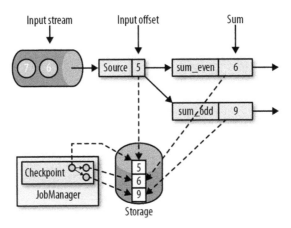

Figure 3-17. A consistent checkpoint of a streaming application

The application has a single source task that consumes a stream of increasing numbers—1, 2, 3, and so on. The stream of numbers is partitioned into a stream of even and odd numbers. Two tasks of a sum operator compute the running sums of all even and odd numbers. The source task stores the current offset of its input stream as state. The sum tasks persist the current sum value as state. In Figure 3-17, Flink took a checkpoint when the input offset was 5, and the sums were 6 and 9.

Recovery from a Consistent Checkpoint

During the execution of a streaming application, Flink periodically takes consistent checkpoints of the application's state. In case of a failure, Flink uses the latest checkpoint to consistently restore the application's state and restarts the processing. Figure 3-18 shows the recovery process.

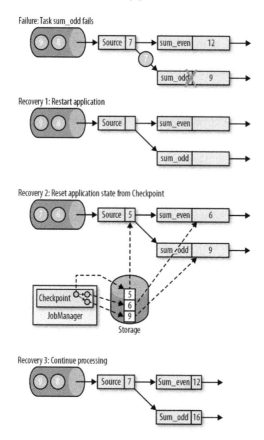

Figure 3-18. Recovering an application from a checkpoint

An application is recovered in three steps:

1. Restart the whole application.
2. Reset the states of all stateful tasks to the latest checkpoint.
3. Resume the processing of all tasks.

This checkpointing and recovery mechanism can provide exactly-once consistency for application state, given that all operators checkpoint and restore all of their states

---

and that all input streams are reset to the position up to which they were consumed when the checkpoint was taken. Whether a data source can reset its input stream depends on its implementation and the external system or interface from which the stream is consumed. For instance, event logs like Apache Kafka can provide records from a previous offset of the stream. In contrast, a stream consumed from a socket cannot be reset because sockets discard data once it has been consumed. Consequently, an application can only be operated under exactly-once state consistency if all input streams are consumed by resettable data sources.

After an application is restarted from a checkpoint, its internal state is exactly the same as when the checkpoint was taken. It then starts to consume and process all data that was processed between the checkpoint and the failure. Although this means Flink processes some messages twice (before and after the failure), the mechanism still achieves *exactly-once state consistency* because the state of all operators was reset to a point that had not seen this data yet.

We have to point out that Flink's checkpointing and recovery mechanism only resets the *internal state* of a streaming application. Depending on the sink operators of an application, some result records might be emitted multiple times to downstream systems, such as an event log, a filesystem, or a database, during the recovery. For some storage systems, Flink provides sink functions that feature exactly-once output, for example, by committing emitted records on checkpoint completion. Another approach that works for many storage systems is idempotent updates. The challenges of end-to-end exactly-once applications and approaches to address them are discussed in detail in "Application Consistency Guarantees" on page 184.

Flink's Checkpointing Algorithm

Flink's recovery mechanism is based on consistent application checkpoints. The naive approach to taking a checkpoint from a streaming application—to pause, checkpoint, and resume the application—is not practical for applications that have even moderate latency requirements due to its "stop-the-world" behavior. Instead, Flink implements checkpointing based on the Chandy–Lamport algorithm for distributed snapshots. The algorithm does not pause the complete application but decouples checkpointing from processing, so that some tasks continue processing while others persist their state. In the following, we explain how this algorithm works.

Flink's checkpointing algorithm uses a special type of record called a *checkpoint barrier*. Similar to watermarks, checkpoint barriers are injected by source operators into the regular stream of records and cannot overtake or be passed by other records. A checkpoint barrier carries a checkpoint ID to identify the checkpoint it belongs to and logically splits a stream into two parts. All state modifications due to records that precede a barrier are included in the barrier's checkpoint and all modifications due to records that follow the barrier are included in a later checkpoint.

We use an example of a simple streaming application to explain the algorithm step by step. The application consists of two source tasks that each consume a stream of increasing numbers. The output of the source tasks is partitioned into streams of even and odd numbers. Each partition is processed by a task that computes the sum of all received numbers and forwards the updated sum to a sink. The application is depicted in Figure 3-19.

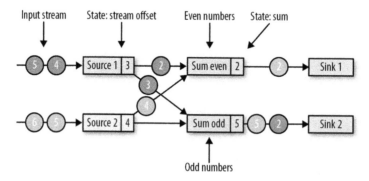

Figure 3-19. Streaming application with two stateful sources, two stateful tasks, and two stateless sinks

A checkpoint is initiated by the JobManager by sending a message with a new checkpoint ID to each data source task as shown in Figure 3-20.

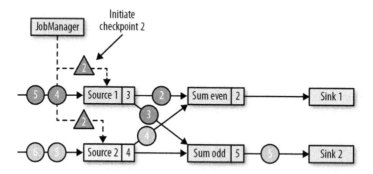

Figure 3-20. JobManager initiates a checkpoint by sending a message to all sources

When a data source task receives the message, it pauses emitting records, triggers a checkpoint of its local state at the state backend, and broadcasts checkpoint barriers with the checkpoint ID via all outgoing stream partitions. The state backend notifies the task once its state checkpoint is complete and the task acknowledges the checkpoint at the JobManager. After all barriers are sent out, the source continues its regular operations. By injecting the barrier into its output stream, the source function defines the stream position on which the checkpoint is taken. Figure 3-21 shows the streaming application after both source tasks checkpointed their local state and emitted checkpoint barriers.

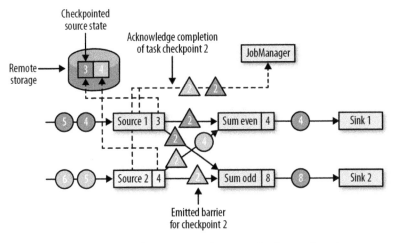

Figure 3-21. Sources checkpoint their state and emit a checkpoint barrier

The checkpoint barriers emitted by the source tasks are shipped to the connected tasks. Similar to watermarks, checkpoint barriers are broadcasted to all connected parallel tasks to ensure that each task receives a barrier from each of its input streams. When a task receives a barrier for a new checkpoint, it waits for the arrival of barriers from all its input partitions for the checkpoint. While it is waiting, it continues processing records from stream partitions that did not provide a barrier yet. Records that arrive on partitions that forwarded a barrier already cannot be processed and are buffered. The process of waiting for all barriers to arrive is called *barrier alignment*, and it is depicted in Figure 3-22.

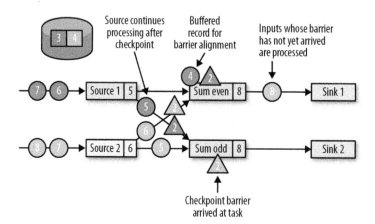

Figure 3-22. Tasks wait to receive a barrier on each input partition; records from input streams for which a barrier already arrived are buffered; all other records are regularly processed

As soon as a task has received barriers from all its input partitions, it initiates a checkpoint at the state backend and broadcasts the checkpoint barrier to all of its downstream connected tasks as shown in Figure 3-23.

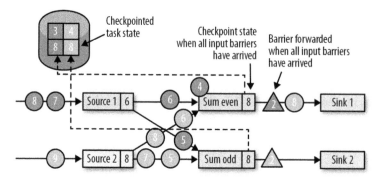

Figure 3-23. Tasks checkpoint their state once all barriers have been received, then they forward the checkpoint barrier

Once all checkpoint barriers have been emitted, the task starts to process the buffered records. After all buffered records have been emitted, the task continues processing its input streams. Figure 3-24 shows the application at this point.

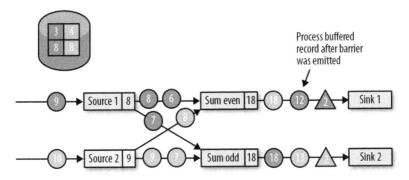

Figure 3-24. Tasks continue regular processing after the checkpoint barrier is forwarded

Eventually, the checkpoint barriers arrive at a sink task. When a sink task receives a barrier, it performs a barrier alignment, checkpoints its own state, and acknowledges the reception of the barrier to the JobManager. The JobManager records the checkpoint of an application as completed once it has received a checkpoint acknowledgement from all tasks of the application. Figure 3-25 shows the final step of the checkpointing algorithm. The completed checkpoint can be used to recover the application from a failure as described before.

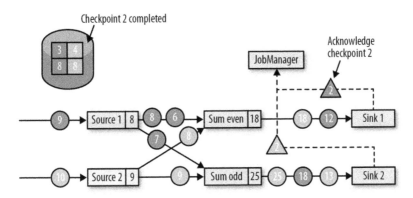

Figure 3-25. Sinks acknowledge the reception of a checkpoint barrier to the JobManager and a checkpoint is complete when all tasks have acknowledged the successful checkpointing of their state

Performace Implications of Checkpointing

Flink's checkpointing algorithm produces consistent distributed checkpoints from streaming applications without stopping the whole application. However, it can increase the processing latency of an application. Flink implements tweaks that can alleviate the performance impact under certain conditions.

While a task checkpoints its state, it is blocked and its input is buffered. Since state can become quite large and checkpointing requires writing the data over the network to a remote storage system, taking a checkpoint can easily take several seconds to minutes—much too long for latency-sensitive applications. In Flink's design it is the responsibility of the state backend to perform a checkpoint. How exactly the state of a task is copied depends on the implementation of the state backend. For example, the FileSystem state backend and the RocksDB state backend support *asynchronous* checkpoints. When a checkpoint is triggered, the state backend creates a local copy of the state. When the local copy is finished, the task continues its regular processing. A background thread asynchronously copies the local snapshot to the remote storage and notifies the task once it completes the checkpoint. Asynchronous checkpointing significantly reduces the time until a task continues to process data. In addition, the RocksDB state backend also features *incremental* checkpointing, which reduces the amount of data to transfer.

Another technique to reduce the checkpointing algorithm's impact on the processing latency is to tweak the barrier alignment step. For applications that require very low latency and can tolerate at-least-once state guarantees, Flink can be configured to process all arriving records during buffer alignment instead of buffering those for which the barrier has already arrived. Once all barriers for a checkpoint have arrived, the operator checkpoints the state, which might now also include modifications caused by records that would usually belong to the next checkpoint. In case of a failure, these records will be processed again, which means the checkpoint provides at-least-once instead of exactly-once consistency guarantees.

Savepoints

Flink's recovery algorithm is based on state checkpoints. Checkpoints are periodically taken and automatically discarded according to a configurable policy. Since the purpose of checkpoints is to ensure an application can be restarted in case of a failure, they are deleted when an application is explicitly canceled.[4] However, consistent snapshots of the state of an application can be used for many more things than just failure recovery.

One of Flink's most valued and unique features are savepoints. In principle, savepoints are created using the same algorithm as checkpoints and hence are basically checkpoints with some additional metadata. Flink does not automatically take a savepoint, so a user (or external scheduler) has to explicitly trigger its creation. Flink also

---

4 It is also possible to configure an application to retain its last checkpoint when it is canceled.

does not automatically clean up savepoints. Chapter 10 describes how to trigger and dispose savepoints.

Using savepoints

Given an application and a compatible savepoint, you can start the application from the savepoint. This will initialize the state of the application to the state of the savepoint and run the application from the point at which the savepoint was taken. While this behavior seems to be exactly the same as recovering an application from a failure using a checkpoint, failure recovery is actually just a special case. It starts the same application with the same configuration on the same cluster. Starting an application from a savepoint allows you to do much more.

- You can start a *different but compatible* application from a savepoint. Hence, you can fix bugs in your application logic and reprocess as many events as your streaming source can provide in order to repair your results. Modified applications can also be used to run A/B tests or what-if scenarios with different business logic. Note that the application and the savepoint must be compatible—the application must be able to load the state of the savepoint.

- You can start the same application with a *different parallelism* and scale the application out or in.

- You can start the same application on a *different cluster*. This allows you to migrate an application to a newer Flink version or to a different cluster or datacenter.

- You can use a savepoint to *pause* an application and *resume* it later. This gives the possibility to release cluster resources for higher-priority applications or when input data is not continuously produced.

- You can also just take a savepoint to *version* and *archive* the state of an application.

Since savepoints are such a powerful feature, many users periodically create savepoints to be able to go back in time. One of the most interesting applications of savepoints we have seen in the wild is continuously migrating a streaming application to the datacenter that provides the lowest instance prices.

Starting an application from a savepoint

All of the previously mentioned use cases for savepoints follow the same pattern. First, a savepoint of a running application is taken and then it is used to restore the state in a starting application. In this section, we describe how Flink initializes the state of an application started from a savepoint.

An application consists of multiple operators. Each operator can define one or more keyed and operator states. Operators are executed in parallel by one or more operator tasks. Hence, a typical application consists of multiple states that are distributed across multiple operator tasks that can run on different TaskManager processes.

Figure 3-26 shows an application with three operators, each running with two tasks. One operator (OP-1) has a single operator state (OS-1) and another operator (OP-2) has two keyed states (KS-1 and KS-2). When a savepoint is taken, the states of all tasks are copied to a persistent storage location.

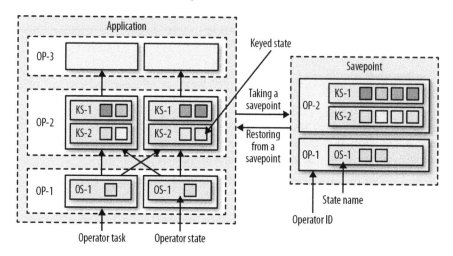

Figure 3-26. Taking a savepoint from an application and restoring an application from a savepoint

The state copies in the savepoint are organized by an operator identifier and a state name. The operator identifier and state name are required to be able to map the state data of a savepoint to the states of the operators of a starting application. When an application is started from a savepoint, Flink redistributes the savepoint data to the tasks of the corresponding operators.

 Note that the savepoint does not contain information about operator tasks. That is because the number of tasks might change when an application is started with different parallelism. We discussed Flink's strategies to scale stateful operators earlier in this section.

If a modified application is started from a savepoint, a state in the savepoint can only be mapped to the application if it contains an operator with a corresponding identifier and state name. By default, Flink assigns unique operator identifiers. However, the identifier of an operator is deterministically generated based on the identifiers of its preceding operators. Hence, the identifier of an operator changes when one of its predecessors changes, for example, when an operator is added or removed. As a consequence, an application with default operator identifiers is very limited in how it can be evolved without losing state. Therefore, we strongly recommend manually assigning unique identifiers to operators and not relying on Flink's default assignment. We describe how to assign operator identifiers in detail in "Specifying Unique Operator Identifiers" on page 168.

Summary

In this chapter we discussed Flink's high-level architecture and the internals of its networking stack, event-time processing mode, state management, and failure recovery mechanism. This information will come in handy when designing advanced streaming applications, setting up and configuring clusters, and operating streaming applications as well as reasoning about their performance.

## CHAPTER 4

Setting Up a Development Environment for Apache Flink

Now that we have all that knowledge, it's time to get our hands dirty and start developing Flink applications! In this chapter, you will learn how to set up an environment to develop, run, and debug Flink applications. We will start by discussing the required software and where you can get the code examples of this book. Using these examples, we will show how Flink applications are executed and debugged in an IDE. Finally, we show how to bootstrap a Flink Maven project, the starting point for a new application.

Required Software

First, let's discuss the software you need to develop Flink applications. You can develop and execute Flink applications on Linux, macOS, and Windows. However, UNIX-based setups enjoy the richest tooling support because this environment is preferred by most Flink developers. We will be assuming a UNIX-based setup in the rest of this chapter. As a Windows user you can use the Windows subsystem for Linux (WSL), Cygwin, or a Linux virtual machine to run Flink in a UNIX environment.

Flink's DataStream API is available for Java and Scala. Hence, a Java JDK is required to implement Flink DataStream applications—Java JDK 8 (or higher). A Java JRE is not sufficient.

We assume the following software is installed as well, although it is not strictly required to develop Flink applications:

- Apache Maven 3.x. The code examples of the book use Maven build management. Moreover, Flink provides Maven archetypes to bootstrap new Flink Maven projects.
- An IDE for Java and/or Scala development. Common choices are IntelliJ IDEA, Eclipse, or Netbeans with the appropriate plugins (such as for Maven, Git, and Scala support). We recommend using IntelliJ IDEA. You can follow the instructions at the IntelliJ IDEA website (*http://bit.ly/1yi9UP3*)to download and install it.

Run and Debug Flink Applications in an IDE

Even though Flink is a distributed data processing system, you will typically develop and run initial tests on your local machine. This makes development easier and simplifies cluster deployment, as you can run the exact same code in a cluster environment without making any changes. In the following, we describe how to obtain the code examples we use here, how to import them into IntelliJ, how to run an example application, and how to debug it.

Import the Book's Examples in an IDE

The code examples of this book are hosted on GitHub. At the book's GitHub page (*http://github.com/streaming-with-flink*), you will find one repository with Scala examples and one repository with Java examples. We will be using the Scala repository for the setup, but you should be able to follow the same instructions if you prefer Java.

Open a terminal and run the following Git command to clone the `examples-scala` repository to your local machine:[1]

```
> git clone https://github.com/streaming-with-flink/examples-scala
```

---

[1] We also provide an `examples-Java` repository (*https://github.com/streaming-with-flink/examples-java*) with all the examples implemented in Java.

You can also download the source code of the examples as a zip-archive from GitHub:

```
> wget https://github.com/streaming-with-flink/examples-scala/archive/master.zip
> unzip master.zip
```

The book examples are provided as a Maven project. You will find the source code in the src/ directory, grouped by chapter:

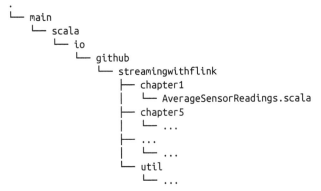

Now open your IDE and import the Maven project. The import steps are similar for most IDEs. In the following, we explain this step in detail for IntelliJ.

Navigate to File -> New -> Project from Existing Sources, select the book examples folder *examples-scala*, and click OK. Make sure that "Import project from external model" and "Maven" are selected and click Next.

A project import wizard will guide you though the next steps, such as selecting the Maven project to import (there should only be one), selecting the SDK, and naming the project. Figures 4-1 to 4-3 illustrate the import process.

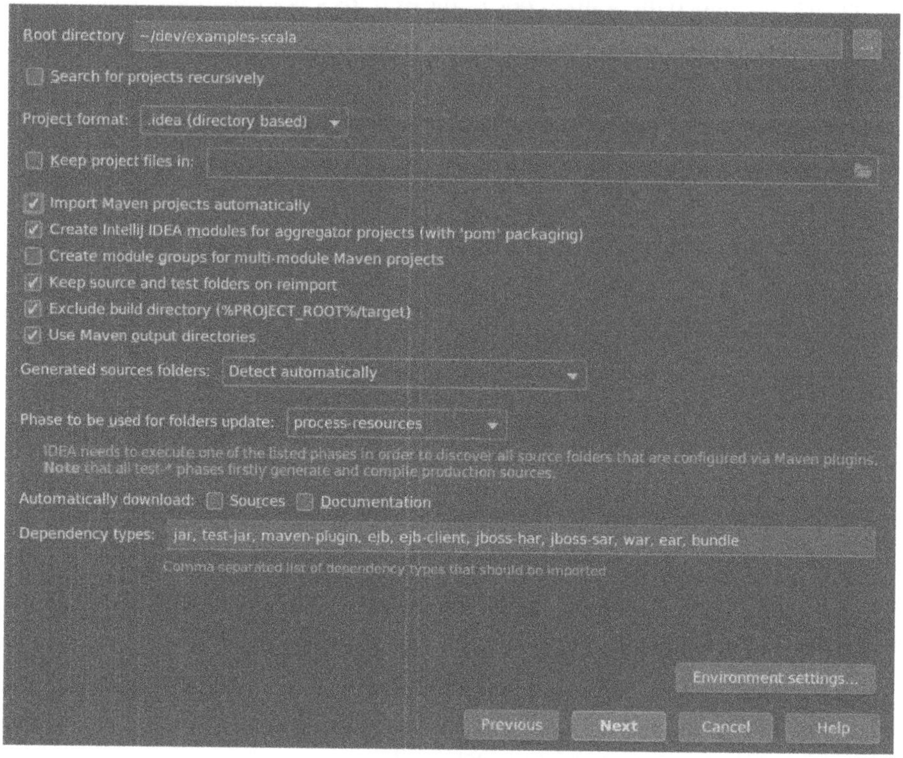

Figure 4-1. Import the book examples repository into IntelliJ

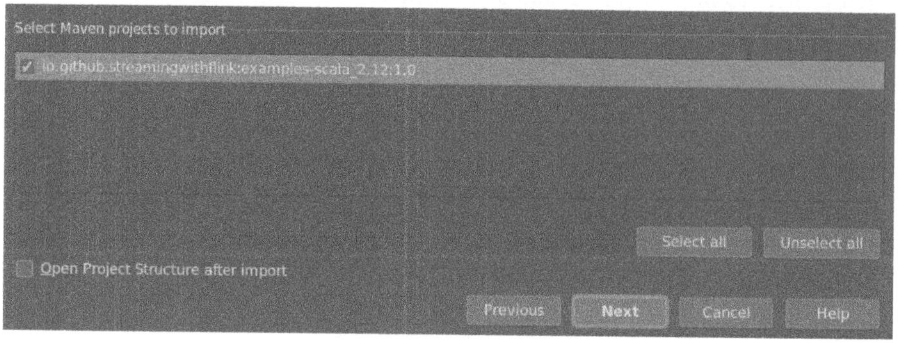

Figure 4-2. Select the Maven project to import

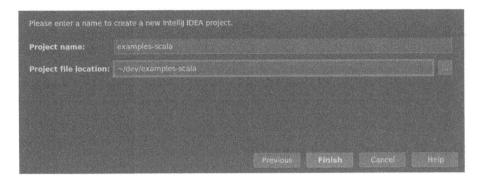

Please enter a name to create a new IntelliJ IDEA project.

Project name: examples-scala

Project file location: ~/dev/examples-scala

| | | Previous | Finish | Cancel | Help |

Figure 4-3. Give your project a name and click Finish

That's it! You should now be able to browse and inspect the code of the book examples.

Run Flink Applications in an IDE

Next, let's run one of the book example applications in your IDE. Search for the `AverageSensorReadings` class and open it. As discussed in "A Quick Look at Flink" on page 12, the program generates read events for multiple thermal sensors, converts the temperature of the events from Fahrenheit to Celsius, and computes the average temperature of each sensor every second. The results of the program are emitted to standard output. Just like many DataStream applications, the source, sink, and operators of the program are assembled in the `main()` method of the `AverageSensorRead ings` class.

To start the application, run the `main()` method. The output of the program is written to the standard out (or console) window of your IDE. The output starts with a few log statements about the states that parallel operator tasks go through, such as SCHEDULING, DEPLOYING, and RUNNING. Once all tasks are up and running, the program starts to produce its results, which should look similar to the following lines:

```
2> SensorReading(sensor_31,1515014051000,23.924656183848732)
4> SensorReading(sensor_32,1515014051000,4.118569049862492)
1> SensorReading(sensor_38,1515014051000,14.781835420242471)
3> SensorReading(sensor_34,1515014051000,23.871433252250583)
```

The program will continue to generate new events, process them, and emit new results every second until you terminate it.

Now let's quickly discuss what is happening under the hood. As explained in "Components of a Flink Setup" on page 38, a Flink application is submitted to the JobManager (master), which distributes execution tasks to one or more TaskManagers (workers). Since Flink is a distributed system, the JobManager and TaskManagers typically run as separate JVM processes on different machines. Usually, the program's `main()` method assembles the dataflow and submits it to a remote JobManager when the `StreamExecutionEnvironment.execute()` method is called.

However, there is also a mode in which the call of the `execute()` method starts a Job-Manager and a TaskManager (by default with as many slots as available CPU threads) as separate threads within the same JVM. Consequently, the whole Flink application is multithreaded and executed within the same JVM process. This mode is used to execute a Flink program within an IDE.

Debug Flink Applications in an IDE

Due to the single JVM execution mode, it is also possible to debug Flink applications in an IDE almost like any other program in your IDE. You can define breakpoints in the code and debug your application as you would normally do.

However, there are a few things to consider when debugging a Flink application in an IDE:

- Unless you specify a parallelism, a program is executed by as many threads as the number of CPU threads of your development machine. Hence, you should be aware that you might debug a multithreaded program.

- In contrast to executing a Flink program by sending it to a remote JobManager, the program is executed in a single JVM. Therefore, certain issues, such as class-loading issues, cannot be properly debugged.

- Although a program is executed in a single JVM, records are serialized for cross-thread communication and possibly state persistence.

Bootstrap a Flink Maven Project

Importing the `examples-scala` repository into your IDE to experiment with Flink is a good first step. However, you should also know how to create a new Flink project from scratch.

Flink provides Maven archetypes to generate Maven projects for Java or Scala Flink applications. Open a terminal and run the following command to create a Flink Maven Quickstart Scala project as a starting point for your Flink application:

```
mvn archetype:generate                              \
    -DarchetypeGroupId=org.apache.flink             \
    -DarchetypeArtifactId=flink-quickstart-scala    \
    -DarchetypeVersion=1.7.1                         \
    -DgroupId=org.apache.flink.quickstart           \
    -DartifactId=flink-scala-project                 \
    -Dversion=0.1                                    \
```

```
-Dpackage=org.apache.flink.quickstart              \
-DinteractiveMode=false
```

This will generate a Maven project for Flink 1.7.1 in a folder called *flink-scala-project*. You can change the Flink version, group and artifact IDs, version, and generated package by changing the respective parameters of the above *mvn* command. The generated folder contains a *src/* folder and a *pom.xml* file. The *src/* folder has the following structure:

```
src/
└── main
    ├── resources
    │   └── log4j.properties
    └── scala
        └── org
            └── apache
                └── flink
                    └── quickstart
                        ├── BatchJob.scala
                        └── StreamingJob.scala
```

The project contains two skeleton files, *BatchJob.scala* and *StreamingJob.scala*, as a starting point for your own programs. You can also delete them if you do not need them.

You can import the project in your IDE following the steps we described in the previous section or you can execute the following command to build a JAR file:

```
mvn clean package -Pbuild-jar
```

If the command completed successfully, you will find a new *target* folder in your project folder. The folder contains a file *flink-scala-project-0.1.jar*, which is the JAR file of your Flink application. The generated *pom.xml* file also contains instructions on how to add new dependencies to your project.

Summary

In this chapter you learned how to set up an environment to develop and debug Flink DataStream applications and how to generate a Maven project using Flink's Maven archetype. The obvious next step is to learn how to actually implement a DataStream program.

Chapter 5 will introduce you to the basics of the DataStream API, and Chapters 6, 7, and 8 will introduce everything you need to know about time-based operators, stateful functions, and source and sink connectors.

The DataStream API (v1.7)

This chapter introduces the basics of Flink's DataStream API. We show the structure and components of a typical Flink streaming application, discuss Flink's type systems and the supported data types, and present data and partitioning transformations. Window operators, time-based transformations, stateful operators, and connectors are discussed in the next chapters. After reading this chapter, you will know how to implement a stream processing application with basic functionality. Our code examples use Scala for conciseness, but the Java API is mostly analogous (exceptions or special cases will be pointed out). We also provide complete example applications implemented in Java and Scala in our GitHub repositories (*https://github.com/ streaming-with-flink/*).

Hello, Flink!

Let's start with a simple example to get a first impression of what it is like to write streaming applications with the DataStream API. We will use this example to showcase the basic structure of a Flink program and introduce some important features of the DataStream API. Our example application ingests a stream of temperature measurements from multiple sensors.

First, let's have a look at the data type we will be using to represent sensor readings:

```
case class SensorReading(
    id: String,
    timestamp: Long,
    temperature: Double)
```

The program in Example 5-1 converts the temperatures from Fahrenheit to Celsius and computes the average temperature every 5 seconds for each sensor.

Example 5-1. Compute the average temperature every 5 seconds for a stream of sensors

```scala
// Scala object that defines the DataStream program in the main() method.
object AverageSensorReadings {

  // main() defines and executes the DataStream program
  def main(args: Array[String]) {

    // set up the streaming execution environment
    val env = StreamExecutionEnvironment.getExecutionEnvironment

    // use event time for the application
    env.setStreamTimeCharacteristic(TimeCharacteristic.EventTime)

    // create a DataStream[SensorReading] from a stream source
    val sensorData: DataStream[SensorReading] = env
      // ingest sensor readings with a SensorSource SourceFunction
      .addSource(new SensorSource)
      // assign timestamps and watermarks (required for event time)
      .assignTimestampsAndWatermarks(new SensorTimeAssigner)

    val avgTemp: DataStream[SensorReading] = sensorData
      // convert Fahrenheit to Celsius with an inline lambda function
      .map( r => {
          val celsius = (r.temperature - 32) * (5.0 / 9.0)
          SensorReading(r.id, r.timestamp, celsius)
        } )
      // organize readings by sensor id
      .keyBy(_.id)
      // group readings in 5 second tumbling windows
      .timeWindow(Time.seconds(5))
      // compute average temperature using a user-defined function
      .apply(new TemperatureAverager)

    // print result stream to standard out
    avgTemp.print()

    // execute application
    env.execute("Compute average sensor temperature")
  }
}
```

You have probably already noticed that Flink programs are defined and submitted for execution in regular Scala or Java methods. Most commonly, this is done in a static main method. In our example, we define the AverageSensorReadings object and include most of the application logic inside main().

To structure a typical Flink streaming application:

1. Set up the execution environment.

---

2. Read one or more streams from data sources.

3. Apply streaming transformations to implement the application logic.

4. Optionally output the result to one or more data sinks.

5. Execute the program.

We now look at these parts in detail.

Set Up the Execution Environment

The first thing a Flink application needs to do is set up its *execution environment*. The execution environment determines whether the program is running on a local machine or on a cluster. In the DataStream API, the execution environment of an application is represented by the `StreamExecutionEnvironment`. In our example, we retrieve the execution environment by calling the static `getExecutionEnvironment()` method. This method returns a local or remote environment, depending on the context in which the method is invoked. If the method is invoked from a submission client with a connection to a remote cluster, a remote execution environment is returned. Otherwise, it returns a local environment.

It is also possible to explicitly create local or remote execution environments as follows:

```
// create a local stream execution environment
val localEnv: StreamExecutionEnvironment.createLocalEnvironment()

// create a remote stream execution environment
val remoteEnv = StreamExecutionEnvironment.createRemoteEnvironment(
   "host",                  // hostname of JobManager
   1234,                    // port of JobManager process
   "path/to/jarFile.jar")   // JAR file to ship to the JobManager
```

Next, we use `env.setStreamTimeCharacteristic(TimeCharacteristic.EventTime)` to instruct our program to interpret time semantics using event time. The execution environment offers more configuration options, such as setting the program parallelism and enabling fault tolerance.

Read an Input Stream

Once the execution environment has been configured, it is time to do some actual work and start processing streams. The `StreamExecutionEnvironment` provides methods to create stream sources that ingest data streams into the application. Data streams can be ingested from sources such as message queues or files, or also be generated on the fly.

In our example, we use:

```
val sensorData: DataStream[SensorReading] =
  env.addSource(new SensorSource)
```

to connect to the source of the sensor measurements and create an initial `DataStream` of type `SensorReading`. Flink supports many data types, which we describe in the next section. Here, we use a Scala case class as the data type that we defined before. A `SensorReading` contains the sensor ID, a timestamp denoting when the measurement was taken, and the measured temperature. The `assignTimestampsAndWatermarks(new SensorTimeAssigner)` method assigns the timestamps and watermarks that are required for event time. The implementation details of `SensorTimeAssigner` do not concern us right now.

Apply Transformations

Once we have a `DataStream`, we can apply a transformation on it. There are different types of transformations. Some transformations can produce a new `DataStream`, possibly of a different type, while other transformations do not modify the records of the `DataStream` but reorganize it by partitioning or grouping. The logic of an application is defined by chaining transformations.

In our example, we first apply a `map()` transformation that converts the temperature of each sensor reading to Celsius. Then, we use the `keyBy()` transformation to partition the sensor readings by their sensor ID. Next, we define a `timeWindow()` transformation, which groups the sensor readings of each sensor ID partition into tumbling windows of 5 seconds:

```
val avgTemp: DataStream[SensorReading] = sensorData
  .map( r => {
      val celsius = (r.temperature - 32) * (5.0 / 9.0)
      SensorReading(r.id, r.timestamp, celsius)
    } )
  .keyBy(_.id)
  .timeWindow(Time.seconds(5))
  .apply(new TemperatureAverager)
```

Window transformations are described in detail in "Window Operators" on page 122. Finally, we apply a user-defined function that computes the average temperature on each window. We discuss the implementation of a user-defined function in a later section of this chapter.

Output the Result

Streaming applications usually emit their results to some external system, such as Apache Kafka, a filesystem, or a database. Flink provides a well-maintained collection of stream sinks that can be used to write data to different systems. It is also possible to implement your own streaming sinks. There are also applications that do not emit results but keep them internally to serve them via Flink's queryable state feature.

In our example, the result is a `DataStream[SensorReading]` record. Every record contains an average temperature of a sensor over a period of 5 seconds. The result stream is written to the standard output by calling `print()`:

```
avgTemp.print()
```

 Note that the choice of a streaming sink affects the end-to-end consistency of an application, whether the result of the application is provided with at-least once or exactly-once semantics. The end-to-end consistency of the application depends on the integration of the chosen stream sinks with Flink's checkpointing algorithm. We will discuss this topic in more detail in "Application Consistency Guarantees" on page 184.

Execute

When the application has been completely defined, it can be executed by calling `StreamExecutionEnvironment.execute()`. This is the last call in our example:

```
env.execute("Compute average sensor temperature")
```

Flink programs are executed lazily. That is, the API calls that create stream sources and transformations do not immediately trigger any data processing. Instead, the API calls construct an execution plan in the execution environment, which consists of the stream sources created from the environment and all transformations that were transitively applied to these sources. Only when `execute()` is called does the system trigger the execution of the program.

The constructed plan is translated into a JobGraph and submitted to a JobManager for execution. Depending on the type of execution environment, a JobManager is started as a local thread (local execution environment) or the JobGraph is sent to a remote JobManager. If the JobManager runs remotely, the JobGraph must be shipped together with a JAR file that contains all classes and required dependencies of the application.

Transformations

In this section we give an overview of the basic transformations of the DataStream API. Time-related operators such as window operators and other specialized transformations are described in later chapters. A stream transformation is applied on one or more streams and converts them into one or more output streams. Writing a Data-

Stream API program essentially boils down to combining such transformations to create a dataflow graph that implements the application logic.

Most stream transformations are based on user-defined functions. The functions encapsulate the user application logic and define how the elements of the input stream are transformed into the elements of the output stream. Functions, such as `MapFunction` in the following, are defined as classes that implement a transformation-specific function interface:

```scala
class MyMapFunction extends MapFunction[Int, Int] {
  override def map(value: Int): Int =  value + 1
}
```

The function interface defines the transformation method that needs to be implemented by the user, such as the `map()` method in the example above.

Most function interfaces are designed as SAM (single abstract method) interfaces and they can be implemented as Java 8 lambda functions. The Scala DataStream API also has built-in support for lambda functions. When presenting the transformations of the DataStream API, we show the interfaces for all function classes, but mostly use lambda functions instead of function classes in code examples for brevity.

The DataStream API provides transformations for the most common data transformation operations. If you are familiar with batch data processing APIs, functional programming languages, or SQL you will find the API concepts very easy to grasp. We present the transformations of the DataStream API in four categories:

1. Basic transformations are transformations on individual events.

2. `KeyedStream` transformations are transformations that are applied to events in the context of a key.

3. Multistream transformations merge multiple streams into one stream or split one stream into multiple streams.

4. Distribution transformations reorganize stream events.

Basic Transformations

Basic transformations process individual events, meaning that each output record was produced from a single input record. Simple value conversions, splitting of records, or filtering of records are examples of common basic functions. We explain their semantics and show code examples.

Map

The map transformation is specified by calling the `DataStream.map()` method and produces a new `DataStream`. It passes each incoming event to a user-defined mapper that returns exactly one output event, possibly of a different type. Figure 5-1 shows a map transformation that converts every square into a circle.

Figure 5-1. A map operation that transforms every square into a circle of the same color

The `MapFunction` is typed to the types of the input and output events and can be specified using the `MapFunction` interface. It defines the `map()` method that transforms an input event into exactly one output event:

```
// T: the type of input elements
// O: the type of output elements
MapFunction[T, O]
    > map(T): O
```

The following is a simple mapper that extracts the first field (`id`) of each `SensorReading` in the input stream:

```
val readings: DataStream[SensorReading] = ...
val sensorIds: DataStream[String] = readings.map(new MyMapFunction)

class MyMapFunction extends MapFunction[SensorReading, String] {
  override def map(r: SensorReading): String = r.id
}
```

When using the Scala API or Java 8, the mapper can also be expressed as a lambda function:

```
val readings: DataStream[SensorReading] = ...
val sensorIds: DataStream[String] = readings.map(r => r.id)
```

Filter

The filter transformation drops or forwards events of a stream by evaluating a boolean condition on each input event. A return value of `true` preserves the input event and forwards it to the output, and `false` results in dropping the event. A filter transformation is specified by calling the `DataStream.filter()` method and produces a new `DataStream` of the same type as the input `DataStream`. Figure 5-2 shows a filter operation that only preserves white squares.

Figure 5-2. A filter operation that only retains white values

The boolean condition is implemented as a function either using the `FilterFunction` interface or a lambda function. The `FilterFunction` interface is typed to the type of the input stream and defines the `filter()` method that is called with an input event and returns a boolean:

```
// T: the type of elements
FilterFunction[T]
    > filter(T): Boolean
```

The following example shows a filter that drops all sensor measurements with temperature below 25°F:

```
val readings: DataStream[SensorReadings] = ...
val filteredSensors = readings
    .filter( r =>  r.temperature >= 25 )
```

FlatMap

The flatMap transformation is similar to map, but it can produce zero, one, or more output events for each incoming event. In fact, the flatMap transformation is a generalization of filter and map and can be used to implement both those operations. Figure 5-3 shows a flatMap operation that differentiates its output based on the color of the incoming event. If the input is a white square, it outputs the event unmodified. Black squares are duplicated, and gray squares are filtered out.

Figure 5-3. A flatMap operation that outputs white squares, duplicates black squares, and drops gray squares

The flatMap transformation applies a function on each incoming event. The corresponding `FlatMapFunction` defines the `flatMap()` method, which may return zero, one, or more events as results by passing them to the `Collector` object:

```
// T: the type of input elements
// O: the type of output elements
FlatMapFunction[T, O]
    > flatMap(T, Collector[O]): Unit
```

This example shows a flatMap transformation commonly found in data processing tutorials. The function is applied on a stream of sentences, splits each sentence by the space character, and emits each resulting word as an individual record:

```
val sentences: DataStream[String] = ...
val words: DataStream[String] = sentences
  .flatMap(id => id.split(" "))
```

KeyedStream Transformations

A common requirement of many applications is to process groups of events that share a certain property together. The DataStream API features the abstraction of a KeyedStream, which is a DataStream that has been logically partitioned into disjoint substreams of events that share the same key.

Stateful transformations that are applied on a KeyedStream read from and write to state in the context of the currently processed event's key. This means that all events with the same key access the same state and thus can be processed together.

> Note that stateful transformations and keyed aggregates have to be used with care. If the key domain is continuously growing—for example, because the key is a unique transaction ID—you have to clean up state for keys that are no longer active to avoid memory problems. Refer to "Implementing Stateful Functions" on page 154, which discusses stateful functions in detail.

A KeyedStream can be processed using the map, flatMap, and filter transformations that you saw earlier. In the following, we will use a keyBy transformation to convert a DataStream into a KeyedStream and keyed transformations such as rolling aggregations and reduce.

keyBy

The keyBy transformation converts a DataStream into a KeyedStream by specifying a key. Based on the key, the events of the stream are assigned to partitions, so that all events with the same key are processed by the same task of the subsequent operator. Events with different keys can be processed by the same task, but the keyed state of a task's function is always accessed in the scope of the current event's key.

Considering the color of the input event as the key, Figure 5-4 assigns black events to one partition and all other events to another partition.

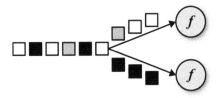

Figure 5-4. A keyBy operation that partitions events based on color

The keyBy() method receives an argument that specifies the key (or keys) to group by and returns a KeyedStream. There are different ways to specify keys. We cover them in "Defining Keys and Referencing Fields" on page 102. The following code declares the id field as the key of a stream of SensorReading records:

```
val readings: DataStream[SensorReading] = ...
val keyed: KeyedStream[SensorReading, String] = readings
  .keyBy(r => r.id)
```

The lambda function r => r.id extracts the id field of a sensor reading r.

Rolling aggregations

Rolling aggregation transformations are applied on a KeyedStream and produce a DataStream of aggregates, such as sum, minimum, and maximum. A rolling aggregate operator keeps an aggregated value for every observed key. For each incoming event, the operator updates the corresponding aggregate value and emits an event with the updated value. A rolling aggregation does not require a user-defined function but receives an argument that specifies on which field the aggregate is computed. The DataStream API provides the following rolling aggregation methods:

sum()
    A rolling sum of the input stream on the specified field.

min()
    A rolling minimum of the input stream on the specified field.

max()
    A rolling maximum of the input stream on the specified field.

minBy()
    A rolling minimum of the input stream that returns the event with the lowest value observed so far.

maxBy()
    A rolling maximum of the input stream that returns the event with the highest value observed so far.

It is not possible to combine multiple rolling aggregation methods—only a single rolling aggregate can be computed at a time.

Consider the following example of keying a stream of Tuple3[Int, Int, Int] on the first field and computing a rolling sum on the second field:

```
val inputStream: DataStream[(Int, Int, Int)] = env.fromElements(
  (1, 2, 2), (2, 3, 1), (2, 2, 4), (1, 5, 3))

val resultStream: DataStream[(Int, Int, Int)] = inputStream
  .keyBy(0) // key on first field of the tuple
  .sum(1)   // sum the second field of the tuple in place
```

In this example the tuple input stream is keyed by the first field and the rolling sum is computed on the second field. The output of the example is (1,2,2) followed by (1,7,2) for the key "1" and (2,3,1) followed by (2,5,1) for the key "2." The first field is the common key, the second field is the sum, and the third field is not defined.

Only Use Rolling Aggregations on Bounded Key Domains

The rolling aggregate operator keeps a state for every key that is processed. Since this state is never cleaned up, you should only apply a rolling aggregations operator on a stream with a bounded key domain.

Reduce

The reduce transformation is a generalization of the rolling aggregation. It applies a ReduceFunction on a KeyedStream, which combines each incoming event with the current reduced value, and produces a DataStream. A reduce transformation does not change the type of the stream. The type of the output stream is the same as the type of the input stream.

The function can be specified with a class that implements the ReduceFunction interface. ReduceFunction defines the reduce() method, which takes two input events and returns an event of the same type:

```
// T: the element type
ReduceFunction[T]
    > reduce(T, T): T
```

In the example below, the stream is keyed by language and the result is a continuously updated list of words per language:

```
val inputStream: DataStream[(String, List[String])] = env.fromElements(
  ("en", List("tea")), ("fr", List("vin")), ("en", List("cake")))

val resultStream: DataStream[(String, List[String])] = inputStream
  .keyBy(0)
  .reduce((x, y) => (x._1, x._2 ::: y._2))
```

The lambda reduce function forwards the first tuple field (the key field) and concatenates the List[String] values of the second tuple field.

Only Use Rolling Reduce on Bounded Key Domains

The rolling reduce operator keeps a state for every key that is processed. Since this state is never cleaned up, you should only apply a rolling reduce operator on a stream with a bounded key domain.

Multistream Transformations

Many applications ingest multiple streams that need to be jointly processed or split a stream in order to apply different logic to different substreams. In the following, we discuss the DataStream API transformations that process multiple input streams or emit multiple output streams.

Union

The `DataStream.union()` method merges two or more `DataStream`s of the same type and produces a new `DataStream` of the same type. Subsequent transformations process the elements of all input streams. Figure 5-5 shows a union operation that merges black and gray events into a single output stream.

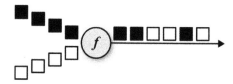

Figure 5-5. A union operation that merges two input streams into one

The events are merged in a FIFO fashion—the operator does not produce a specific order of events. Moreover, the union operator does not perform duplication elimination. Every input event is emitted to the next operator.

The following shows how to union three streams of type `SensorReading` into a single stream:

```
val parisStream: DataStream[SensorReading] = ...
val tokyoStream: DataStream[SensorReading] = ...
val rioStream: DataStream[SensorReading] = ...
val allCities: DataStream[SensorReading] = parisStream
  .union(tokyoStream, rioStream)
```

Connect, coMap, and coFlatMap

Combining events of two streams is a very common requirement in stream processing. Consider an application that monitors a forest area and outputs an alert whenever there is a high risk of fire. The application receives the stream of temperature sensor readings you have seen previously and an additional stream of smoke level measurements. When the temperature is over a given threshold and the smoke level is high, the application emits a fire alert.

The DataStream API provides the connect transformation to support such use cases.[1] The DataStream.connect() method receives a DataStream and returns a Connected Streams object, which represents the two connected streams:

```
// first stream
val first: DataStream[Int] = ...
// second stream
val second: DataStream[String] = ...

// connect streams
val connected: ConnectedStreams[Int, String] = first.connect(second)
```

The ConnectedStreams object provides map() and flatMap() methods that expect a CoMapFunction and CoFlatMapFunction as argument respectively.[2]

Both functions are typed on the types of the first and second input stream and on the type of the output stream and define two methods—one for each input. map1() and flatMap1() are called to process an event of the first input and map2() and flat Map2() are invoked to process an event of the second input:

```
// IN1: the type of the first input stream
// IN2: the type of the second input stream
// OUT: the type of the output elements
CoMapFunction[IN1, IN2, OUT]
    > map1(IN1): OUT
    > map2(IN2): OUT

// IN1: the type of the first input stream
// IN2: the type of the second input stream
// OUT: the type of the output elements
CoFlatMapFunction[IN1, IN2, OUT]
    > flatMap1(IN1, Collector[OUT]): Unit
    > flatMap2(IN2, Collector[OUT]): Unit
```

A Function Cannot Choose Which ConnectedStreams to Read

It is not possible to control the order in which the methods of a CoMapFunction or CoFlatMapFunction are called. Instead, a method is called as soon as an event has arrived via the corresponding input.

Joint processing of two streams usually requires that events of both streams are deterministically routed based on some condition to be processed by the same parallel instance of an operator. By default, connect() does not establish a relationship

---

1 Flink features dedicated operators for time-based stream joins, which are discussed in Chapter 6. The connect transformation and the cofunctions discussed in this section are more generic.

2 You can also apply a CoProcessFunction to ConnectedStreams. We discuss CoProcessFunction in Chapter 6.

between the events of both streams so events of both streams are randomly assigned to operator instances. This behavior yields nondeterministic results and is usually undesirable. In order to achieve deterministic transformations on ConnectedStreams, connect() can be combined with keyBy() or broadcast(). We first show the keyBy() case:

```
val one: DataStream[(Int, Long)] = ...
val two: DataStream[(Int, String)] = ...

// keyBy two connected streams
val keyedConnect1: ConnectedStreams[(Int, Long), (Int, String)] = one
  .connect(two)
  .keyBy(0, 0) // key both input streams on first attribute

// alternative: connect two keyed streams
val keyedConnect2: ConnectedStreams[(Int, Long), (Int, String)] = one.keyBy(0)
  .connect(two.keyBy(0)
```

Regardless of whether you keyBy() ConnectedStreams or you connect() two Keyed Streams, the connect() transformation will route all events from both streams with the same key to the same operator instance. Note that the keys of both streams should refer to the same class of entities, just like a join predicate in a SQL query. An operator that is applied on a connected and keyed stream has access to keyed state.[3]

The next example shows how to connect a (nonkeyed) DataStream with a broadcasted stream:

```
val first: DataStream[(Int, Long)] = ...
val second: DataStream[(Int, String)] = ...

// connect streams with broadcast
val keyedConnect: ConnectedStreams[(Int, Long), (Int, String)] = first
  // broadcast second input stream
  .connect(second.broadcast())
```

All events of the broadcasted stream are replicated and sent to all parallel operator instances of the subsequent processing function. The events of the nonbroadcasted stream are simply forwarded. Hence, the elements of both input streams can be jointly processed.

---

3 See Chapter 8 for details on keyed state.

You can use broadcast state to connect a keyed and a broadcast stream. Broadcast state is an improved version of the broadcast()-connect() transformation. It also supports connecting a keyed and a broadcasted stream and storing the broadcasted events in managed state. This allows you to implement operators that are dynamically configured via a data stream (e.g., to add or remove filtering rules or update machine-learning models). The broadcast state is discussed in detail in "Using Connected Broadcast State" on page 160.

Split and select

Split is the inverse transformation to the union transformation. It divides an input stream into two or more output streams of the same type as the input stream. Each incoming event can be routed to zero, one, or more output streams. Hence, split can also be used to filter or replicate events. Figure 5-6 shows a split operator that routes all white events into a separate stream than the rest.

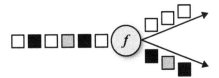

Figure 5-6. A split operation that splits the input stream into a stream of white events and a stream of others

The DataStream.split() method receives an OutputSelector that defines how stream elements are assigned to named outputs. The OutputSelector defines the select() method that is called for each input event and returns a java.lang.Itera ble[String]. The String values that are returned for a record specify the output streams to which the record is routed.

```
// IN: the type of the split elements
OutputSelector[IN]
    > select(IN): Iterable[String]
```

The DataStream.split() method returns a SplitStream, which provides a select() method to select one or more streams from the SplitStream by specifying the output names.

Example 5-2 splits a stream of numbers into a stream of large numbers and a stream of small numbers.

Example 5-2. Split a tuple stream into a stream with large numbers and a stream with small numbers.

```scala
val inputStream: DataStream[(Int, String)] = ...

val splitted: SplitStream[(Int, String)] = inputStream
  .split(t => if (t._1 > 1000) Seq("large") else Seq("small"))

val large: DataStream[(Int, String)] = splitted.select("large")
val small: DataStream[(Int, String)] = splitted.select("small")
val all: DataStream[(Int, String)] = splitted.select("small", "large")
```

One restriction of the split transformation is that all outgoing streams are of the same type as the input type. In "Emitting to Side Outputs" on page 119, we present the side-output feature of the process functions, which can emit multiple streams of different types from a function.

Distribution Transformations

Partitioning transformations correspond to the data exchange strategies we introduced in "Data Exchange Strategies" on page 19. These operations define how events are assigned to tasks. When building applications with the DataStream API the system automatically chooses data partitioning strategies and routes data to the correct destination depending on the operation semantics and the configured parallelism. Sometimes it is necessary or desirable to control the partitioning strategies at the application level or define custom partitioners. For instance, if we know that the load of the parallel partitions of a DataStream is skewed, we might want to rebalance the data to evenly distribute the computation load of subsequent operators. Alternatively, the application logic might require that all tasks of an operation receive the same data or that events be distributed following a custom strategy. In this section, we present DataStream methods that enable users to control partitioning strategies or define their own.

Note that keyBy() is different from the distribution transformations discussed in this section. All transformations in this section produce a DataStream whereas keyBy() results in a KeyedStream, on which transformation with access to keyed state can be applied.

Random

The random data exchange strategy is implemented by the DataStream.shuffle() method. The method distributes records randomly according to a uniform distribution to the parallel tasks of the following operator.

Round-Robin

The rebalance() method partitions the input stream so that events are evenly distributed to successor tasks in a round-robin fashion. Figure 5-7 illustrates the round-robin distribution transformation.

Rescale

The rescale() method also distributes events in a round-robin fashion, but only to a subset of successor tasks. In essence, the rescale partitioning strategy offers a way to perform a lightweight load rebalance when the number of sender and receiver tasks is not the same. The rescale transformation is more efficient if the number of receiver tasks is a multitude of the number of sender tasks or vice versa.

The fundamental difference between rebalance() and rescale() lies in the way task connections are formed. While rebalance() will create communication channels between all sending tasks to all receiving tasks, rescale() will only create channels from each task to some of the tasks of the downstream operator. The connection pattern of the rescale distribution transformation is shown in Figure 5-7.

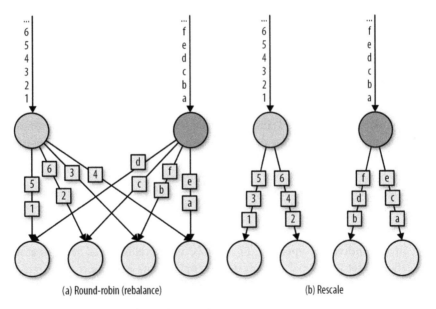

Figure 5-7. Rebalance and rescale transformations

Broadcast

The broadcast() method replicates the input data stream so that all events are sent to all parallel tasks of the downstream operator.

Global

The global() method sends all events of the input data stream to the first parallel task of the downstream operator. This partitioning strategy must be used with care, as routing all events to the same task might impact application performance.

Custom

When none of the predefined partitioning strategies is suitable, you can define your own by using the partitionCustom() method. This method receives a Partitioner object that implements the partitioning logic and the field or key position on which the stream is to be partitioned. The following example partitions a stream of integers so that all negative numbers are sent to the first task and all other numbers are sent to a random task:

```scala
val numbers: DataStream[(Int)] = ...
numbers.partitionCustom(myPartitioner, 0)

object myPartitioner extends Partitioner[Int] {
  val r = scala.util.Random

  override def partition(key: Int, numPartitions: Int): Int = {
    if (key < 0) 0 else r.nextInt(numPartitions)
  }
}
```

Setting the Parallelism

Flink applications are executed in parallel in a distributed environment such as a cluster of machines. When a DataStream program is submitted to the JobManager for execution, the system creates a dataflow graph and prepares the operators for execution. Each operator is parallelized into one or multiple tasks. Each task will process a subset of the operator's input stream. The number of parallel tasks of an operator is called the parallelism of the operator. It determines how much the operator's processing effort can be distributed and also how much data it can process.

The parallelism of an operator can be controlled at the level of the execution environment or per individual operator. By default, the parallelism of all operators of an application is set as the parallelism of the application's execution environment. The parallelism of the environment (and thus also the default parallelism of all operators) is automatically initialized based on the context in which the application is started. If the application runs in a local execution environment the parallelism is set to match the number of CPU cores. When submitting an application to a running Flink cluster, the environment parallelism is set to the default parallelism of the cluster unless it is explicitly specified via the submission client (see "Running and Managing Streaming Applications" on page 245 for more details).

In general, it is a good idea to define the parallelism of your operators relative to the default parallelism of the environment. This allows you to easily scale the application by adjusting its parallelism via the submission client. You can access the default parallelism of the environment as shown in the following example:

```
val env: StreamExecutionEnvironment.getExecutionEnvironment
// get default parallelism as configured in the cluster config or
//   explicitly specified via the submission client.
val defaultP = env.env.getParallelism
```

You can also override the default parallelism of the environment, but you will no longer be able to control the parallelism of your application via the submission client:

```
val env: StreamExecutionEnvironment.getExecutionEnvironment
// set parallelism of the environment
env.setParallelism(32)
```

The default parallelism of an operator can be overridden by specifying it explicitly. In the following example, the source operator will be executed with the default parallelism of the environment, the map transformation has double as many tasks as the source, and the sink operation will always be executed by two parallel tasks:

```
val env = StreamExecutionEnvironment.getExecutionEnvironment

// get default parallelism
val defaultP = env.getParallelism

// the source runs with the default parallelism
val result: = env.addSource(new CustomSource)
  // the map parallelism is set to double the default parallelism
  .map(new MyMapper).setParallelism(defaultP * 2)
  // the print sink parallelism is fixed to 2
  .print().setParallelism(2)
```

When you submit the application via a submission client and specify the parallelism to be 16, the source will run with a parallelism of 16, the mapper will run with 32 tasks, and the sink will run with 2 tasks. If you run the application in a local environment—or example, from your IDE—on a machine with 8 cores, the source task will run with 8 tasks, the mapper with 16 tasks, and the sink with 2 tasks.

Types

Flink DataStream applications process streams of events that are represented as data objects. Functions are called with data objects and emit data objects. Internally, Flink needs to be able to handle these objects. They need to be serialized and deserialized to ship them over the network or write them into or read them from state backends, checkpoints, and savepoints. In order to do this efficiently, Flink requires detailed knowledge of the types of data the application processes. Flink uses the concept of type information to represent data types and generate specific serializers, deserializers, and comparators for every data type.

Flink also features a type extraction system that analyzes the input and return types of functions to automatically obtain type information and hence serializers and deserializers. However, in certain situations, such as lambda functions or generic types, it is necessary to explicitly provide type information to make an application work or improve its performance.

In this section, we discuss the types supported by Flink, how to create type information for a data type, and how to help Flink's type system with hints if it cannot automatically infer the return type of a function.

Supported Data Types

Flink supports all common data types that are available in Java and Scala. The most widely used types can be grouped into the following categories:

- Primitives
- Java and Scala tuples
- Scala case classes
- POJOs, including classes generated by Apache Avro
- Some special types

Types that are not specially handled are treated as generic types and serialized using the Kryo serialization framework (*https://github.com/EsotericSoftware/kryo*).

Only Use Kryo as a Fallback Solution

Note that you should avoid using Kryo if possible. Since Kryo is a general-purpose serializer it is usually not very efficient. Flink provides configuration options to improve the efficiency by preregistering classes to Kryo. Moreover, Kryo does not provide a good migration path to evolve data types.

Let's look at each type category.

Primitives

All Java and Scala primitive types, such as Int (or Integer for Java), String, and Double, are supported. Here is an example that processes a stream of Long values and increments each element:

```
val numbers: DataStream[Long] = env.fromElements(1L, 2L, 3L, 4L)
numbers.map( n => n + 1)
```

Java and Scala tuples

Tuples are composite data types that consist of a fixed number of typed fields.

The Scala DataStream API uses regular Scala tuples. The following example filters a `DataStream` of tuples with two fields:

```scala
// DataStream of Tuple2[String, Integer] for Person(name, age)
val persons: DataStream[(String, Integer)] = env.fromElements(
  ("Adam", 17),
  ("Sarah", 23))

// filter for persons of age > 18
persons.filter(p => p._2 > 18)
```

Flink provides efficient implementations of Java tuples. Flink's Java tuples can have up to 25 fields, with each length is implemented as a separate class—`Tuple1`, `Tuple2`, up to `Tuple25`. The tuple classes are strongly typed.

We can rewrite the filtering example in the Java DataStream API as follows:

```java
// DataStream of Tuple2<String, Integer> for Person(name, age)
DataStream<Tuple2<String, Integer>> persons = env.fromElements(
  Tuple2.of("Adam", 17),
  Tuple2.of("Sarah", 23));

// filter for persons of age > 18
persons.filter(p -> p.f1 > 18);
```

Tuple fields can be accessed by the name of their public fields—`f0`, `f1`, `f2`, etc., as shown earlier—or by position using the `getField(int pos)` method, where indexes start at 0:

```java
Tuple2<String, Integer> personTuple = Tuple2.of("Alex", "42");
Integer age = personTuple.getField(1); // age = 42
```

In contrast to their Scala counterparts, Flink's Java tuples are mutable, so the values of fields can be reassigned. Functions can reuse Java tuples in order to reduce the pressure on the garbage collector. The following example shows how to update a field of a Java tuple:

```java
personTuple.f1 = 42;        // set the 2nd field to 42
personTuple.setField(43, 1); // set the 2nd field to 43
```

Scala case classes

Flink supports Scala case classes. Case class fields are accessed by name. In the following, we define a case class `Person` with two fields: `name` and `age`. As for the tuples, we filter the `DataStream` by age:

```scala
case class Person(name: String, age: Int)

val persons: DataStream[Person] = env.fromElements(
  Person("Adam", 17),
  Person("Sarah", 23))
```

```
// filter for persons with age > 18
persons.filter(p => p.age > 18)
```

POJOs

Flink analyzes each type that does not fall into any category and checks to see if it can be identified and handled as a POJO type. Flink accepts a class as a POJO if it satisfies the following conditions:

- It is a public class.
- It has a public constructor without any arguments—a default constructor.
- All fields are public or accessible through getters and setters. The getter and setter functions must follow the default naming scheme, which is Y getX() and setX(Y x) for a field x of type Y.
- All fields have types that are supported by Flink.

For example, the following Java class will be identified as a POJO by Flink:

```
public class Person {
  // both fields are public
  public String name;
  public int age;

  // default constructor is present
  public Person() {}

  public Person(String name, int age) {
      this.name = name;
      this.age = age;
  }
}

DataStream<Person> persons = env.fromElements(
  new Person("Alex", 42),
  new Person("Wendy", 23));
```

Avro-generated classes are automatically identified by Flink and handled as POJOs.

Arrays, Lists, Maps, Enums, and other special types

Flink supports several special-purpose types, such as primitive and object Array types; Java's ArrayList, HashMap, and Enum types; and Hadoop Writable types. Moreover, it provides type information for Scala's Either, Option, and Try types, and Flink's Java version of the Either type.

Creating Type Information for Data Types

The central class in Flink's type system is TypeInformation. It provides the system with the necessary information it needs to generate serializers and comparators. For instance, when you join or group by some key, TypeInformation allows Flink to perform the semantic check of whether the fields used as keys are valid.

When an application is submitted for execution, Flink's type system tries to automatically derive the TypeInformation for every data type that is processed by the framework. A so-called type extractor analyzes the generic types and return types of all functions to obtain the respective TypeInformation objects. Hence, you might use Flink for a while without ever needing to worry about TypeInformation for your data types. However, sometimes the type extractor fails or you might want to define your own types and tell Flink how to handle them efficiently. In such cases, you need to generate a TypeInformation for a specific data type.

Flink provides two utility classes for Java and Scala with static methods to generate a TypeInformation. For Java, the helper class is org.apache.flink.api.common.type info.Types, and it is used as shown in the following examples:

```
// TypeInformation for primitive types
TypeInformation<Integer> intType = Types.INT;

// TypeInformation for Java Tuples
TypeInformation<Tuple2<Long, String>> tupleType =
  Types.TUPLE(Types.LONG, Types.STRING);

// TypeInformation for POJOs
TypeInformation<Person> personType = Types.POJO(Person.class);
```

TypeInformation's helper class is org.apache.flink.api.scala.typeutils.Types for the Scala API, and it is used as shown in the following:

```
// TypeInformation for primitive types
val stringType: TypeInformation[String] = Types.STRING

// TypeInformation for Scala Tuples
val tupleType: TypeInformation[(Int, Long)] = Types.TUPLE[(Int, Long)]

// TypeInformation for case classes
val caseClassType: TypeInformation[Person] = Types.CASE_CLASS[Person]
```

Type Information in the Scala API

In the Scala API, Flink uses Scala compiler macros that generate TypeInformation objects for all data types at compile time. To access the createTypeInformation macro function, make sure to always add the following import statement to your Scala application:

```
import org.apache.flink.streaming.api.scala._
```

Explicitly Providing Type Information

In most cases, Flink can automatically infer types and generate the correct `TypeInfor` `mation`. Flink's type extractor leverages reflection and analyzes function signatures and subclass information to derive the correct output type of a user-defined function. Sometimes, though, the necessary information cannot be extracted (e.g., because of Java erasing generic type information). Moreover, in some cases Flink might not choose the `TypeInformation` that generates the most efficient serializers and deserializers. Hence, you might need to explicitly provide `TypeInformation` objects to Flink for some of the data types used in your application.

There are two ways to provide `TypeInformation`. First, you can extend a function class to explicitly provide the `TypeInformation` of its return type by implementing the `ResultTypeQueryable` interface. The following example shows a `MapFunction` that provides its return type:

```
class Tuple2ToPersonMapper extends MapFunction[(String, Int), Person]
    with ResultTypeQueryable[Person] {

  override def map(v: (String, Int)): Person = Person(v._1, v._2)

  // provide the TypeInformation for the output data type
  override def getProducedType: TypeInformation[Person] = Types.CASE_CLASS[Person]
}
```

In the Java DataStream API, you can also use the `returns()` method to explicitly specify the return type of an operator when defining the dataflow as shown in the following:

```
DataStream<Tuple2<String, Integer>> tuples = ...
DataStream<Person> persons = tuples
  .map(t -> new Person(t.f0, t.f1))
  // provide TypeInformation for the map lambda function's return type
  .returns(Types.POJO(Person.class));
```

Defining Keys and Referencing Fields

Some of the transformations you saw in the previous section require a key specification or field reference on the input stream type. In Flink, keys are not predefined in the input types like in systems that work with key-value pairs. Instead, keys are defined as functions over the input data. Therefore, it is not necessary to define data types to hold keys and values, which avoids a lot of boilerplate code.

In the following, we discuss different methods to reference fields and define keys on data types.

Field Positions

If the data type is a tuple, keys can be defined by simply using the field position of the corresponding tuple element. The following example keys the input stream by the second field of the input tuple:

```
val input: DataStream[(Int, String, Long)] = ...
val keyed = input.keyBy(1)
```

Composite keys consisting of more than one tuple field can also be defined. In this case, the positions are provided as a list, one after the other. We can key the input stream by the second and third fields as follows:

```
val keyed2 = input.keyBy(1, 2)
```

Field Expressions

Another way to define keys and select fields is by using `String`-based field expressions. Field expressions work for tuples, POJOs, and case classes. They also support the selection of nested fields.

In the introductory example of this chapter, we defined the following case class:

```
case class SensorReading(
    id: String,
    timestamp: Long,
    temperature: Double)
```

To key the stream by sensor ID we can pass the field name `id` to the `keyBy()` function:

```
val sensorStream: DataStream[SensorReading] = ...
val keyedSensors = sensorStream.keyBy("id")
```

POJO or case class fields are selected by their field name like in the above example. Tuple fields are referenced either by their field name (1-offset for Scala tuples, 0-offset for Java tuples) or by their 0-offset field index:

```
val input: DataStream[(Int, String, Long)] = ...
val keyed1 = input.keyBy("2") // key by 3rd field
val keyed2 = input.keyBy("_1") // key by 1st field

DataStream<Tuple3<Integer, String, Long>> javaInput = ...
javaInput.keyBy("f2") // key Java tuple by 3rd field
```

Nested fields in POJOs and tuples are selected by denoting the nesting level with a "." (period character). Consider the following case classes:

```
case class Address(
    address: String,
    zip: String
    country: String)
```

```
case class Person(
  name: String,
  birthday: (Int, Int, Int), // year, month, day
  address: Address)
```

If we want to reference a person's ZIP code, we can use a field expression:

```
val persons: DataStream[Person] = ...
persons.keyBy("address.zip") // key by nested POJO field
```

It is also possible to nest expressions on mixed types. The following expression accesses the field of a tuple nested in a POJO:

```
persons.keyBy("birthday._1") // key by field of nested tuple
```

A full data type can be selected using the wildcard field expression "_" (underscore character):

```
persons.keyBy("birthday._") // key by all fields of nested tuple
```

Key Selectors

A third option to specify keys are KeySelector functions. A KeySelector function extracts a key from an input event:

```
// T: the type of input elements
// KEY: the type of the key
KeySelector[IN, KEY]
  > getKey(IN): KEY
```

The introductory example actually uses a simple KeySelector function in the keyBy() method:

```
val sensorData: DataStream[SensorReading] = ...
val byId: KeyedStream[SensorReading, String] = sensorData
  .keyBy(r => r.id)
```

A KeySelector function receives an input item and returns a key. The key does not necessarily have to be a field of the input event but can be derived using arbitrary computations. In the following, the KeySelector function returns the maximum of the tuple fields as the key:

```
val input : DataStream[(Int, Int)] = ...
val keyedStream = input.keyBy(value => math.max(value._1, value._2))
```

Compared to field positions and field expressions, an advantage of KeySelector functions is that the resulting key is strongly typed due to the generic types of the KeySelector class.

Implementing Functions

You've seen user-defined functions in action in the code examples of this chapter so far. In this section, we explain the different ways in which you can define and parametrize functions in the DataStream API in more detail.

Function Classes

Flink exposes all interfaces for user-defined functions, such as `MapFunction`, `Filter Function`, and `ProcessFunction`, as interfaces or abstract classes.

A function is implemented by implementing the interface or extending the abstract class. In the following example, we implement a `FilterFunction` that filters for strings that contain the word `"flink"`:

```
class FlinkFilter extends FilterFunction[String] {
  override def filter(value: String): Boolean = {
    value.contains("flink")
  }
}
```

An instance of the function class can then be passed as an argument to the filter transformation:

```
val flinkTweets = tweets.filter(new FlinkFilter)
```

Functions can also be implemented as anonymous classes:

```
val flinkTweets = tweets.filter(
  new RichFilterFunction[String] {
    override def filter(value: String): Boolean = {
      value.contains("flink")
    }
  })
```

Functions can receive parameters through their constructor. We can parametrize the above example and pass the `String` `"flink"` as a parameter to the `KeywordFilter` constructor as shown below:

```
val tweets: DataStream[String] = ???
val flinkTweets = tweets.filter(new KeywordFilter("flink"))

class KeywordFilter(keyWord: String) extends FilterFunction[String] {
  override def filter(value: String): Boolean = {
    value.contains(keyWord)
  }
}
```

When a program is submitted for execution, all function objects are serialized using Java serialization and shipped to all parallel tasks of their corresponding operators. Therefore, all configuration values are preserved after the object is deserialized.

Functions Must Be Java Serializable

Flink serializes all function objects with Java serialization to ship them to the worker processes. Everything contained in a user function must be `Serializable`.

If your function requires a nonserializable object instance, you can either implement it as a rich function and initialize the nonserializable field in the `open()` method or override the Java serialization and deserialization methods.

Lambda Functions

Most DataStream API methods accept lambda functions. Lambda functions are available for Scala and Java and offer a simple and concise way to implement application logic when no advanced operations such as accessing state and configuration are required. The following example show a lambda function that filters tweets containing the word "flink":

```
val tweets: DataStream[String] = ...
// a filter lambda function that checks if tweets contains the word "flink"
val flinkTweets = tweets.filter(_.contains("flink"))
```

Rich Functions

Oftentimes there is a need to initialize a function before it processes the first record or to retrieve information about the context in which it is executed. The DataStream API provides rich functions that expose more functionality than the regular functions discussed until now.

There are rich versions of all the DataStream API transformation functions, and you can use them in the same places you can use a regular function or lambda function. Rich functions can be parameterized just like regular function classes. The name of a rich function starts with `Rich` followed by the transformation name—`RichMapFunction`, `RichFlatMapFunction`, and so on.

When using a rich function, you can implement two additional methods to the function's lifecycle:

- The `open()` method is an initialization method for the rich function. It is called once per task before a transformation method like filter or map is called. `open()` is typically used for setup work that needs to be done only once. Note that the `Configuration` parameter is only used by the DataSet API and not by the DataStream API. Hence, it should be ignored.

- The `close()` method is a finalization method for the function and it is called once per task after the last call of the transformation method. Thus, it is commonly used for cleanup and releasing resources.

In addition, the method `getRuntimeContext()` provides access to the function's `Run timeContext`. The `RuntimeContext` can be used to retrieve information such as the function's parallelism, its subtask index, and the name of the task that executes the function. Further, it includes methods for accessing partitioned state. Stateful stream processing in Flink is discussed in detail in "Implementing Stateful Functions" on page 154. The following example code shows how to use the methods of a `RichFlat MapFunction`. Example 5-3 shows the methods of a RichFLatMapFunction

Example 5-3. The open() and close() methods of a RichFlatMapFunction.

```
class MyFlatMap extends RichFlatMapFunction[Int, (Int, Int)] {
  var subTaskIndex = 0

  override def open(configuration: Configuration): Unit = {
    subTaskIndex = getRuntimeContext.getIndexOfThisSubtask
    // do some initialization
    // e.g., establish a connection to an external system
  }

  override def flatMap(in: Int, out: Collector[(Int, Int)]): Unit = {
    // subtasks are 0-indexed
    if(in % 2 == subTaskIndex) {
      out.collect((subTaskIndex, in))
    }
    // do some more processing
  }

  override def close(): Unit = {
    // do some cleanup, e.g., close connections to external systems
  }
}
```

Including External and Flink Dependencies

Adding external dependencies is a common requirement when implementing Flink applications. There are many popular libraries out there, such as Apache Commons or Google Guava, for various use cases. Moreover, most Flink applications depend on one or more of Flink's connectors to ingest data from or emit data to external systems, like Apache Kafka, filesystems, or Apache Cassandra. Some applications also leverage Flink's domain-specific libraries, such as the Table API, SQL, or the CEP library. Consequently, most Flink applications do not only depend on Flink's DataStream API dependency and the Java SDK but also on additional third-party and Flink-internal dependencies.

When an application is executed, all of its dependencies must be available to the application. By default, only the core API dependencies (DataStream and DataSet APIs) are loaded by a Flink cluster. All other dependencies an application requires must be explicitly provided.

The reason for this is to keep the number of default dependencies low.[4] Most connectors and libraries rely on one or more libraries, which typically have several additional transitive dependencies. Often, these include frequently used libraries, such as Apache Commons or Google's Guava. Many problems originate from incompatibilities among different versions of the same library that are pulled in from different connectors or directly from the user application.

There are two ways to ensure all dependencies are available to an application when it is executed:

1. Bundle all dependencies into the application JAR file. This yields a self-contained, yet typically quite large, application JAR file.

2. The JAR file of a dependency can be added to the *./lib* folder of a Flink setup. In this case, the dependencies are loaded into the classpath when Flink processes are started. A dependency that is added to the classpath like this is available to (and might interfere with) all applications that run on the Flink setup.

Building a so-called fat JAR file is the preferred way to handle application dependencies. The Flink Maven archetypes we introduced in "Bootstrap a Flink Maven Project" on page 76 generate Maven projects that are configured to produce application-fat JARs that include all required dependencies. Dependencies included in the classpath of Flink processes by default are automatically excluded from the JAR file. The *pom.xml* file of a generated Maven project contains comments that explain how to add additional dependencies.

Summary

In this chapter we introduced the basics of Flink's DataStream API. We examined the structure of Flink programs and learned how to combine data and partitioning transformations to build streaming applications. We also looked into supported data types and different ways to specify keys and user-defined functions. If you take a step back and read the introductory example once more, you hopefully have a better idea about what is going on. In Chapter 6, things are going to get even more interesting—we will learn how to enrich our programs with window operators and time semantics.

---

4 Flink also aims to keep its own external dependencies to a minimum and hides most of them (including transitive dependencies) from user applications to prevent version conflicts.

## CHAPTER 6

Time-Based and Window Operators

In this chapter, we will cover DataStream API methods for time handling and time-based operators, like windows. As you learned in "Time Semantics", Flink's time-based operators can be applied with different notions of time.

First, we will learn how to define time characteristics, timestamps, and watermarks. Then, we will cover the process functions, low-level transformations that provide access to timestamps and watermarks and can register timers. Next, we will get to use Flink's window API, which provides built-in implementations of the most common window types. You will also get an introduction to custom, user-defined window operations and core windowing constructs, such as assigners, triggers, and evictors. Finally, we will discuss how to join streams on time and strategies to handle late events.

Configuring Time Characteristics

To define time operations in a distributed stream processing application, it is important to understand the meaning of time. When you specify a window to collect events in one-minute buckets, which events exactly will each bucket contain? In the Data-Stream API, you can use the *time characteristic* to tell Flink how to define time when you are creating windows. The time characteristic is a property of the `StreamExecutionEnvironment` and it takes the following values:

`ProcessingTime`
    specifies that operators determine the current time of the data stream according to the system clock of the machine where they are being executed. Processing-time windows trigger based on machine time and include whatever elements happen to have arrived at the operator until that point in time. In general, using processing time for window operations results in nondeterministic results

because the contents of the windows depend on the speed at which the elements arrive. This setting offers very low latency because processing tasks do not have to wait for watermarks to advance the event time.

EventTime

specifies that operators determine the current time by using information from the data itself. Each event carries a timestamp and the logical time of the system is defined by watermarks. As you learned in "Timestamps" on page 47, timestamps either exist in the data before entering the data processing pipeline, or are assigned by the application at the sources. An event-time window triggers when the watermarks declare that all timestamps for a certain time interval have been received. Event-time windows compute deterministic results even when events arrive out of order. The window result will not depend on how fast the stream is read or processed.

IngestionTime

specifies the processing time of the source operator as an event time timestamp to each ingested record and automatically generates watermarks. It is a hybrid of EventTime and ProcessingTime. The ingestion time of an event is the time it entered the stream processor. Ingestion time does not offer much practical value compared to event time as it does not provide deterministic results and has similar performance as event time.

Example 6-1 shows how to set the time characteristic by revisiting the sensor streaming application code you wrote in "Hello, Flink!" on page 79.

Example 6-1. Setting the time characteristic to event time

```
object AverageSensorReadings {

  // main() defines and executes the DataStream program
  def main(args: Array[String]) {
    // set up the streaming execution environment
    val env = StreamExecutionEnvironment.getExecutionEnvironment

    // use event time for the application
    env.setStreamTimeCharacteristic(TimeCharacteristic.EventTime)

    // ingest sensor stream
    val sensorData: DataStream[SensorReading] = env.addSource(...)
  }
}
```

Setting the time characteristic to EventTime enables timestamp and watermark handling, and as a result, event-time operations. Of course, you can still use processing-time windows and timers if you choose the EventTime time characteristic.

In order to use processing time, replace `TimeCharacteristic.EventTime` with `TimeCharacteristic.ProcessingTime`.

Assigning Timestamps and Generating Watermarks

As discussed in "Event-Time Processing" on page 47, your application needs to provide two important pieces of information to Flink in order to operate in event time. Each event must be associated with a timestamp that typically indicates when the event actually happened. Event-time streams also need to carry watermarks from which operators infer the current event time.

Timestamps and watermarks are specified in milliseconds since the epoch of `1970-01-01T00:00:00Z`. A watermark tells operators that no more events with a timestamp less than or equal to the watermark are expected. Timestamps and watermarks can be either assigned and generated by a `SourceFunction` or using an explicit user-defined timestamp assigner and watermark generator. Assigning timestamps and generating watermarks in a `SourceFunction` is discussed in "Source Functions, Timestamps, and Watermarks" on page 204. Here we explain how to do this with a user-defined function.

Overriding Source-Generated Timestamps and Watermarks

If a timestamp assigner is used, any existing timestamps and watermarks will be overwritten.

The DataStream API provides the `TimestampAssigner` interface to extract timestamps from elements after they have been ingested into the streaming application. Typically, the timestamp assigner is called right after the source function because most assigners make assumptions about the order of elements with respect to their timestamps when generating watermarks. Since elements are typically ingested in parallel, any operation that causes Flink to redistribute elements across parallel stream partitions, such as parallelism changes, `keyBy()`, or other explicit redistributions, mixes up the timestamp order of the elements.

It is best practice to assign timestamps and generate watermarks as close to the sources as possible or even within the `SourceFunction`. Depending on the use case, it is possible to apply an initial filtering or transformation on the input stream before assigning timestamps if such operations do not induce a redistribution of elements.

To ensure that event-time operations behave as expected, the assigner should be called before any event-time dependent transformation (e.g., before the first event-time window).

Timestamp assigners behave like other transformation operators. They are called on a stream of elements and produce a new stream of timestamped elements and watermarks. Timestamp assigners do not change the data type of a DataStream.

The code in Example 6-2 shows how to use a timestamp assigner. In this example, after reading the stream, we first apply a filter transformation and then call the assignTimestampsAndWatermarks() method where we define the timestamp assigner MyAssigner().

Example 6-2. Using a timestamp assigner

```
val env = StreamExecutionEnvironment.getExecutionEnvironment

// set the event time characteristic
env.setStreamTimeCharacteristic(TimeCharacteristic.EventTime)

// ingest sensor stream
val readings: DataStream[SensorReading] = env
  .addSource(new SensorSource)
  // assign timestamps and generate watermarks
  .assignTimestampsAndWatermarks(new MyAssigner())
```

In the example above, MyAssigner can either be of type AssignerWithPeriodicWatermarks or AssignerWithPunctuatedWatermarks. These two interfaces extend the TimestampAssigner interface provided by the DataStream API. The first interface defines assigners that emit watermarks periodically while the second injects watermarks based on a property of the input events. We describe both interfaces in detail next.

Assigner with periodic watermarks

Assigning watermarks periodically means that we instruct the system to emit watermarks and advance the event time in fixed intervals of machine time. The default interval is set to two hundred milliseconds, but it can be configured using the ExecutionConfig.setAutoWatermarkInterval() method:

```
val env = StreamExecutionEnvironment.getExecutionEnvironment
env.setStreamTimeCharacteristic(TimeCharacteristic.EventTime)
// generate watermarks every 5 seconds
env.getConfig.setAutoWatermarkInterval(5000)
```

In the preceding example, you instruct the program to emit watermarks every 5 seconds. Actually, every 5 seconds, Flink invokes the getCurrentWatermark() method of AssignerWithPeriodicWatermarks. If the method returns a nonnull value with a timestamp larger than the timestamp of the previous watermark, the new watermark is forwarded. This check is necessary to ensure event time continuously increases; otherwise no watermark is produced.

Example 6-3 shows an assigner with periodic timestamps that produces watermarks by keeping track of the maximum element timestamp it has seen so far. When asked for a new watermark, the assigner returns a watermark with the maximum timestamp minus a 1-minute tolerance interval.

Example 6-3. A periodic watermark assigner

```scala
class PeriodicAssigner
    extends AssignerWithPeriodicWatermarks[SensorReading] {

  val bound: Long = 60 * 1000     // 1 min in ms
  var maxTs: Long = Long.MinValue // the maximum observed timestamp

  override def getCurrentWatermark: Watermark = {
    // generated watermark with 1 min tolerance
    new Watermark(maxTs - bound)
  }

  override def extractTimestamp(
      r: SensorReading,
      previousTS: Long): Long = {
    // update maximum timestamp
    maxTs = maxTs.max(r.timestamp)
    // return record timestamp
    r.timestamp
  }
}
```

The DataStream API provides implementations for two common cases of timestamp assigners with periodic watermarks. If your input elements have timestamps that are monotonically increasing, you can use the shortcut method `assignAscending TimeStamps`. This method uses the current timestamp to generate watermarks, since no earlier timestamps can appear. The following shows how to generate watermarks for ascending timestamps:

```scala
val stream: DataStream[SensorReading] = ...
val withTimestampsAndWatermarks = stream
  .assignAscendingTimestamps(e => e.timestamp)
```

The other common case of periodic watermark generation is when you know the maximum lateness that you will encounter in the input stream—the maximum difference between an element's timestamp and the largest timestamp of all perviously ingested elements. For such cases, Flink provides the `BoundedOutOfOrder nessTimeStampExtractor`, which takes the maximum expected lateness as an argument:

```scala
val stream: DataStream[SensorReading] = ...
val output = stream.assignTimestampsAndWatermarks(
```

```
new BoundedOutOfOrdernessTimestampExtractor[SensorReading](
    Time.seconds(10))(e =>.timestamp)
```

In the preceding code, elements are allowed to be late up to 10 seconds. This means if the difference between an element's event time and the maximum timestamp of all previous elements is greater than 10 seconds, the element might arrive for processing after its corresponding computation has completed and the result has been emitted. Flink offers different strategies to handle such late events, and we discuss those later in "Handling Late Data" on page 148.

Assigner with punctuated watermarks

Sometimes the input stream contains special tuples or markers that indicate the stream's progress. Flink provides the AssignerWithPunctuatedWatermarks interface for such cases, or when watermarks can be defined based on some other property of the input elements. It defines the checkAndGetNextWatermark() method, which is called for each event right after extractTimestamp(). This method can decide to generate a new watermark or not. A new watermark is emitted if the method returns a nonnull watermark that is larger than the latest emitted watermark.

Example 6-4 shows a punctuated watermark assigner that emits a watermark for every reading it receives from the sensor with the ID "sensor_1".

Example 6-4. A punctuated watermark assigner

```
class PunctuatedAssigner
    extends AssignerWithPunctuatedWatermarks[SensorReading] {

  val bound: Long = 60 * 1000 // 1 min in ms

  override def checkAndGetNextWatermark(
      r: SensorReading,
      extractedTS: Long): Watermark = {
    if (r.id == "sensor_1") {
      // emit watermark if reading is from sensor_1
      new Watermark(extractedTS - bound)
    } else {
      // do not emit a watermark
      null
    }
  }

  override def extractTimestamp(
      r: SensorReading,
      previousTS: Long): Long = {
    // assign record timestamp
    r.timestamp
  }
}
```

Watermarks, Latency, and Completeness

So far we have discussed how to generate watermarks using a `TimestampAssigner`. What we have not discussed yet is the effect that watermarks have on your streaming application.

Watermarks are used to balance latency and result completeness. They control how long to wait for data to arrive before performing a computation, such as finalizing a window computation and emitting the result. An operator based on event time uses watermarks to determine the completeness of its ingested records and the progress of its operation. Based on the received watermarks, the operator computes a point in time up to which it expects to have received relevant input records.

However, the reality is that we can never have perfect watermarks because that would mean we are always certain there are no delayed records. In practice, you need to make an educated guess and use heuristics to generate watermarks in your applications. You need to use whatever information you have about the sources, the network, and the partitions to estimate progress and an upper bound for the lateness of your input records. Estimates mean there is room for errors, in which case you might generate watermarks that are inaccurate, resulting in late data or an unnecessary increase in the application's latency. With this in mind, you can use watermarks to balance result latency and result completeness.

If you generate loose watermarks—where the watermarks are far behind the timestamps of the processed records—you increase the latency of the produced results. You may have been able to generate a result earlier but you had to wait for the watermark. Moreover the state size typically increases because the application needs to buffer more data until it can perform a computation. However, you can be quite certain all relevant data is available when you perform a computation.

On the other hand, if you generate very tight watermarks—watermarks that might be larger than the timestamps of some later records—time-based computations might be performed before all relevant data has arrived. While this might yield incomplete or inaccurate results, the results are produced in a timely fashion with lower latency.

Unlike batch applications, which are built around the premise that all data is available, the latency/completeness tradeoff is a fundamental characteristic of stream processing applications, which process unbounded data as it arrives. Watermarks are a powerful way to control the behavior of an application with respect to time. Besides watermarks, Flink has many features to tweak the exact behavior of time-based operations, such as process functions and window triggers, and offers different ways to handle late data, which are discussed in "Handling Late Data" on page 148.

Process Functions

Even though time information and watermarks are crucial to many streaming applications, you might have noticed that we cannot access them through the basic DataStream API transformations we have seen so far. For example, a MapFunction does not have access to timestamps or the current event time.

The DataStream API provides a family of low-level transformations, the process functions, which can also access record timestamps and watermarks and register timers that trigger at a specific time in the future. Moreover, process functions feature side outputs to emit records to multiple output streams. Process functions are commonly used to build event-driven applications and to implement custom logic for which predefined windows and transformations might not be suitable. For example, most operators for Flink's SQL support are implemented using process functions.

Currently, Flink provides eight different process functions: ProcessFunction, Keyed ProcessFunction, CoProcessFunction, ProcessJoinFunction, BroadcastProcess Function, KeyedBroadcastProcessFunction, ProcessWindowFunction, and ProcessAllWindowFunction. As indicated by name, these functions are applicable in different contexts. However, they have a very similar feature set. We will continue discussing these common features by looking in detail at the KeyedProcessFunction.

The KeyedProcessFunction is a very versatile function and can be applied to a Keyed Stream. The function is called for each record of the stream and returns zero, one, or more records. All process functions implement the RichFunction interface and hence offer open(), close(), and getRuntimeContext() methods. Additionally, a KeyedPro cessFunction[KEY, IN, OUT] provides the following two methods:

1. processElement(v: IN, ctx: Context, out: Collector[OUT]) is called for each record of the stream. As usual, result records are emitted by passing them to the Collector. The Context object is what makes a process function special. It gives access to the timestamp and the key of the current record and to a TimerService. Moreover, the Context can emit records to side outputs.

2. onTimer(timestamp: Long, ctx: OnTimerContext, out: Collector[OUT]) is a callback function that is invoked when a previously registered timer triggers. The timestamp argument gives the timestamp of the firing timer and the Collec tor allows records to be emitted. The OnTimerContext provides the same services as the Context object of the processElement() method and also returns the time domain (processing time or event time) of the firing trigger.

TimerService and Timers

The TimerService of the Context and OnTimerContext objects offers the following methods:

- currentProcessingTime(): Long returns the current processing time.
- currentWatermark(): Long returns the timestamp of the current watermark.
- registerProcessingTimeTimer(timestamp: Long): Unit registers a processing time timer for the current key. The timer will fire when the processing time of the executing machine reaches the provided timestamp.
- registerEventTimeTimer(timestamp: Long): Unit registers an event-time timer for the current key. The timer will fire when the watermark is updated to a timestamp that is equal to or larger than the timer's timestamp.
- deleteProcessingTimeTimer(timestamp: Long): Unit deletes a processing-time timer that was previously registered for the current key. If no such timer exists, the method has no effect.
- deleteEventTimeTimer(timestamp: Long): Unit deletes an event-time timer that was previously registered for the current key. If no such timer exists, the method has no effect.

When a timer fires, the onTimer() callback function is called. The processElement() and onTimer() methods are synchronized to prevent concurrent access and manipulation of state.

Timers on Nonkeyed Streams

Timers can only be registered on keyed streams. A common use case for timers is to clear keyed state after some period of inactivity for a key or to implement custom time-based windowing logic. To use timers on a nonkeyed stream, you can create a keyed stream by using a KeySelector with a constant dummy key. Note that this will move all data to a single task such that the operator would be effectively executed with a parallelism of 1.

For each key and timestamp, exactly one timer can be registered, which means each key can have multiple timers but only one for each timestamp. By default, a KeyedProcessFunction holds the timestamps of all timers in a priority queue on the heap. However, you can configure the RocksDB state backend to also store the timers.

Timers are checkpointed along with any other state of the function. If an application needs to recover from a failure, all processing-time timers that expired while the application was restarting will fire immediately when the application resumes. This is also true for processing-time timers that are persisted in a savepoint. Timers are always asynchronously checkpointed, with one exception. If you are using the

RocksDB state backend with incremental checkpoints and storing the timers on the heap (default setting), they are checkpointed synchronously. In that case, it is recommended to not use timers excessively, to avoid long checkpointing times.

 Timers that are registered for a timestamp in the past are not silently dropped but processed as well. Processing-time timers fire immediately after the registering method returns. Event-time timers fire when the next watermark is processed.

The following code shows how to apply a KeyedProcessFunction to a KeyedStream. The function monitors the temperatures of sensors and emits a warning if the temperature of a sensor monotonically increases for a period of 1 second in processing time:

```
val warnings = readings
  // key by sensor id
  .keyBy(_.id)
  // apply ProcessFunction to monitor temperatures
  .process(new TempIncreaseAlertFunction)
```

The implementation of the TempIncreaseAlterFunction is shown in Example 6-5.

Example 6-5. A KeyedProcessFunction that emits a warning if the temperature of a sensor monotonically increases for 1 second in processing time

```
/** Emits a warning if the temperature of a sensor
  * monotonically increases for 1 second (in processing time).
  */
class TempIncreaseAlertFunction
    extends KeyedProcessFunction[String, SensorReading, String] {
  // stores temperature of last sensor reading
  lazy val lastTemp: ValueState[Double] = getRuntimeContext.getState(
      new ValueStateDescriptor[Double]("lastTemp", Types.of[Double]))
  // stores timestamp of currently active timer
  lazy val currentTimer: ValueState[Long] = getRuntimeContext.getState(
      new ValueStateDescriptor[Long]("timer", Types.of[Long]))

  override def processElement(
      r: SensorReading,
      ctx: KeyedProcessFunction[String, SensorReading, String]#Context,
      out: Collector[String]): Unit = {
    // get previous temperature
    val prevTemp = lastTemp.value()
    // update last temperature
    lastTemp.update(r.temperature)

    val curTimerTimestamp = currentTimer.value();
    if (prevTemp == 0.0 || r.temperature < prevTemp) {
```

```scala
      // temperature decreased; delete current timer
      ctx.timerService().deleteProcessingTimeTimer(curTimerTimestamp)
      currentTimer.clear()
    } else if (r.temperature > prevTemp && curTimerTimestamp == 0) {
      // temperature increased and we have not set a timer yet
      // set processing time timer for now + 1 second
      val timerTs = ctx.timerService().currentProcessingTime() + 1000
      ctx.timerService().registerProcessingTimeTimer(timerTs)
      // remember current timer
      currentTimer.update(timerTs)
    }
  }

  override def onTimer(
      ts: Long,
      ctx: KeyedProcessFunction[String, SensorReading, String]#OnTimerContext,
      out: Collector[String]): Unit = {
    out.collect("Temperature of sensor '" + ctx.getCurrentKey +
      "' monotonically increased for 1 second.")
    currentTimer.clear()
  }
}
```

Emitting to Side Outputs

Most operators of the DataStream API have a single output—they produce one result stream with a specific data type. Only the split operator allows splitting a stream into multiple streams of the same type. Side outputs are a feature of process functions to emit multiple streams from a function with possibly different types. A side output is identified by an OutputTag[X] object, where X is the type of the resulting side output stream. Process functions can emit a record to one or more side outputs via the Context object.

Example 6-6 shows how to emit data from a ProcessFunction via DataStream of a side output.

Example 6-6. Applying a ProcessFunction that emits to a side output

```scala
val monitoredReadings: DataStream[SensorReading] = readings
  // monitor stream for readings with freezing temperatures
  .process(new FreezingMonitor)

// retrieve and print the freezing alarms side output
monitoredReadings
  .getSideOutput(new OutputTag[String]("freezing-alarms"))
  .print()

// print the main output
readings.print()
```

Example 6-7 shows the FreezingMonitor function that monitors a stream of sensor readings and emits a warning to a side output for readings with a temperature below 32°F.

Example 6-7. A ProcessFunction that emits records to a side output

```scala
/** Emits freezing alarms to a side output for readings
  * with a temperature below 32F. */
class FreezingMonitor extends ProcessFunction[SensorReading, SensorReading] {

  // define a side output tag
  lazy val freezingAlarmOutput: OutputTag[String] =
    new OutputTag[String]("freezing-alarms")

  override def processElement(
      r: SensorReading,
      ctx: ProcessFunction[SensorReading, SensorReading]#Context,
      out: Collector[SensorReading]): Unit = {
    // emit freezing alarm if temperature is below 32F
    if (r.temperature < 32.0) {
      ctx.output(freezingAlarmOutput, s"Freezing Alarm for ${r.id}")
    }
    // forward all readings to the regular output
    out.collect(r)
  }
}
```

CoProcessFunction

For low-level operations on two inputs, the DataStream API also provides the CoProcessFunction. Similar to a CoFlatMapFunction, a CoProcessFunction offers a transformation method for each input, processElement1() and processElement2(). Similar to the ProcessFunction, both methods are called with a Context object that gives access to the element or timer timestamp, a TimerService, and side outputs. The CoProcessFunction also provides an onTimer() callback method. Example 6-8 shows how to apply a CoProcessFunction to combine two streams.

Example 6-8. Applying a CoProcessFunction

```scala
// ingest sensor stream
val sensorData: DataStream[SensorReading] = ...

// filter switches enable forwarding of readings
val filterSwitches: DataStream[(String, Long)] = env
  .fromCollection(Seq(
    ("sensor_2", 10 * 1000L), // forward sensor_2 for 10 seconds
    ("sensor_7", 60 * 1000L)) // forward sensor_7 for 1 minute
  )
```

```
val forwardedReadings = readings
  // connect readings and switches
  .connect(filterSwitches)
  // key by sensor ids
  .keyBy(_.id, _._1)
  // apply filtering CoProcessFunction
  .process(new ReadingFilter)
```

The implementation of a `ReadingFilter` function that dynamically filters a stream of sensor readings based on a stream of filter switches is shown in Example 6-9.

Example 6-9. Implementation of a CoProcessFunction that dynamically filters a stream of sensor readings

```
class ReadingFilter
    extends CoProcessFunction[SensorReading, (String, Long), SensorReading] {

  // switch to enable forwarding
  lazy val forwardingEnabled: ValueState[Boolean] = getRuntimeContext.getState(
      new ValueStateDescriptor[Boolean]("filterSwitch", Types.of[Boolean]))

  // hold timestamp of currently active disable timer
  lazy val disableTimer: ValueState[Long] = getRuntimeContext.getState(
      new ValueStateDescriptor[Long]("timer", Types.of[Long]))

  override def processElement1(
      reading: SensorReading,
      ctx: CoProcessFunction[SensorReading, (String, Long), SensorReading]#Context,
      out: Collector[SensorReading]): Unit = {
    // check if we may forward the reading
    if (forwardingEnabled.value()) {
      out.collect(reading)
    }
  }

  override def processElement2(
      switch: (String, Long),
      ctx: CoProcessFunction[SensorReading, (String, Long), SensorReading]#Context,
      out: Collector[SensorReading]): Unit = {
    // enable reading forwarding
    forwardingEnabled.update(true)
    // set disable forward timer
    val timerTimestamp = ctx.timerService().currentProcessingTime() + switch._2
    val curTimerTimestamp = disableTimer.value()
      if (timerTimestamp > curTimerTimestamp) {
      // remove current timer and register new timer
      ctx.timerService().deleteEventTimeTimer(curTimerTimestamp)
      ctx.timerService().registerProcessingTimeTimer(timerTimestamp)
      disableTimer.update(timerTimestamp)
    }
```

```
    }

    override def onTimer(
        ts: Long,
        ctx: CoProcessFunction[SensorReading, (String, Long), SensorReading]
                            #OnTimerContext,
        out: Collector[SensorReading]): Unit = {
      // remove all state; forward switch will be false by default
      forwardingEnabled.clear()
      disableTimer.clear()
    }
}
```

Window Operators

Windows are common operations in streaming applications. They enable transformations such as aggregations on *bounded intervals* of an unbounded stream. Typically, these intervals are defined using time-based logic. Window operators provide a way to group events in buckets of finite size and apply computations on the bounded contents of these buckets. For example, a window operator can group the events of a stream into windows of 5 minutes and count for each window how many events have been received.

The DataStream API provides built-in methods for the most common window operations as well as a very flexible windowing mechanism to define custom windowing logic. In this section, we show you how to define window operators, present the built-in window types of the DataStream API, discuss the functions that can be applied on a window, and finally explain how to define custom windowing logic.

Defining Window Operators

Window operators can be applied on a keyed or a nonkeyed stream. Window operators on keyed windows are evaluated in parallel, and nonkeyed windows are processed in a single thread.

To create a window operator, you need to specify two window components:

1. A *window assigner* that determines how the elements of the input stream are grouped into windows. A window assigner produces a WindowedStream (or All WindowedStream if applied on a nonkeyed DataStream).
2. A *window function* that is applied on a WindowedStream (or AllWindowedStream) and processes the elements that are assigned to a window.

The following code shows how to specify a window assigner and a window function on a keyed or nonkeyed stream:

```
// define a keyed window operator
stream
```

```
    .keyBy(...)
    .window(...)                      // specify the window assigner
    .reduce/aggregate/process(...) // specify the window function

// define a nonkeyed window-all operator
stream
    .windowAll(...)                   // specify the window assigner
    .reduce/aggregate/process(...) // specify the window function
```

In the remainder of the chapter we focus on keyed windows only. Nonkeyed windows (also called all-windows in the DataStream API) behave exactly the same, except that they collect all data and are not evaluated in parallel.

> Note that you can customize a window operator by providing a custom trigger or evictor and declaring strategies to deal with late elements. Custom window operators are discussed in detail later in this section.

Built-in Window Assigners

Flink provides built-in window assigners for the most common windowing use cases. All assigners we discuss here are time-based and were introduced in "Operations on Data Streams" on page 22. Time-based window assigners assign an element based on its event-time timestamp or the current processing time to windows. Time windows have a start and an end timestamp.

All built-in window assigners provide a default trigger that triggers the evaluation of a window once the (processing or event) time passes the end of the window. It is important to note that a window is created when the first element is assigned to it. Flink will never evaluate empty windows.

Count-Based Windows

In addition to time-based windows, Flink also supports count-based windows—windows that group a fixed number of elements in the order in which they arrive at the window operator. Since they depend on the ingestion order, count-based windows are not deterministic. Moreover, they can cause issues if they are used without a custom trigger that discards incomplete and stale windows at some point.

Flink's built-in window assigners create windows of type `TimeWindow`. This window type essentially represents a time interval between the two timestamps, where start is inclusive and end is exclusive. It exposes methods to retrieve the window boundaries, to check whether windows intersect, and to merge overlapping windows.

In the following, we show the different built-in window assigners of the DataStream API and how to use them to define window operators.

Tumbling windows

A tumbling window assigner places elements into nonoverlapping, fixed-size windows, as shown in Figure 6-1.

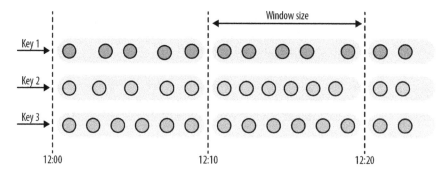

Figure 6-1. A tumbling window assigner places elements into fixed-size, nonoverlapping windows

The Datastream API provides two assigners—TumblingEventTimeWindows and Tum blingProcessingTimeWindows—for tumbling event-time and processing-time windows, respectively. A tumbling window assigner receives one parameter, the window size in time units; this can be specified using the of(Time size) method of the assigner. The time interval can be set in milliseconds, seconds, minutes, hours, or days.

The following code shows how to define event-time and processing-time tumbling windows on a stream of sensor data measurements:

```
val sensorData: DataStream[SensorReading] = ...

val avgTemp = sensorData
  .keyBy(_.id)
  // group readings in 1s event-time windows
  .window(TumblingEventTimeWindows.of(Time.seconds(1)))
  .process(new TemperatureAverager)

val avgTemp = sensorData
  .keyBy(_.id)
  // group readings in 1s processing-time windows
  .window(TumblingProcessingTimeWindows.of(Time.seconds(1)))
  .process(new TemperatureAverager)
```

The window definition looked a bit different in our first DataStream API example, "Operations on Data Streams" on page 22. There, we defined an event-time tumbling window using the timeWindow(size) method, which is a shortcut for either window. (TumblingEventTimeWindows.of(size)) or for window.(TumblingProcessing TimeWindows.of(size)) depending on the configured time characteristic. The following code shows how to use this shortcut:

```
val avgTemp = sensorData
  .keyBy(_.id)
  // shortcut for window.(TumblingEventTimeWindows.of(size))
  .timeWindow(Time.seconds(1))
  .process(new TemperatureAverager)
```

By default, tumbling windows are aligned to the epoch time, 1970-01-01-00:00:00.000. For example, an assigner with a size of one hour will define windows at 00:00:00, 01:00:00, 02:00:00, and so on. Alternatively, you can specify an offset as a second parameter in the assigner. The following code shows windows with an offset of 15 minutes that start at 00:15:00, 01:15:00, 02:15:00, and so on:

```
val avgTemp = sensorData
  .keyBy(_.id)
  // group readings in 1 hour windows with 15 min offset
  .window(TumblingEventTimeWindows.of(Time.hours(1), Time.minutes(15)))
  .process(new TemperatureAverager)
```

Sliding windows

The sliding window assigner assigns elements to fixed-sized windows that are shifted by a specified slide interval, as shown in Figure 6-2.

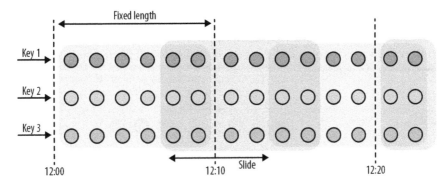

Figure 6-2. A sliding window assigner places elements into fixed-size, possibly overlapping windows

For a sliding window, you have to specify a window size and a slide interval that defines how frequently a new window is started. When the slide interval is smaller than the window size, the windows overlap and elements can be assigned to more than one window. If the slide is larger than the window size, some elements might not be assigned to any window and hence may be dropped.

The following code shows how to group the sensor readings in sliding windows of 1 hour size with a 15-minute slide interval. Each reading will be added to four windows. The DataStream API provides event-time and processing-time assigners, as well as shortcut methods, and a time interval offset can be set as the third parameter to the window assigner:

```
// event-time sliding windows assigner
val slidingAvgTemp = sensorData
  .keyBy(_.id)
  // create 1h event-time windows every 15 minutes
  .window(SlidingEventTimeWindows.of(Time.hours(1), Time.minutes(15)))
  .process(new TemperatureAverager)

// processing-time sliding windows assigner
val slidingAvgTemp = sensorData
  .keyBy(_.id)
  // create 1h processing-time windows every 15 minutes
  .window(SlidingProcessingTimeWindows.of(Time.hours(1), Time.minutes(15)))
  .process(new TemperatureAverager)

// sliding windows assigner using a shortcut method
val slidingAvgTemp = sensorData
  .keyBy(_.id)
  // shortcut for window.(SlidingEventTimeWindow.of(size, slide))
  .timeWindow(Time.hours(1), Time(minutes(15)))
  .process(new TemperatureAverager)
```

Session windows

A session window assigner places elements into nonoverlapping windows of activity of varying size. The boundaries of session windows are defined by gaps of inactivity, time intervals in which no record is received. Figure 6-3 illustrates how elements are assigned to session windows.

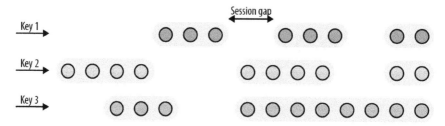

Figure 6-3. A session window assigner places elements into varying size windows defined by a session gap

The following examples show how to group the sensor readings into session windows where each session is defined by a 15-minute period of inactivity:

```
// event-time session windows assigner
val sessionWindows = sensorData
  .keyBy(_.id)
    // create event-time session windows with a 15 min gap
  .window(EventTimeSessionWindows.withGap(Time.minutes(15)))
  .process(...)

// processing-time session windows assigner
val sessionWindows = sensorData
  .keyBy(_.id)
    // create processing-time session windows with a 15 min gap
  .window(ProcessingTimeSessionWindows.withGap(Time.minutes(15)))
  .process(...)
```

Since the start and the end of a session window depend on the received elements, a window assigner cannot immediately assign all the elements to the correct window. Instead, the SessionWindows assigner initially maps each incoming element into its own window with the element's timestamp as the start time and the session gap as the window size. Subsequently, it merges all windows with overlapping ranges.

Applying Functions on Windows

Window functions define the computation that is performed on the elements of a window. There are two types of functions that can be applied on a window:

1. *Incremental aggregation functions* are directly applied when an element is added to a window and hold and update a single value as window state. These functions are typically very space-efficient and eventually emit the aggregated value as a result. ReduceFunction and AggregateFunction are incremental aggregation functions.
2. *Full window functions* collect all elements of a window and iterate over the list of all collected elements when they are evaluated. Full window functions usually require more space but allow for more complex logic than incremental aggregation functions. The ProcessWindowFunction is a full window function.

In this section, we discuss the different types of functions that can be applied on a window to perform aggregations or arbitrary computations on the window's contents. We also show how to jointly apply incremental aggregation and full window functions in a window operator.

ReduceFunction

The ReduceFunction was introduced in "KeyedStream Transformations" on page 87 when discussing running aggregations on keyed streams. A ReduceFunction accepts two values of the same type and combines them into a single value of the same type. When applied on a windowed stream, ReduceFunction incrementally aggregates the elements that are assigned to a window. A window only stores the current result of the aggregation—a single value of the ReduceFunction's input (and output) type. When a new element is received, the ReduceFunction is called with the new element and the current value that is read from the window's state. The window's state is replaced by the ReduceFunction's result.

The advantages of applying ReduceFunction on a window are the constant and small state size per window and the simple function interface. However, the applications for ReduceFunction are limited and usually restricted to simple aggregations since the input and output type must be the same.

Example 6-10 shows a reduce lambda function that computes the mininum temperature per sensor every 15 seconds.

Example 6-10. Applying a reduce lambda function on a WindowedStream

```
val minTempPerWindow: DataStream[(String, Double)] = sensorData
  .map(r => (r.id, r.temperature))
  .keyBy(_._1)
  .timeWindow(Time.seconds(15))
  .reduce((r1, r2) => (r1._1, r1._2.min(r2._2)))
```

AggregateFunction

Similar to ReduceFunction, AggregateFunction is also incrementally applied to the elements that are applied to a window. Moreover, the state of a window operator with an AggregateFunction also consists of a single value.

While the interface of the AggregateFunction is much more flexible, it is also more complex to implement compared to the interface of the ReduceFunction. The following code shows the interface of the AggregateFunction:

```
public interface AggregateFunction<IN, ACC, OUT> extends Function, Serializable {

    // create a new accumulator to start a new aggregate.
    ACC createAccumulator();

    // add an input element to the accumulator and return the accumulator.
    ACC add(IN value, ACC accumulator);

    // compute the result from the accumulator and return it.
    OUT getResult(ACC accumulator);

    // merge two accumulators and return the result.
    ACC merge(ACC a, ACC b);
}
```

The interface defines an input type, IN, an accumulator of type ACC, and a result type OUT. In contrast to the ReduceFunction, the intermediate data type and the output type do not depend on the input type.

Example 6-11 shows how to use an AggregateFunction to compute the average temperature of sensor readings per window. The accumulator maintains a running sum and count and the getResult() method computes the average value.

Example 6-11. Applying an AggregateFunction on a WindowedStream

```scala
val avgTempPerWindow: DataStream[(String, Double)] = sensorData
  .map(r => (r.id, r.temperature))
  .keyBy(_._1)
  .timeWindow(Time.seconds(15))
  .aggregate(new AvgTempFunction)


// An AggregateFunction to compute the average tempeature per sensor.
// The accumulator holds the sum of temperatures and an event count.
class AvgTempFunction
    extends AggregateFunction
  [(String, Double), (String, Double, Int), (String, Double)] {

  override def createAccumulator() = {
    ("", 0.0, 0)
  }

  override def add(in: (String, Double), acc: (String, Double, Int)) = {
    (in._1, in._2 + acc._2, 1 + acc._3)
  }

  override def getResult(acc: (String, Double, Int)) = {
    (acc._1, acc._2 / acc._3)
  }

  override def merge(acc1: (String, Double, Int), acc2: (String, Double, Int)) = {
    (acc1._1, acc1._2 + acc2._2, acc1._3 + acc2._3)
  }
}
```

ProcessWindowFunction

ReduceFunction and AggregateFunction are incrementally applied on events that are assigned to a window. However, sometimes we need access to all elements of a window to perform more complex computations, such as computing the median of values in a window or the most frequently occurring value. For such applications, neither the ReduceFunction nor the AggregateFunction are suitable. Flink's DataStream API offers the ProcessWindowFunction to perform arbitrary computations on the contents of a window.

The DataStream API of Flink 1.7 features the WindowFunction interface. WindowFunction has been superseded by ProcessWindow Function and will not be discussed here.

The following code shows the interface of the ProcessWindowFunction:

```
public abstract class ProcessWindowFunction<IN, OUT, KEY, W extends Window>
    extends AbstractRichFunction {

  // Evaluates the window
  void process(
    KEY key, Context ctx, Iterable<IN> vals, Collector<OUT> out) throws Exception;

  // Deletes any custom per-window state when the window is purged
  public void clear(Context ctx) throws Exception {}

  // The context holding window metadata
  public abstract class Context implements Serializable {

    // Returns the metadata of the window
    public abstract W window();

    // Returns the current processing time
    public abstract long currentProcessingTime();

    // Returns the current event-time watermark
    public abstract long currentWatermark();

    // State accessor for per-window state
    public abstract KeyedStateStore windowState();

    // State accessor for per-key global state
    public abstract KeyedStateStore globalState();

    // Emits a record to the side output identified by the OutputTag.
    public abstract <X> void output(OutputTag<X> outputTag, X value);
  }
}
```

The process() method is called with the key of the window, an Iterable to access the elements of the window, and a Collector to emit results. Moreover, the method has a Context parameter similar to other process methods. The Context object of the ProcessWindowFunction gives access to the metadata of the window, the current processing time and watermark, state stores to manage per-window and per-key global states, and side outputs to emit records.

We already discussed some of the features of the Context object when introducing the process functions, such as access to the current processing and event-time and side outputs. However, `ProcessWindowFunction`'s `Context` object also offers unique features. The metadata of the window typically contains information that can be used as an identifier for a window, such as the start and end timestamps in the case of a time window.

Another feature are per-window and per-key global states. Global state refers to the keyed state that is not scoped to any window, while per-window state refers to the window instance that is currently being evaluated. Per-window state is useful to maintain information that should be shared between multiple invocations of the `pro` `cess()` method on the same window, which can happen due to configuring allowed lateness or using a custom trigger. A `ProcessWindowFunction` that utilizes per-window state needs to implement its `clear()` method to clean up any window-specific state before the window is purged. Global state can be used to share information between multiple windows on the same key.

Example 6-12 groups the sensor reading stream into tumbling windows of 5 seconds and uses a `ProcessWindowFunction` to compute the lowest and highest temperature that occur within the window. It emits one record for each window consisting of the window's start and end timestamp and the minimum and maximum temperature.

Example 6-12. Computing the minimum and maximum temperature per sensor and window using a ProcessWindowFunction

```
// output the lowest and highest temperature reading every 5 seconds
val minMaxTempPerWindow: DataStream[MinMaxTemp] = sensorData
  .keyBy(_.id)
  .timeWindow(Time.seconds(5))
  .process(new HighAndLowTempProcessFunction)


case class MinMaxTemp(id: String, min: Double, max:Double, endTs: Long)

/**
 * A ProcessWindowFunction that computes the lowest and highest temperature
 * reading per window and emits them together with the
 * end timestamp of the window.
 */
class HighAndLowTempProcessFunction
    extends ProcessWindowFunction[SensorReading, MinMaxTemp, String, TimeWindow] {

  override def process(
      key: String,
      ctx: Context,
      vals: Iterable[SensorReading],
      out: Collector[MinMaxTemp]): Unit = {

    val temps = vals.map(_.temperature)
    val windowEnd = ctx.window.getEnd
```

```
    out.collect(MinMaxTemp(key, temps.min, temps.max, windowEnd))
  }
}
```

Internally, a window that is evaluated by ProcessWindowFunction stores all assigned events in a ListState.[1] By collecting all events and providing access to window metadata and other features, ProcessWindowFunction can address many more use cases than ReduceFunction or AggregateFunction. However, the state of a window that collects all events can become significantly larger than the state of a window whose elements are incrementally aggregated.

Incremental aggregation and ProcessWindowFunction

ProcessWindowFunction is a very powerful window function, but you need to use it with caution since it typically holds more data in state than incrementally aggregating functions. Quite often the logic that needs to be applied on a window can be expressed as an incremental aggregation, but it also needs access to window metadata or state.

If you have incremental aggregation logic but also need access to window metadata, you can combine a ReduceFunction or AggregateFunction, which perform incremental aggregation, with a ProcessWindowFunction, which provides access to more functionality. Elements that are assigned to a window will be immediately aggregated and when the trigger of the window fires, the aggregated result will be handed to ProcessWindowFunction. The Iterable parameter of the ProcessWindowFunction.process() method will only provide a single value, the incrementally aggregated result.

In the DataStream API this is done by providing a ProcessWindowFunction as a second parameter to the reduce() or aggregate() methods as shown in the following code:

```
input
  .keyBy(...)
  .timeWindow(...)
  .reduce(
    incrAggregator: ReduceFunction[IN],
    function: ProcessWindowFunction[IN, OUT, K, W])

input
  .keyBy(...)
  .timeWindow(...)
  .aggregate(
```

---

1 ListState and its performance characteristics are discussed in detail in Chapter 7.

```
        incrAggregator: AggregateFunction[IN, ACC, V],
        windowFunction: ProcessWindowFunction[V, OUT, K, W])
```

The code in Examples 6-13 and 6-14 shows how to solve the same use case as the code in Example 6-12 with a combination of a ReduceFunction and a ProcessWindowFunction, emitting every 5 seconds the minimun and maximum temperature per sensor and the end timestamp of each window.

Example 6-13. Applying a ReduceFunction for incremental aggregation and a ProcessWindowFunction for finalizing the window result

```
case class MinMaxTemp(id: String, min: Double, max:Double, endTs: Long)

val minMaxTempPerWindow2: DataStream[MinMaxTemp] = sensorData
  .map(r => (r.id, r.temperature, r.temperature))
  .keyBy(_._1)
  .timeWindow(Time.seconds(5))
  .reduce(
    // incrementally compute min and max temperature
    (r1: (String, Double, Double), r2: (String, Double, Double)) => {
      (r1._1, r1._2.min(r2._2), r1._3.max(r2._3))
    },
    // finalize result in ProcessWindowFunction
    new AssignWindowEndProcessFunction()
  )
```

As you can see in Example 6-13, the ReduceFunction and ProcessWindowFunction are both defined in the reduce() method call. Since the aggregation is performed by the ReduceFunction, the ProcessWindowFunction only needs to append the window end timestamp to the incrementally computed result as shown in Example 6-14.

Example 6-14. Implementation of a ProcessWindowFunction that assigns the window end timestamp to an incrementally computed result

```
class AssignWindowEndProcessFunction
  extends
  ProcessWindowFunction[(String, Double, Double), MinMaxTemp, String, TimeWindow] {

  override def process(
      key: String,
      ctx: Context,
      minMaxIt: Iterable[(String, Double, Double)],
      out: Collector[MinMaxTemp]): Unit = {

    val minMax = minMaxIt.head
    val windowEnd = ctx.window.getEnd
    out.collect(MinMaxTemp(key, minMax._2, minMax._3, windowEnd))
  }
}
```

Customizing Window Operators

Window operators defined using Flink's built-in window assigners can address many common use cases. However, as you start writing more advanced streaming applications, you might find yourself needing to implement more complex windowing logic, such as windows that emit early results and update their results if late elements are encountered, or windows that start and end when specific records are received.

The DataStream API exposes interfaces and methods to define custom window operators by allowing you to implement your own assigners, triggers, and evictors. Along with the previously discussed window functions, these components work together in a window operator to group and process elements in windows.

When an element arrives at a window operator, it is handed to the `WindowAssigner`. The assigner determines to which windows the element needs to be routed. If a window does not exist yet, it is created.

If the window operator is configured with an incremental aggregation function, such as a `ReduceFunction` or `AggregateFunction`, the newly added element is immediately aggregated and the result is stored as the contents of the window. If the window operator does not have an incremental aggregation function, the new element is appended to a `ListState` that holds all assigned elements.

Every time an element is added to a window, it is also passed to the trigger of the window. The trigger defines (fires) when a window is considered ready for evaluation and when a window is purged and its contents are cleared. A trigger can decide based on assigned elements or registered timers (similar to a process function) to evaluate or purge the contents of its window at specific points in time.

What happens when a trigger fires depends on the configured functions of the window operator. If the operator is configured just with an incremental aggregation function, the current aggregation result is emitted. This case is shown in Figure 6-4.

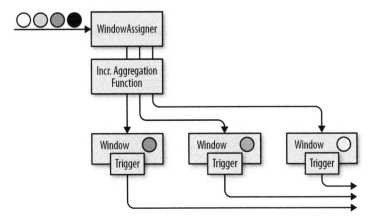

Figure 6-4. A window operator with an incremental aggregation function (the single circle in each window represents its aggregated window state)

If the operator only has a full window function, the function is applied on all elements of the window and the result is emitted as shown in Figure 6-5.

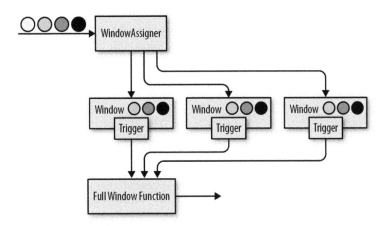

Figure 6-5. A window operator with a full window function (the circles in each window represent its collected raw input records)

Finally, if the operator has an incremental aggregation function and a full window function, the full window function is applied on the aggregated value and the result is emitted. Figure 6-6 depicts this case.

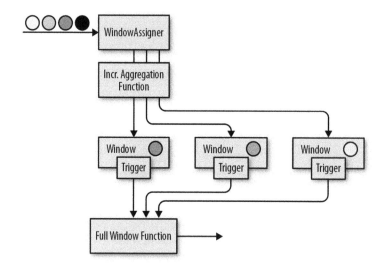

Figure 6-6. A window operator with an incremental aggregation and full window function (the single circle in each window represents its aggregated window state)

The evictor is an optional component that can be injected before or after a `Process WindowFunction` is called. An evictor can remove collected elements from the contents of a window. Since it has to iterate over all elements, it can only be used if no incremental aggregation function is specified.

The following code shows how to define a window operator with a custom trigger and evictor:

```
stream
  .keyBy(...)
  .window(...)                  // specify the window assigner
  [.trigger(...)]               // optional: specify the trigger
  [.evictor(...)]               // optional: specify the evictor
  .reduce/aggregate/process(...) // specify the window function
```

While evictors are optional components, each window operator needs a trigger to decide when to evaluate its windows. In order to provide a concise window operator API, each `WindowAssigner` has a default trigger that is used unless an explicit trigger is defined.

Note that an explicitly specified trigger overrides the existing trigger and does not complement it—the window will only be evaluated based on the trigger that was last defined.

In the following sections, we discuss the lifecycle of windows and introduce the interfaces to define custom window assigners, triggers, and evictors.

Window lifecycle

A window operator creates and typically also deletes windows while it processes incoming stream elements. As discussed before, elements are assigned to windows by a WindowAssigner, a trigger decides when to evalute a window, and a window function performs the actual window evaluation. In this section, we discuss the lifecycle of a window—when it is created, what information it consists of, and when it is deleted.

A window is created when the WindowAssigner assigns the first element to it. Consequently, there is no window without at least one element. A window consists of different pieces of state as follows:

Window content
> The window content holds the elements that have been assigned to the window or the result of the incremental aggregation in case the window operator has a ReduceFunction or AggregateFunction.

Window object
> The WindowAssigner returns zero, one, or multiple window objects. The window operator groups elements based on the returned objects. Hence, a window object holds the information used to distinguish windows from each other. Each window object has an end timestamp that defines the point in time after which the window and its state can be deleted.

Timers of a trigger
> A trigger can register timers to be called back at certain points in time—for example, to evaluate a window or purge its contents. These timers are maintained by the window operator.

Custom-defined state in a trigger
> A trigger can define and use custom, per-window and per-key state. This state is completely controlled by the trigger and not maintained by the window operator.

The window operator deletes a window when the end time of the window, defined by the end timestamp of the window object, is reached. Whether this happens with processing-time or event-time semantics depends on the value returned by the WindowAssigner.isEventTime() method.

When a window is deleted, the window operator automatically clears the window content and discards the window object. Custom-defined trigger state and registered trigger timers are not cleared because this state is opaque to the window operator. Hence, a trigger must clear all of its state in the Trigger.clear() method to prevent leaking state.

Window assigners

The WindowAssigner determines for each arriving element to which windows it is assigned. An element can be added to zero, one, or multiple windows. The following shows the WindowAssigner interface:

```
public abstract class WindowAssigner<T, W extends Window>
    implements Serializable {

  // Returns a collection of windows to which the element is assigned
  public abstract Collection<W> assignWindows(
    T element,
    long timestamp,
    WindowAssignerContext context);

  // Returns the default Trigger of the WindowAssigner
  public abstract Trigger<T, W> getDefaultTrigger(
    StreamExecutionEnvironment env);

  // Returns the TypeSerializer for the windows of this WindowAssigner
  public abstract TypeSerializer<W> getWindowSerializer(
    ExecutionConfig executionConfig);

  // Indicates whether this assigner creates event-time windows
  public abstract boolean isEventTime();

  // A context that gives access to the current processing time
  public abstract static class WindowAssignerContext {

    // Returns the current processing time
    public abstract long getCurrentProcessingTime();
  }
}
```

A WindowAssigner is typed to the type of the incoming elements and the type of the windows to which the elements are assigned. It also needs to provide a default trigger that is used if no explicit trigger is specified. The code in Example 6-15 creates a custom assigner for 30-second tumbling event-time windows.

Example 6-15. A window assigner for tumbling event-time windows

```
/** A custom window that groups events into 30-second tumbling windows. */
class ThirtySecondsWindows
    extends WindowAssigner[Object, TimeWindow] {

  val windowSize: Long = 30 * 1000L

  override def assignWindows(
      o: Object,
      ts: Long,
      ctx: WindowAssigner.WindowAssignerContext): java.util.List[TimeWindow] = {
```

```
  // rounding down by 30 seconds
  val startTime = ts - (ts % windowSize)
  val endTime = startTime + windowSize
  // emitting the corresponding time window
  Collections.singletonList(new TimeWindow(startTime, endTime))
}

override def getDefaultTrigger(
    env: environment.StreamExecutionEnvironment): Trigger[Object, TimeWindow] = {
  EventTimeTrigger.create()
}

override def getWindowSerializer(
    executionConfig: ExecutionConfig): TypeSerializer[TimeWindow] = {
  new TimeWindow.Serializer
}

override def isEventTime = true
}
```

The GlobalWindows Assigner

The GlobalWindows assigner maps all elements to the same global window. Its default trigger is the NeverTrigger that, as the name suggests, never fires. Consequently, the GlobalWindows assigner requires a custom trigger and possibly an evictor to selectively remove elements from the window state.

The end timestamp of GlobalWindows is Long.MAX_VALUE. Consequently, GlobalWindows will never be completely cleaned up. When applied on a KeyedStream with an evolving key space, Global Windows will maintain some state for each key. It should only be used with care.

In addition to the WindowAssigner interface there is also the MergingWindowAssigner interface that extends WindowAssigner. The MergingWindowAssigner is used for window operators that need to merge existing windows. One example for such an assigner is the EventTimeSessionWindows assigner we discussed before, which works by creating a new window for each arriving element and merging overlapping windows afterward.

When merging windows, you need to ensure that the state of all merging windows and their triggers is also appropriately merged. The Trigger interface features a callback method that is invoked when windows are merged to merge state that is associated with the windows. Merging of windows is discussed in more detail in the next section.

Triggers

Triggers define when a window is evaluated and its results are emitted. A trigger can decide to fire based on progress in time- or data-specific conditions, such as element count or certain observed element values. For example, the default triggers of the previously discussed time windows fire when the processing time or the watermark exceed the timestamp of the window's end boundary.

Triggers have access to time properties and timers, and can work with state. Hence, they are as powerful as process functions. For example, you can implement triggering logic to fire when the window receives a certain number of elements, when an element with a specific value is added to the window, or after detecting a pattern on added elements like "two events of the same type within 5 seconds." A custom trigger can also be used to compute and emit early results from an event-time window, before the watermark reaches the window's end timestamp. This is a common strategy to produce (incomplete) low-latency results despite using a conservative watermarking strategy.

Every time a trigger is called it produces a `TriggerResult` that determines what should happen to the window. `TriggerResult` can take one of the following values:

CONTINUE
    No action is taken.

FIRE
    If the window operator has a `ProcessWindowFunction`, the function is called and the result is emitted. If the window only has an incremetal aggregation function (`ReduceFunction` or `AggregateFunction`) the current aggregation result is emitted. The state of the window is not changed.

PURGE
    The content of the window is completely discarded and the window including all metadata is removed. Also, the `ProcessWindowFunction.clear()` method is invoked to clean up all custom per-window state.

FIRE_AND_PURGE
    FIRE_AND_PURGE: Evaluates the window first (FIRE) and subsequently removes all state and metadata (PURGE).

The possible `TriggerResult` values enable you to implement sophisticated windowing logic. A custom trigger may fire several times, computing new or updated results or purging a window without emitting a result if a certain condition is fulfilled. The next block of code shows the `Trigger` API:

```
public abstract class Trigger<T, W extends Window> implements Serializable {

    // Called for every element that gets added to a window
```

```
  TriggerResult onElement(
    T element, long timestamp, W window, TriggerContext ctx);

  // Called when a processing-time timer fires
  public abstract TriggerResult onProcessingTime(
    long timestamp, W window, TriggerContext ctx);

  // Called when an event-time timer fires
  public abstract TriggerResult onEventTime(
    long timestamp, W window, TriggerContext ctx);

  // Returns true if this trigger supports merging of trigger state
  public boolean canMerge();

  // Called when several windows have been merged into one window
  // and the state of the triggers needs to be merged
  public void onMerge(W window, OnMergeContext ctx);

  // Clears any state that the trigger might hold for the given window
  // This method is called when a window is purged
  public abstract void clear(W window, TriggerContext ctx);
}

// A context object that is given to Trigger methods to allow them
// to register timer callbacks and deal with state
public interface TriggerContext {

  // Returns the current processing time
  long getCurrentProcessingTime();

  // Returns the current watermark time
  long getCurrentWatermark();

  // Registers a processing-time timer
  void registerProcessingTimeTimer(long time);

  // Registers an event-time timer
  void registerEventTimeTimer(long time);

  // Deletes a processing-time timer
  void deleteProcessingTimeTimer(long time);

  // Deletes an event-time timer
  void deleteEventTimeTimer(long time);

  // Retrieves a state object that is scoped to the window and the key of the trigger
  <S extends State> S getPartitionedState(StateDescriptor<S, ?> stateDescriptor);
}

// Extension of TriggerContext that is given to the Trigger.onMerge() method
public interface OnMergeContext extends TriggerContext {
  // Merges per-window state of the trigger
```

```
    // The state to be merged must support merging
    void mergePartitionedState(StateDescriptor<S, ?> stateDescriptor);
}
```

As you can see, the Trigger API can be used to implement sophisticated logic by providing access to time and state. There are two aspects of triggers that require special care: cleaning up state and merging triggers.

When using per-window state in a trigger, you need to ensure that this state is properly deleted when the window is deleted. Otherwise, the window operator will accumulate more and more state over time and your application will probably fail at some point. In order to clean up all state when a window is deleted, the `clear()` method of a trigger needs to remove all custom per-window state and delete all processing-time and event-time timers using the `TriggerContext` object. It is not possible to clean up state in a timer callback method, since these methods are not called after a window is deleted.

If a trigger is applied together with a `MergingWindowAssigner`, it needs to be able to handle the case when two windows are merged. In this case, any custom states of the triggers also need to be merged. `canMerge()` declares that a trigger supports merging and the `onMerge()` method needs to implement the logic to perform the merge. If a trigger does not support merging it cannot be used in combination with a `Merging WindowAssigner`.

When triggers are merged, all descriptors of custom states must be provided to the `mergePartitionedState()` method of the `OnMergeContext` object.

 Note that mergable triggers may only use state primitives that can be automatically merged—`ListState`, `ReduceState`, or `Aggrega tingState`.

Example 6-16 shows a trigger that fires early, before the end time of the window is reached. The trigger registers a timer when the first event is assigned to a window, 1 second ahead of the current watermark. When the timer fires, a new timer is registered. Therefore, the trigger fires, at most, every second.

Example 6-16. An early firing trigger

```
/** A trigger that fires early. The trigger fires at most every second. */
class OneSecondIntervalTrigger
    extends Trigger[SensorReading, TimeWindow] {

  override def onElement(
      r: SensorReading,
      timestamp: Long,
```

```scala
        window: TimeWindow,
        ctx: Trigger.TriggerContext): TriggerResult = {

    // firstSeen will be false if not set yet
    val firstSeen: ValueState[Boolean] = ctx.getPartitionedState(
      new ValueStateDescriptor[Boolean]("firstSeen", classOf[Boolean]))

    // register initial timer only for first element
    if (!firstSeen.value()) {
      // compute time for next early firing by rounding watermark to second
      val t = ctx.getCurrentWatermark + (1000 - (ctx.getCurrentWatermark % 1000))
      ctx.registerEventTimeTimer(t)
      // register timer for the window end
      ctx.registerEventTimeTimer(window.getEnd)
      firstSeen.update(true)
    }
    // Continue. Do not evaluate per element
    TriggerResult.CONTINUE
  }

  override def onEventTime(
      timestamp: Long,
      window: TimeWindow,
      ctx: Trigger.TriggerContext): TriggerResult = {
    if (timestamp == window.getEnd) {
      // final evaluation and purge window state
      TriggerResult.FIRE_AND_PURGE
    } else {
      // register next early firing timer
      val t = ctx.getCurrentWatermark + (1000 - (ctx.getCurrentWatermark % 1000))
      if (t < window.getEnd) {
        ctx.registerEventTimeTimer(t)
      }
      // fire trigger to evaluate window
      TriggerResult.FIRE
    }
  }

  override def onProcessingTime(
      timestamp: Long,
      window: TimeWindow,
      ctx: Trigger.TriggerContext): TriggerResult = {
    // Continue. We don't use processing time timers
    TriggerResult.CONTINUE
  }

  override def clear(
      window: TimeWindow,
      ctx: Trigger.TriggerContext): Unit = {

    // clear trigger state
    val firstSeen: ValueState[Boolean] = ctx.getPartitionedState(
```

```
    new ValueStateDescriptor[Boolean]("firstSeen", classOf[Boolean]))
    firstSeen.clear()
  }
}
```

Note that the trigger uses custom state, which is cleaned up using the clear() method. Since we are using a simple nonmergable ValueState, the trigger is not mergable.

Evictors

The Evictor is an optional component in Flink's windowing mechanism. It can remove elements from a window before or after the window function is evaluated.

Example 6-17 shows the Evictor interface.

Example 6-17. The Evictor interface

```
public interface Evictor<T, W extends Window> extends Serializable {

  // Optionally evicts elements. Called before windowing function.
  void evictBefore(
    Iterable<TimestampedValue<T>> elements,
    int size,
    W window,
    EvictorContext evictorContext);

  // Optionally evicts elements. Called after windowing function.
  void evictAfter(
    Iterable<TimestampedValue<T>> elements,
    int size,
    W window,
    EvictorContext evictorContext);

// A context object that is given to Evictor methods.
interface EvictorContext {

  // Returns the current processing time.
  long getCurrentProcessingTime();

  // Returns the current event time watermark.
  long getCurrentWatermark();
}
```

The evictBefore() and evictAfter() methods are called before and after a window function is applied on the content of a window, respectively. Both methods are called with an Iterable that serves all elements that were added to the window, the number of elements in the window (size), the window object, and an EvictorContext that provides access to the current processing time and watermark. Elements are removed

---

from a window by calling the remove() method on the Iterator that can be obtained from the Iterable.

Preaggregation and Evictors

Evictors iterate over a list of elements in a window. They can only be applied if the window collects all added events and does not apply a ReduceFunction or AggregateFunction to incrementally aggregate the window content.

Evictors are often applied on a GlobalWindow for partial cleaning of the window—without purging the complete window state.

Joining Streams on Time

A common requirement when working with streams is to connect or join the events of two streams. Flink's DataStream API features two built-in operators to join streams with a temporal condition: the interval join and the window join. In this section, we describe both operators.

If you cannot express your required join semantics using Flink's built-in join operators, you can implement custom join logic as a CoProcessFunction, BroadcastProcessFunction, or KeyedBroadcastProcessFunction.

Note that you should design such an operator with efficient state access patterns and effective state cleanup strategies.

Interval Join

The interval join joins events from two streams that have a common key and that have timestamps not more than specified intervals apart from each other.

Figure 6-7 shows an interval join of two streams, A and B, that joins an event from A with an event from B if the timestamp of the B event is not less than one hour earlier and not more than 15 minutes later than the timestamp of the A event. The join interval is symmetric, i.e., an event from B joins with all events from A that are no more than 15 minutes earlier and at most one hour later than the B event.

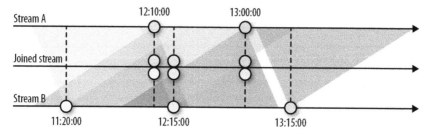

Figure 6-7. An interval join joining two streams A and B

The interval join currently only supports event time and operates with INNER JOIN semantics (events that have no matching event will not be forwarded). An interval join is defined as shown in Example 6-18.

Example 6-18. Using the interval join

```
input1
  .keyBy(…)
  .between(<lower-bound>, <upper-bound>) // bounds with respect to input1
  .process(ProcessJoinFunction) // process pairs of matched events
```

Pairs of joined events are passed into a `ProcessJoinFunction`. The lower and upper bounds are defined as negative and positive time intervals, for example, as `between(Time.hour(-1), Time.minute(15))`. The lower and upper bounds can be arbitrarily chosen as long as the lower bound is smaller than the upper bound; you can join all A events with all B events that have timestamps between one and two hours more than the A event.

An interval join needs to buffer records from one or both inputs. For the first input, all records with timestamps larger than the current watermark—the upper bound— are buffered. For the second input, all records with timestamps larger than the current watermark + the lower bound are buffered. Note that both bounds may be negative. The join in Figure 6-7 stores all records with timestamps larger than the current watermark—15 minutes from stream A—and all records with timestamps larger than the current watermark—one hour from stream B. You should be aware that the storage requirements of the interval join may significantly increase if the event time of both input streams is not synchronized because the watermark is determined by the "slower" stream.

Window Join

As the name suggests, the window join is based on Flink's windowing mechanism. Elements of both input streams are assigned to common windows and joined (or cogrouped) when a window is complete.

Example 6-19 shows how to define a window join.

Example 6-19. Joining two windowed streams

```
input1.join(input2)
    .where(...)        // specify key attributes for input1
    .equalTo(...)      // specify key attributes for input2
    .window(...)       // specify the WindowAssigner
    [.trigger(...)]    // optional: specify a Trigger
    [.evictor(...)]    // optional: specify an Evictor
    .apply(...)        // specify the JoinFunction
```

Figure 6-8 shows how the window join of the DataStream API works.

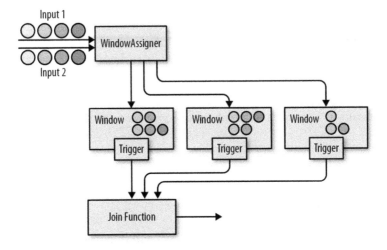

Figure 6-8. Operation of a window join

Both input streams are keyed on their key attributes and the common window assigner maps events of both streams to common windows, meaning a window stores the events of both inputs. When the timer of a window fires, the JoinFunction is called for each combination of elements from the first and the second input—the cross-product. It is also possible to specify a custom trigger and evictor. Since the events of both streams are mapped into the same windows, triggers and evictors behave exactly as in regular window operators.

In addition to joining two streams, it is also possible to cogroup two streams on a window by starting the operator definition with coGroup() instead of join(). The overall logic is the same, but instead of calling a JoinFunction for every pair of events from both inputs, a CoGroupFunction is called once per window with iterators over the elements from both inputs.

It should be noted that joining windowed streams can have unexpected semantics. For instance, assume you join two streams with a join operator that is configured with 1-hour tumbling window. An element of the first input will not be joined with an element of the second input even if they are just 1 second apart from each other but assigned to two different windows.

Handling Late Data

As discussed, watermarks can be used to balance result completeness and result latency. Unless you opt for a very conservative watermark strategy that guarantees that all relevant records will be included at the cost of high latency, your application will most likely have to handle late elements.

A late element is an element that arrives at an operator when a computation to which it would need to contribute has already been performed. In the context of an event-time window operator, an event is late if it arrives at the operator and the window assigner maps it to a window that has already been computed because the operator's watermark passed the end timestamp of the window.

The DataStream API provides different options for how to handle late events:

- Late events can be simply dropped.
- Late events can be redirected into a separate stream.
- Computation results can be updated based on late events and updates have to be emitted.

In the following, we discuss these options in detail and show how they are applied for process functions and window operators.

Dropping Late Events

The easiest way to handle late events is to simply discard them. Dropping late events is the default behavior for event-time window operators. Hence, a late arriving element will not create a new window.

A process function can easily filter out late events by comparing their timestamps with the current watermark.

Redirecting Late Events

Late events can also be redirected into another DataStream using the side-output feature. From there, the late events can be processed or emitted using a regular sink function. Depending on the business requirements, late data can later be integrated into the results of the streaming application with a periodic backfill process.

Example 6-20 shows how to specify a window operator with a side output for late events.

Example 6-20. Defining a window operator with a side output for late events

```
val readings: DataStream[SensorReading] = ???

val countPer10Secs: DataStream[(String, Long, Int)] = readings
  .keyBy(_.id)
  .timeWindow(Time.seconds(10))
  // emit late readings to a side output
  .sideOutputLateData(new OutputTag[SensorReading]("late-readings"))
  // count readings per window
  .process(new CountFunction())

// retrieve the late events from the side output as a stream
val lateStream: DataStream[SensorReading] = countPer10Secs
  .getSideOutput(new OutputTag[SensorReading]("late-readings"))
```

A process function can identify late events by comparing event timestamps with the current watermark and emitting them using the regular side-output API. Example 6-21 shows a `ProcessFunction` that filters out late sensor readings from its input and redirects them to a side-output stream.

Example 6-21. A ProcessFunction that filters out late sensor readings and redirects them to a side output

```
val readings: DataStream[SensorReading] = ???
val filteredReadings: DataStream[SensorReading] = readings
  .process(new LateReadingsFilter)

// retrieve late readings
val lateReadings: DataStream[SensorReading] = filteredReadings
  .getSideOutput(new OutputTag[SensorReading]("late-readings"))


/** A ProcessFunction that filters out late sensor readings and
  * re-directs them to a side output */
class LateReadingsFilter
    extends ProcessFunction[SensorReading, SensorReading] {

  val lateReadingsOut = new OutputTag[SensorReading]("late-readings")

  override def processElement(
      r: SensorReading,
      ctx: ProcessFunction[SensorReading, SensorReading]#Context,
      out: Collector[SensorReading]): Unit = {

    // compare record timestamp with current watermark
```

```
    if (r.timestamp < ctx.timerService().currentWatermark()) {
      // this is a late reading => redirect it to the side output
      ctx.output(lateReadingsOut, r)
    } else {
      out.collect(r)
    }
  }
}
```

Updating Results by Including Late Events

Late events arrive at an operator after a computation to which they should have contributed was completed. Therefore, the operator emits a result that is incomplete or
inaccurate. Instead of dropping or redirecting late events, another strategy is to
recompute an incomplete result and emit an update. However, there are a few issues
that need to be taken into account in order to be able to recompute and update
results.

An operator that supports recomputing and updating of emitted results needs to preserve all state required for the computation after the first result was emitted. However, since it is typically not possible for an operator to retain all state forever, it needs
to purge state at some point. Once the state for a certain result has been purged, the
result cannot be updated anymore and late events can only be dropped or redirected.

In addition to keeping state around, the downstream operators or external systems
that follow an operator, which updates previously emitted results, need to be able to
handle these updates. For example, a sink operator that writes the results and updates
of a keyed window operator to a key-value store could do this by overriding inaccurate results with the latest update using upsert writes. For some use cases it might also
be necessary to distinguish between the first result and an update due to a late event.

The window operator API provides a method to explicitly declare that you expect late
elements. When using event-time windows, you can specify an additional time period
called *allowed lateness*. A window operator with allowed lateness will not delete a
window and its state after the watermark passes the window's end timestamp. Instead,
the operator continues to maintain the complete window for the allowed lateness
period. When a late element arrives within the allowed lateness period it is handled
like an on-time element and handed to the trigger. When the watermark passes the
window's end timestamp plus the lateness interval, the window is finally deleted and
all subsequent late elements are discarded.

Allowed lateness can be specified using the `allowedLateness()` method as
Example 6-22 demonstrates.

Example 6-22. Defining a window operator with an allowed lateness of 5 seconds

```
val readings: DataStream[SensorReading] = ???

val countPer10Secs: DataStream[(String, Long, Int, String)] = readings
  .keyBy(_.id)
  .timeWindow(Time.seconds(10))
  // process late readings for 5 additional seconds
  .allowedLateness(Time.seconds(5))
  // count readings and update results if late readings arrive
  .process(new UpdatingWindowCountFunction)


/** A counting WindowProcessFunction that distinguishes between
  * first results and updates. */
class UpdatingWindowCountFunction
    extends ProcessWindowFunction[
          SensorReading, (String, Long, Int, String), String, TimeWindow] {

  override def process(
      id: String,
      ctx: Context,
      elements: Iterable[SensorReading],
      out: Collector[(String, Long, Int, String)]): Unit = {

    // count the number of readings
    val cnt = elements.count(_ => true)

    // state to check if this is the first evaluation of the window or not
    val isUpdate = ctx.windowState.getState(
      new ValueStateDescriptor[Boolean]("isUpdate", Types.of[Boolean]))

    if (!isUpdate.value()) {
      // first evaluation, emit first result
      out.collect((id, ctx.window.getEnd, cnt, "first"))
      isUpdate.update(true)
    } else {
      // not the first evaluation, emit an update
      out.collect((id, ctx.window.getEnd, cnt, "update"))
    }
  }
}
```

Process functions can also be implemented to support late data. Since state management is always custom and manually done in process functions, Flink does not provide a built-in API to support late data. Instead, you can implement the necessary logic using the building blocks of record timestamps, watermarks, and timers.

Summary

In this chapter you learned how to implement streaming applications that operate on time. We explained how to configure the time characteristics of a streaming application and how to assign timestamps and watermarks. You learned about time-based operators, including Flink's process functions, built-in windows, and custom windows. We also discussed the semantics of watermarks, how to trade off result completeness and result latency, and strategies for handling late events.

## CHAPTER 7

Stateful Operators and Applications

Stateful operators and user functions are common building blocks of stream processing applications. In fact, most nontrivial operations need to memorize records or partial results because data is streamed and arrives over time.[1] Many of Flink's built-in DataStream operators, sources, and sinks are stateful and buffer records or maintain partial results or metadata. For instance, a window operator collects input records for a `ProcessWindowFunction` or the result of applying a `ReduceFunction`, a `Process Function` memorizes scheduled timers, and some sink functions maintain state about transactions to provide exactly-once functionality. In addition to built-in operators and provided sources and sinks, Flink's DataStream API exposes interfaces to register, maintain, and access state in user-defined functions.

Stateful stream processing has implications on many aspects of a stream processor such as failure recovery and memory management as well as the maintenance of streaming applications. Chapters 2 and 3 discussed the foundations of stateful stream processing and related details of Flink's architecture, respectively. Chapter 9 explains how to set up and configure Flink to reliably process stateful applications. Chapter 10 gives guidance on how to operate stateful applications—taking and restoring from application savepoints, rescaling applications, and performing application upgrades.

This chapter focuses on the implementation of stateful user-defined functions and discusses the performance and robustness of stateful applications. Specifically, we explain how to define and interact with different types of state in user-defined functions. We also discuss performance aspects and how to control the size of function

---

1 This differs from batch processing where user-defined functions, such as `GroupReduceFunction`, are called when all data to be processed has been collected.

state. Finally, we show how to configure keyed state as queryable and how to access it from an external application.

Implementing Stateful Functions

In "State Management", we explained that functions can have two types of state, keyed state and operator state. Flink provides multiple interfaces to define stateful functions. In this section, we show how functions with keyed and operator state are implemented.

Declaring Keyed State at RuntimeContext

User functions can employ keyed state to store and access state in the context of a key attribute. For each distinct value of the key attribute, Flink maintains one state instance. The keyed state instances of a function are distributed across all parallel tasks of the function's operator. That means each parallel instance of the function is responsible for a subrange of the key domain and maintains the corresponding state instances. Hence, keyed state is very similar to a distributed key-value map. Consult "State Management" on page 53 for more details on keyed state.

Keyed state can only be used by functions that are applied on a KeyedStream. A Keyed Stream is constructed by calling the DataStream.keyBy() method that defines a key on a stream. A KeyedStream is partitioned on the specified key and remembers the key definition. An operator that is applied on a KeyedStream is applied in the context of its key definition.

Flink provides multiple primitives for keyed state. A state primitive defines the structure of the state for an individual key. The choice of the right state primitive depends on how the function interacts with the state. The choice also affects the performance of a function because each state backend provides its own implementations for these primitives. The following state primitives are supported by Flink:

- ValueState[T] holds a single value of type T. The value can be read using Value State.value() and updated with ValueState.update(value: T).

- ListState[T] holds a list of elements of type T. New elements can be appended to the list by calling ListState.add(value: T) or ListState.addAll(values: java.util.List[T]). The state elements can be accessed by calling List State.get(), which returns an Iterable[T] over all state elements. It is not possible to remove individual elements from ListState, but the list can be updated by calling ListState.update(values: java.util.List[T]). A call to this method will replace existing values with the given list of values.

- MapState[K, V] holds a map of keys and values. The state primitive offers many of the methods of a regular Java Map such as get(key: K), put(key: K, value:

V), `contains(key: K)`, `remove(key: K)`, and iterators over the contained entries, keys, and values.

- `ReducingState[T]` offers the same methods as `ListState[T]` (except for `addAll()` and `update()`), but instead of appending values to a list, `Reducing State.add(value: T)` immediately aggregates `value` using a `ReduceFunction`. The iterator returned by `get()` returns an `Iterable` with a single entry, which is the reduced value.

- `AggregatingState[I, O]` behaves similar to `ReducingState`. However, it uses the more general `AggregateFunction` to aggregate values. `Aggregating State.get()` computes the final result and returns it as an `Iterable` with a single element.

All state primitives can be cleared by calling `State.clear()`.

Example 7-1 shows how to apply a `FlatMapFunction` with a keyed `ValueState` on a stream of sensor measurements. The example application emits an alert event if the temperature measured by a sensor changes by more than a threshold since the last measurement.

Example 7-1. Applying a FlatMapFunction with a keyed ValueState

```
val sensorData: DataStream[SensorReading]  = ???
// partition and key the stream on the sensor ID
val keyedData: KeyedStream[SensorReading, String] = sensorData
  .keyBy(_.id)

// apply a stateful FlatMapFunction on the keyed stream which
// compares the temperature readings and raises alerts
val alerts: DataStream[(String, Double, Double)] = keyedData
  .flatMap(new TemperatureAlertFunction(1.7))
```

A function with keyed state must be applied on a `KeyedStream`. We need to specify the key by calling `keyBy()` on the input stream before we apply the function. When the processing method of a function with keyed input is called, Flink's runtime automatically puts all keyed state objects of the function into the context of the key of the record that is passed by the function call. Therefore, a function can only access the state that belongs to the record it currently processes.

Example 7-2 shows the implementation of a `FlatMapFunction` with a keyed `Value State` that checks whether the measured temperature changed more than a configured threshold.

Example 7-2. Implementing a FlatMapFunction with a keyed ValueState

```scala
class TemperatureAlertFunction(val threshold: Double)
    extends RichFlatMapFunction[SensorReading, (String, Double, Double)] {

  // the state handle object
  private var lastTempState: ValueState[Double] = _

  override def open(parameters: Configuration): Unit = {
    // create state descriptor
    val lastTempDescriptor =
      new ValueStateDescriptor[Double]("lastTemp", classOf[Double])
    // obtain the state handle
    lastTempState = getRuntimeContext.getState[Double](lastTempDescriptor)
  }

  override def flatMap(
      reading: SensorReading,
      out: Collector[(String, Double, Double)]): Unit = {
    // fetch the last temperature from state
    val lastTemp = lastTempState.value()
    // check if we need to emit an alert
    val tempDiff = (reading.temperature - lastTemp).abs
    if (tempDiff > threshold) {
      // temperature changed by more than the threshold
      out.collect((reading.id, reading.temperature, tempDiff))
    }
    // update lastTemp state
    this.lastTempState.update(reading.temperature)
  }
}
```

To create a state object, we have to register a `StateDescriptor` with Flink's runtime via the `RuntimeContext`, which is exposed by `RichFunction` (see "Implementing Functions" on page 105 for a discussion of the `RichFunction` interface). The `StateDescriptor` is specific to the state primitive and includes the name of the state and the data types of the state. The descriptors for `ReducingState` and `AggregatingState` also need a `ReduceFunction` or `AggregateFunction` object to aggregate the added values. The state name is scoped to the operator so that a function can have more than one state object by registering multiple state descriptors. The data types handled by the state are specified as `Class` or `TypeInformation` objects (see "Types" on page 97 for a discussion of Flink's type handling). The data type must be specified because Flink needs to create a suitable serializer. Alternatively, it is also possible to explicitly specify a `TypeSerializer` to control how state is written into a state backend, checkpoint, and savepoint.[2]

Typically, the state handle object is created in the `open()` method of `RichFunction`. `open()` is called before any processing methods, such as `flatMap()` in the case of a `FlatMapFunction`, are called. The state handle object (`lastTempState` in Example 7-2) is a regular member variable of the function class.

 The state handle object only provides access to the state, which is stored an maintained in the state backend. The handle does not hold the state itself.

When a function registers a `StateDescriptor`, Flink checks if the state backend has data for the function and a state with the given name and type. This might happen if the stateful function is restarted to recover from a failure or when an application is started from a savepoint. In both cases, Flink links the newly registered state handle object to the existing state. If the state backend does not contain state for the given descriptor, the state that is linked to the handle is initialized as empty.

The Scala DataStream API offers syntactic shortcuts to define `map` and `flatMap` functions with a single `ValueState`. Example 7-3 shows how to implement the previous example with the shortcut.

Example 7-3. Scala DataStream API shortcut for a FlatMap with a keyed ValueState

```scala
val alerts: DataStream[(String, Double, Double)] = keyedData
  .flatMapWithState[(String, Double, Double), Double] {
    case (in: SensorReading, None) =>
      // no previous temperature defined; just update the last temperature
      (List.empty, Some(in.temperature))
    case (r: SensorReading, lastTemp: Some[Double]) =>
      // compare temperature difference with threshold
      val tempDiff = (r.temperature - lastTemp.get).abs
      if (tempDiff > 1.7) {
        // threshold exceeded; emit an alert and update the last temperature
        (List((r.id, r.temperature, tempDiff)), Some(r.temperature))
      } else {
        // threshold not exceeded; just update the last temperature
        (List.empty, Some(r.temperature))
      }
  }
```

---

2 The serialization format of state is an important aspect when updating an application and is discussed later in this chapter.

The flatMapWithState() method expects a function that accepts a Tuple2. The first field of the tuple holds the input record to flatMap, and the second field holds an Option of the retrieved state for the key of the processed record. Option is not defined if the state has not been initialized yet. The function also returns a Tuple2. The first field is a list of the flatMap results, and the second field is the new value of the state.

Implementing Operator List State with the ListCheckpointed Interface

Operator state is managed per parallel instance of an operator. All events that are processed in the same parallel task of an operator have access to the same state. In "State Management" on page 53, we discussed that Flink supports three types of operator state: list state, list union state, and broadcast state.

A function can work with operator list state by implementing the ListCheckpointed interface. The ListCheckpointed interface does not work with state handles like ValueState or ListState, which are registered at the state backend. Instead, functions implement operator state as regular member variables and interact with the state backend via callback functions of the ListCheckpointed interface. The interface provides two methods:

```
// returns a snapshot the state of the function as a list
snapshotState(checkpointId: Long, timestamp: Long): java.util.List[T]

// restores the state of the function from the provided list
restoreState(java.util.List[T] state): Unit
```

The snapshotState() method is invoked when Flink triggers a checkpoint of the stateful function. The method has two parameters, checkpointId, which is a unique, monotonically increasing identifier for checkpoints, and timestamp, which is the wall-clock time when the master initiated the checkpoint. The method has to return the operator state as a list of serializable state objects.

The restoreState() method is always invoked when the state of a function needs to be initialized—when the job is started (from a savepoint or not) or in the case of a failure. The method is called with a list of state objects and has to restore the state of the operator based on these objects.

Example 7-4 shows how to implement the ListCheckpointed interface for a function that counts temperature measurements that exceed a threshold per partition, for each parallel instance of the function.

Example 7-4. A RichFlatMapFunction with operator list state

```
class HighTempCounter(val threshold: Double)
    extends RichFlatMapFunction[SensorReading, (Int, Long)]
```

```
    with ListCheckpointed[java.lang.Long] {

  // index of the subtask
  private lazy val subtaskIdx = getRuntimeContext
    .getIndexOfThisSubtask
  // local count variable
  private var highTempCnt = 0L

  override def flatMap(
      in: SensorReading,
      out: Collector[(Int, Long)]): Unit = {
    if (in.temperature > threshold) {
      // increment counter if threshold is exceeded
      highTempCnt += 1
      // emit update with subtask index and counter
      out.collect((subtaskIdx, highTempCnt))
    }
  }

  override def restoreState(
      state: util.List[java.lang.Long]): Unit = {
    highTempCnt = 0
    // restore state by adding all longs of the list
    for (cnt <- state.asScala) {
      highTempCnt += cnt
    }
  }

  override def snapshotState(
      chkpntId: Long,
      ts: Long): java.util.List[java.lang.Long] = {
    // snapshot state as list with a single count
    java.util.Collections.singletonList(highTempCnt)
  }
}
```

The function in the above example counts per parallel instance how many temperature measurements exceeded a configured threshold. The function uses operator state
and has a single state variable for each parallel operator instance that is checkpointed
and restored using the methods of the ListCheckpointed interface. Note that the
ListCheckpointed interface is implemented in Java and expects a java.util.List
instead of a Scala native list.

Looking at the example, you might wonder why operator state is handled as a list of
state objects. As discussed in "Scaling Stateful Operators" on page 56, the list structure supports changing the parallelism of functions with operator state. In order to
increase or decrease the parallelism of a function with operator state, the operator
state needs to be redistributed to a larger or smaller number of task instances. This
requires splitting or merging of state objects. Since the logic for splitting and merging

of state is custom for every stateful function, this cannot be automatically done for arbitrary types of state.

By providing a list of state objects, functions with operator state can implement this logic using the snapshotState() and restoreState() methods. The snapshot State() method splits the operator state into multiple parts and the restoreState() method assembles the operator state from possibly multiple parts. When the state of a function is restored, the parts of the state are distributed among all parallel instances of the function and handed to the restoreState() method. If there are more parallel subtasks than state objects, some subtasks are started with no state, and the restoreState() method is called with an empty list.

Looking again at the HighTempCounter function in Example 7-4, we see that each parallel instance of the operator exposes its state as a list with a single entry. If we increased the parallelism of this operator, some of the new subtasks would be initialized with an empty state, and start counting from zero. In order to achieve better state distribution behavior when the HighTempCounter function is rescaled, we can implement the snapshotState() method so that it splits its count into multiple partial counts as shown in Example 7-5.

Example 7-5. Split operator list state for better distribution during rescaling

```
override def snapshotState(
    chkpntId: Long,
    ts: Long): java.util.List[java.lang.Long] = {
  // split count into ten partial counts
  val div = highTempCnt / 10
  val mod = (highTempCnt % 10).toInt
  // return count as ten parts
  (List.fill(mod)(new java.lang.Long(div + 1)) ++
    List.fill(10 - mod)(new java.lang.Long(div))).asJava
}
```

ListCheckpointed Interface Uses Java Serialization

The ListCheckpointed interface uses Java serialization to serialize and deserialize the list of state objects. This can be a problem if you need to update your application because Java serialization does not allow for migrating or configuring a custom serializer. Implement CheckpointedFunction instead of the ListCheckpointed interface if you need to ensure a function's operator state can be evolved.

Using Connected Broadcast State

A common requirement in streaming applications is to distribute the same information to all parallel instances of a function and maintain it as recoverable state. An example is a stream of rules and a stream of events on which the rules are applied. The function that applies the rules ingests two input streams, the event stream and the rules stream. It remembers the rules in an operator state in order to apply them to all events of the event stream. Since each parallel instance of the function must hold all rules in its operator state, the rules stream needs to be broadcasted to ensure each instance of the function receives all rules.

In Flink, such a state is called a broadcast state. Broadcast state can be combined with a regular DataStream or KeyedStream. Example 7-6 shows how to implement a temperature alert application with thresholds that can be dynamically configured via a broadcasted stream.

Example 7-6. Connecting a broadcast stream and keyed event stream

```
val sensorData: DataStream[SensorReading] = ???
val thresholds: DataStream[ThresholdUpdate] = ???
val keyedSensorData: KeyedStream[SensorReading, String] = sensorData.keyBy(_.id)

// the descriptor of the broadcast state
val broadcastStateDescriptor =
  new MapStateDescriptor[String, Double](
    "thresholds", classOf[String], classOf[Double])

val broadcastThresholds: BroadcastStream[ThresholdUpdate] = thresholds
  .broadcast(broadcastStateDescriptor)

// connect keyed sensor stream and broadcasted rules stream
val alerts: DataStream[(String, Double, Double)] = keyedSensorData
  .connect(broadcastThresholds)
  .process(new UpdatableTemperatureAlertFunction())
```

A function with broadcast state is applied on two streams in three steps:

1. You create a BroadcastStream by calling DataStream.broadcast() and providing one or more MapStateDescriptor objects. Each descriptor defines a separate broadcast state of the function that is later applied on the BroadcastStream.

2. You connect the BroadcastStream with a DataStream or KeyedStream. The BroadcastStream must be put as an argument in the connect() method.

3. You apply a function on the connected streams. Depending on whether the other stream is keyed or not, a KeyedBroadcastProcessFunction or BroadcastProcessFunction can be applied.

Example 7-7 shows the implementation of a KeyedBroadcastProcessFunction that supports the dynamic configuration of sensor thresholds at runtime.

Example 7-7. Implementing a KeyedBroadcastProcessFunction

```scala
class UpdatableTemperatureAlertFunction()
    extends KeyedBroadcastProcessFunction
      [String, SensorReading, ThresholdUpdate, (String, Double, Double)] {

  // the descriptor of the broadcast state
  private lazy val thresholdStateDescriptor =
    new MapStateDescriptor[String, Double](
      "thresholds", classOf[String], classOf[Double])

  // the keyed state handle
  private var lastTempState: ValueState[Double] = _

  override def open(parameters: Configuration): Unit = {
    // create keyed state descriptor
    val lastTempDescriptor = new ValueStateDescriptor[Double](
      "lastTemp", classOf[Double])
    // obtain the keyed state handle
    lastTempState = getRuntimeContext.getState[Double](lastTempDescriptor)
  }

  override def processBroadcastElement(
      update: ThresholdUpdate,
      ctx: KeyedBroadcastProcessFunction
        [String, SensorReading, ThresholdUpdate, (String, Double, Double)]#Context,
      out: Collector[(String, Double, Double)]): Unit = {
    // get broadcasted state handle
    val thresholds = ctx.getBroadcastState(thresholdStateDescriptor)

    if (update.threshold != 0.0d) {
      // configure a new threshold for the sensor
      thresholds.put(update.id, update.threshold)
    } else {
      // remove threshold for the sensor
      thresholds.remove(update.id)
    }
  }

  override def processElement(
      reading: SensorReading,
      readOnlyCtx: KeyedBroadcastProcessFunction
        [String, SensorReading, ThresholdUpdate,
        (String, Double, Double)]#ReadOnlyContext,
      out: Collector[(String, Double, Double)]): Unit = {
    // get read-only broadcast state
    val thresholds = readOnlyCtx.getBroadcastState(thresholdStateDescriptor)
    // check if we have a threshold
    if (thresholds.contains(reading.id)) {
      // get threshold for sensor
      val sensorThreshold: Double = thresholds.get(reading.id)
```

```
    // fetch the last temperature from state
    val lastTemp = lastTempState.value()
    // check if we need to emit an alert
    val tempDiff = (reading.temperature - lastTemp).abs
    if (tempDiff > sensorThreshold) {
      // temperature increased by more than the threshold
      out.collect((reading.id, reading.temperature, tempDiff))
    }
  }

    // update lastTemp state
    this.lastTempState.update(reading.temperature)
  }
}
```

BroadcastProcessFunction and KeyedBroadcastProcessFunction differ from a regular CoProcessFunction because the element processing methods are not symmetric. The methods, processElement() and processBroadcastElement(), are called with different context objects. Both context objects offer a method getBroadcastState(MapStateDescriptor) that provides access to a broadcast state handle. However, the broadcast state handle that is returned in the processElement() method provides read-only access to the broadcast state. This is a safety mechanism to ensure the broadcast state holds the same information in all parallel instances. In addition, both context objects also provide access to the event-time timestamp, the current watermark, the current processing time, and the side outputs, similar to the context objects of other process functions.

 The BroadcastProcessFunction and KeyedBroadcastProcess Function differ from each other as well. BroadcastProcessFunc tion does not expose a timer service to register timers and consequently does not offer an onTimer() method. Note that you should not access keyed state from the processBroadcastEle ment() method of KeyedBroadcastProcessFunction. Since the broadcast input does not specify a key, the state backend cannot access a keyed value and will throw an exception. Instead, the context of the KeyedBroadcastProcessFunction.processBroad castElement() method provides a method applyToKeyed State(StateDescriptor, KeyedStateFunction) to apply a KeyedStateFunction to the value of each key in the keyed state referenced by the StateDescriptor.

Broadcasted Events Might Not Arrive in Deterministic Order

The order in which the broadcasted events arrive at the different parallel tasks of the broadcast state operator might differ if the operator that emits the broadcasted messages runs with a parallelism larger than 1.

Consequently, you should either ensure the value of the broadcast state does not depend on the order in which the broadcasted messages are received or ensure the parallelism of the broadcasting operator is set to 1.

Using the CheckpointedFunction Interface

The CheckpointedFunction interface is the lowest-level interface to specify stateful functions. It provides hooks to register and maintain keyed state and operator state and is the only interface that gives access to operator list union state—the operator state that is fully replicated in the case of a recovery or savepoint restart.[3]

The CheckpointedFunction interface defines two methods, initializeState() and snapshotState(), which work similar to the methods of the ListCheckpointed interface for operator list state. The initializeState() method is called when a parallel instance of CheckpointedFunction is created. This happens when an application is started or when a task is restarted due to a failure. The method is called with a FunctionInitializationContext object that provides access to an Operator StateStore and a KeyedStateStore object. The state stores are responsible for registering function state with Flink's runtime and returning the state objects, such as ValueState, ListState, or BroadcastState. Each state is registered with a name that must be unique for the function. When a function registers state, the state store tries to initialize the state by checking if the state backend holds state for the function registered under the given name. If the task is restarted due to a failure or from a savepoint, the state will be initialized from the saved data. If the application is not started from a checkpoint or savepoint, the state will be initially empty.

The snapshotState() method is called immediately before a checkpoint is taken and receives a FunctionSnapshotContext object as the parameter. FunctionSnapshotCon text gives access to the unique identifier of the checkpoint and the timestamp when the JobManager initiates the checkpoint. The purpose of the snapshotState() method is to ensure all state objects are updated before the checkpoint is done. Moreover, in combination with the CheckpointListener interface, the snapshotState() method can be used to consistently write data to external datastores by synchronizing with Flink's checkpoints.

---

3 See Chapter 3 for details on how operator list union state is distributed.

Example 7-8 shows how the CheckpointedFunction interface is used to create a function with keyed and operator state that counts per key and operator instance how many sensor readings exceed a specified threshold.

Example 7-8. A function implementing the CheckpointedFunction interface

```scala
class HighTempCounter(val threshold: Double)
    extends FlatMapFunction[SensorReading, (String, Long, Long)]
    with CheckpointedFunction {

  // local variable for the operator high temperature cnt
  var opHighTempCnt: Long = 0
  var keyedCntState: ValueState[Long] = _
  var opCntState: ListState[Long] = _

  override def flatMap(
      v: SensorReading,
      out: Collector[(String, Long, Long)]): Unit = {
    // check if temperature is high
    if (v.temperature > threshold) {
      // update local operator high temp counter
      opHighTempCnt += 1
      // update keyed high temp counter
      val keyHighTempCnt = keyedCntState.value() + 1
      keyedCntState.update(keyHighTempCnt)
      // emit new counters
      out.collect((v.id, keyHighTempCnt, opHighTempCnt))
    }
  }

  override def initializeState(initContext: FunctionInitializationContext): Unit = {
    // initialize keyed state
    val keyCntDescriptor = new ValueStateDescriptor[Long]("keyedCnt", classOf[Long])
    keyedCntState = initContext.getKeyedStateStore.getState(keyCntDescriptor)
    // initialize operator state
    val opCntDescriptor = new ListStateDescriptor[Long]("opCnt", classOf[Long])
    opCntState = initContext.getOperatorStateStore.getListState(opCntDescriptor)
    // initialize local variable with state
    opHighTempCnt = opCntState.get().asScala.sum
  }

  override def snapshotState(
      snapshotContext: FunctionSnapshotContext): Unit = {
    // update operator state with local state
    opCntState.clear()
    opCntState.add(opHighTempCnt)
  }
}
```

Receiving Notifications About Completed Checkpoints

Frequent synchronization is a major reason for performance limitations in distributed systems. Flink's design aims to reduce synchronization points. Checkpoints are implemented based on barriers that flow with the data and therefore avoid global synchronization across all operators of an application.

Due to its checkpointing mechanism, Flink can achieve very good performance. However, another implication is that the state of an application is never in a consistent state except for the logical points in time when a checkpoint is taken. For some operators it can be important to know whether a checkpoint completed or not. For example, sink functions that aim to write data to external systems with exactly-once guarantees must only emit records that were received before a successful checkpoint to ensure the received data will not be recomputed in the case of a failure.

As discussed in "Checkpoints, Savepoints, and State Recovery" on page 58, a checkpoint is only successful if all operator tasks successfully checkpointed their states to the checkpoint storage. Hence, only the JobManager can determine whether a checkpoint is successful or not. Operators that need to be notified about completed checkpoints can implement the CheckpointListener interface. This interface provides the notifyCheckpointComplete(long chkpntId) method, which might be called when the JobManager registers a checkpoint as completed—when all operators successfully copied their state to the remote storage.

 Note that Flink does not guarantee that the notifyCheckpointCom plete() method is called for each completed checkpoint. It is possible that a task misses the notification. This needs to be taken into account when implementing the interface.

Enabling Failure Recovery for Stateful Applications

Streaming applications are supposed to run continuously and must recover from failures, such as failing machines or processes. Most streaming applications require that failures not affect the correctness of the computed results.

In "Checkpoints, Savepoints, and State Recovery", we explained Flink's mechanism to create consistent checkpoints of a stateful application, a snapshot of the state of all built-in and user-defined stateful functions at a point in time when all operators processed all events up to a specific position in the application's input streams. In order to provide fault tolerance for an application, the JobManager initiates checkpoints at regular intervals.

Applications need to explicitly enable the periodic checkpointing mechanism via the StreamExecutionEnvironment as shown in Example 7-9.

Example 7-9. Enabling checkpointing for an application

```
val env = StreamExecutionEnvironment.getExecutionEnvironment

// set checkpointing interval to 10 seconds (10000 milliseconds)
env.enableCheckpointing(10000L)
```

The checkpointing interval is an important parameter that affects the overhead of the checkpointing mechanism during regular processing and the time it takes to recover from a failure. A shorter checkpointing interval causes higher overhead during regular processing but can enable faster recovery because less data needs to be reprocessed.

Flink provides more tuning knobs to configure the checkpointing behavior, such as the choice of consistency guarantees (exactly-once or at-least-once), the number of concurrent checkpoints, and a timeout to cancel long-running checkpoints, as well as several state backend–specific options. We discuss these options in more detail in "Tuning Checkpointing and Recovery" on page 263.

Ensuring the Maintainability of Stateful Applications

The state of an application that was running for several weeks can be expensive or even impossible to recompute. At the same time, long-running applications need to be maintained. Bugs need to be fixed, functionality adjusted, added, or removed, or the parallelism of the operator needs to be adjusted to account for higher or lower data rates. Therefore, it is important that application state can be migrated to a new version of the application or be redistributed to more or fewer operator tasks.

Flink features savepoints to maintain applications and their states. However, it requires that all stateful operators of the initial version of an application specify two parameters to ensure the application can be properly maintained in the future. These parameters are a unique operator identifier and the maximum parallelism (for operators with keyed state). In the following we describe how to set these parameters.

Operator Unique Identifiers and Maximum Parallelism Are Baked into Savepoints

The unique identifier and maximum parallelism of operators are baked into a savepoint and cannot be changed. It is not possible to start an application from a previously taken savepoint if the identifiers or the maximum parallelism of operators were changed.

Once you change operator identifiers or the maximum parallelism, you cannot start an application from a savepoint but have to start it from scratch without any state initialization.

Specifying Unique Operator Identifiers

Unique identifiers should be specified for every operator of an application. The identifiers are written into a savepoint as metadata with the actual state data of an operator. When an application is started from a savepoint, the identifiers are used to map a state in the savepoint to the corresponding operator of the started application. Savepoint state can only be restored to an operator of a started application if their identifiers are identical.

If you do not explicitly set unique identifiers to the operators of your stateful application, you will face significant limitations when you have to evolve the application. We discuss the importance of unique operator identifiers and the mapping of savepoint state in more detail in "Savepoints" on page 66.

We strongly recommend assigning unique identifiers to every operator of an application. You can set the identifier with the uid() method as shown in Example 7-10.

Example 7-10. Setting a unique identifier for an operator

```
val alerts: DataStream[(String, Double, Double)] = keyedSensorData
  .flatMap(new TemperatureAlertFunction(1.1))
  .uid("TempAlert")
```

Defining the Maximum Parallelism of Keyed State Operators

The maximum parallelism parameter of an operator defines the number of key groups into which the keyed state of the operator is split. The number of key groups limits the maximum number of parallel tasks to which keyed state can be scaled. "Scaling Stateful Operators" on page 56 discusses key groups and how keyed state is scaled out and in. The maximum parallelism can be set for all operators of an application via the StreamExecutionEnvironment or per operator using the setMaxParallel ism() method as shown in Example 7-11.

Example 7-11. Setting the maximum parallelism of operators

```
val env = StreamExecutionEnvironment.getExecutionEnvironment

// set the maximum parallelism for this application
env.setMaxParallelism(512)

val alerts: DataStream[(String, Double, Double)] = keyedSensorData
  .flatMap(new TemperatureAlertFunction(1.1))
  // set the maximum parallelism for this operator and
  // override the application-wide value
  .setMaxParallelism(1024)
```

The default maximum parallelism of an operator depends on the operator's parallelism in the application's first version:

- If the parallelism is less than or equal to 128, the maximum parallelism is 128.
- If the operator's parallelism is larger than 128, the maximum parallelism is computed as the minimum of `nextPowerOfTwo(parallelism + (parallelism / 2))` and 2^{15}.

Performance and Robustness of Stateful Applications

The way operators interact with state has implications on the robustness and performance of an application. There are several aspects that affect the behavior of an application such as the choice of the state backend that locally maintains the state and performs checkpoints, the configuration of the checkpointing algorithm, and the size of the application's state. In this section, we discuss aspects that need to be taken into account to ensure robust execution behavior and consistent performance of long-running applications.

Choosing a State Backend

In "State Backends" on page 55, we explained that Flink maintains application state in a state backend. The state backend is responsible for storing the local state of each task instance and persisting it to remote storage when a checkpoint is taken. Because local state can be maintained and checkpointed in different ways, state backends are pluggable—two applications can use different state backend implementations to maintain their states. The choice of the state backend has implications on the robustness and performance of a stateful application. Each state backend provides implementations for the different state primitives, such as `ValueState`, `ListState`, and `MapState`.

Currently, Flink offers three state backends, the `MemoryStateBackend`, the `FsState Backend`, and the `RocksDBStateBackend`:

- `MemoryStateBackend` stores state as regular objects on the heap of the TaskManager JVM process. For example, `MapState` is backed by a Java `HashMap` object. While this approach provides very low latencies to read or write state, it has implications on the robustness of an application. If the state of a task instance grows too large, the JVM and all task instances running on it can be killed due to an `OutOfMemoryError`. Moreover, this approach can suffer from garbage collection pauses because it puts many long-lived objects on the heap. When a checkpoint is taken, `MemoryStateBackend` sends the state to the JobManager, which stores it in its heap memory. Hence, the total state of an application must fit into the JobManager's memory. Since its memory is volatile, the state is lost in case of a JobManager failure. Due to these limitations, MemoryStateBackend is only recommended for development and debugging purposes.

- FsStateBackend stores the local state on the TaskManager's JVM heap, just like MemoryStateBackend. However, instead of checkpointing the state to the JobManager's volatile memory, FsStateBackend writes the state to a remote and persistent file system. Hence, FsStateBackend provides in-memory speed for local accesses and fault tolerance in the case of failures. However, it is limited by the size of the TaskManager memory and might suffer from garbage collection pauses.

- RocksDBStateBackend stores all state into local RocksDB instances. RocksDB is an embedded key-value store that persists data to the local disk. In order to read and write data from and to RocksDB, it needs to be de/serialized. The RocksDBStateBackend also checkpoints the state to a remote and persistent file system. Because it writes data to disk and supports incremental checkpoints (more on this in "Checkpoints, Savepoints, and State Recovery" on page 58), RocksDBStateBackend is a good choice for applications with very large state. Users have reported applications with state sizes of multiple terabytes leveraging RocksDBStateBackend. However, reading and writing data to disk and the overhead of de/serializing objects result in lower read and write performance compared to maintaining state on the heap.

Since StateBackend is a public interface, it is also possible to implement a custom state backend. Example 7-12 shows how to configure a state backend (here, RocksDBStateBackend) for an application and all its stateful functions.

Example 7-12. Configuring RocksDBStateBackend for an application

```
val env = StreamExecutionEnvironment.getExecutionEnvironment

val checkpointPath: String = ???
// configure path for checkpoints on the remote filesystem
val backend = new RocksDBStateBackend(checkpointPath)

// configure the state backend
env.setStateBackend(backend)
```

We discuss in "Tuning Checkpointing and Recovery" on page 263 how to use and configure state backends in your application.

Choosing a State Primitive

The performance of a stateful operator (built-in or user-defined) depends on several aspects, including the data types of the state, the state backend of the application, and the chosen state primitives.

For state backends that de/serialize state objects when reading or writing, such as RocksDBStateBackend, the choice of the state primitive (ValueState, ListState, or MapState) can have a major impact on the performance of an application. For instance, ValueState is completely deserialized when it is accessed and serialized when it is updated. The ListState implementation of RocksDBStateBackend deserializes all list entries before constructing Iterable to read the values. However, adding a single value to ListState—appending it to the end of the list—is a cheap operation because only the appended value is serialized. MapState of RocksDBStateBackend allows reading and writing values per key—only those keys and values are de/serialized that are read or written. When iterating over the entry set of MapState, the serialized entries are prefetched from RocksDB and only deserialized when a key or value is actually accessed.

For example, with RocksDBStateBackend it is more efficient to use MapState[X, Y] instead of ValueState[HashMap[X, Y]]. ListState[X] has an advantage over Value State[List[X]] if elements are frequently appended to the list and the elements of the list are less frequently accessed.

Another good practice is to update state only once per function call. Since checkpoints are synchronized with function invocations, multiple state updates do not provide any benefits but can cause additional serialization overhead when updating state several times in a single function call.

Preventing Leaking State

Streaming applications are often designed to run continuously for months or years. If the state of an application is continuously increasing, it will at some point grow too large and kill the application unless action is taken to scale the application to more resources. In order to prevent increasing resource consumption of an application over time, it is important that the size of the operator state be controlled. Since the handling of state directly affects the semantics of an operator, Flink cannot automatically clean up state and free storage. Instead, all stateful operators must control the size of their state and have to ensure it is not infinitely growing.

A common reason for growing state is keyed state on an evolving key domain. In this scenario, a stateful function receives records with keys that are only active for a certain period of time and are never received after that. A typical example is a stream of click events where clicks have a session id attribute that expires after some time. In such a case, a function with keyed state would accumulate state for more and more keys. As the key space evolves, the state of expired keys becomes stale and useless. A solution for this problem is to remove the state of expired keys. However, a function with keyed state can only access the state of a key if it received a record with that key. In many cases, a function does not know if a record will be the last one for a key. Hence, it will not be able to evict the state for the key because it might receive another record for the key.

This problem does not only exist for custom stateful functions but also for some of the built-in operators of the DataStream API. For example, computing running aggregates on a KeyedStream, either with the built-in aggregations functions such as min, max, sum, minBy, or maxBy or with a custom ReduceFunction or AggregateFunction, keeps the state for each key and never discards it. Consequently, these functions should only be used if the key values are from a constant and bounded domain. Other examples are windows with count-based triggers, which process and clean their state when a certain number of records has been received. Windows with time-based triggers (both processing time and event time) are not affected by this because they trigger and purge their state based on time.

This means that you should take application requirements and the properties of its input data, such as key domain, into account when designing and implementing stateful operators. If your application requires keyed state for a moving key domain, it should ensure the state of keys is cleared when it is not needed anymore. This can be done by registering timers for a point of time in the future.[4] Similar to state, timers are registered in the context of the currently active key. When the timer fires, a callback method is called and the context of timer's key is loaded. Hence, the callback method has full access to the key's state and can also clear it. The functions that offer support to register timers are the Trigger interface for windows and the process function. Both were covered in Chapter 6.

Example 7-13 shows a KeyedProcessFunction that compares two subsequent temperature measurements and raises an alert if the difference is greater than a certain threshold. This is the same use case as in the keyed state example before, but the KeyedProcessFunction also clears the state for keys (i.e., sensors) that have not provided any new temperature measurements within one hour of event time.

Example 7-13. A stateful KeyedProcessFunction that cleans its state

```
class SelfCleaningTemperatureAlertFunction(val threshold: Double)
    extends KeyedProcessFunction[String, SensorReading, (String, Double, Double)] {

  // the keyed state handle for the last temperature
  private var lastTempState: ValueState[Double] = _
```

---

4 Timers can be based on event time or processing time.

```scala
  // the keyed state handle for the last registered timer
  private var lastTimerState: ValueState[Long] = _

  override def open(parameters: Configuration): Unit = {
    // register state for last temperature
    val lastTempDesc = new ValueStateDescriptor[Double]("lastTemp", classOf[Double])
    lastTempState = getRuntimeContext.getState[Double](lastTempDescriptor)
    // register state for last timer
    val lastTimerDesc = new ValueStateDescriptor[Long]("lastTimer", classOf[Long])
    lastTimerState = getRuntimeContext.getState(timestampDescriptor)
  }

  override def processElement(
      reading: SensorReading,
      ctx: KeyedProcessFunction
        [String, SensorReading, (String, Double, Double)]#Context,
      out: Collector[(String, Double, Double)]): Unit = {

    // compute timestamp of new clean up timer as record timestamp + one hour
    val newTimer = ctx.timestamp() + (3600 * 1000)
    // get timestamp of current timer
    val curTimer = lastTimerState.value()
    // delete previous timer and register new timer
    ctx.timerService().deleteEventTimeTimer(curTimer)
    ctx.timerService().registerEventTimeTimer(newTimer)
    // update timer timestamp state
    lastTimerState.update(newTimer)

    // fetch the last temperature from state
    val lastTemp = lastTempState.value()
    // check if we need to emit an alert
    val tempDiff = (reading.temperature - lastTemp).abs
    if (tempDiff > threshold) {
      // temperature increased by more than the threshold
      out.collect((reading.id, reading.temperature, tempDiff))
    }

    // update lastTemp state
    this.lastTempState.update(reading.temperature)
  }

  override def onTimer(
      timestamp: Long,
      ctx: KeyedProcessFunction
        [String, SensorReading, (String, Double, Double)]#OnTimerContext,
      out: Collector[(String, Double, Double)]): Unit = {

    // clear all state for the key
    lastTempState.clear()
    lastTimerState.clear()
  }
}
```

The state-cleaning mechanism implemented by the above `KeyedProcessFunction` works as follows. For each input event, the `processElement()` method is called. Before comparing the temperature measurements and updating the last temperature, the method updates the clean-up timer by deleting the previous timer and registering a new one. The clean-up time is computed by adding one hour to the timestamp of the current record. In order to be able to delete the currently registered timer, its timestamp is stored in an additional `ValueState[Long]` called `lastTimerState`. After that, the method compares the temperatures, possibly emits an alert, and updates its state.

Since our `KeyedProcessFunction` always updates the registered timer by deleting the current timer and registering a new one, only a single timer is registered per key. Once that timer fires, the `onTimer()` method is called. The method clears all state associated with the key, the last temperature and the last timer state.

Evolving Stateful Applications

It is often necessary to fix a bug or to evolve the business logic of a long-running stateful streaming application. Consequently, a running application needs to be replaced by an updated version usually without losing the state of the application.

Flink supports such updates by taking a savepoint of a running application, stopping it, and starting a new version of the application from the savepoint.[5] However, updating an application while preserving its state is only possible for certain application changes—the original application and its new version need to be savepoint compatible. In the following, we explain how applications can be evolved while preserving savepoint compatibility.

In "Savepoints", we explained that each state in a savepoint can be addressed by a composite identifier consisting of a unique operator identifier and the state name declared by the state descriptor.

Implement Your Applications With Evolution in Mind

It is important to understand that the initial design of an application determines if and how it can be modified later on in a savepoint-compatible way. Many changes will not be possible if the original version was not designed with updates in mind. Assigning unique identifiers to operators is mandatory for most application changes.

---

5 Chapter 10 explains how to take savepoints of running applications and how to start a new application from an existing savepoint.

When an application is started from a savepoint, the operators of the started application are initialized by looking up the corresponding states from the savepoint using operator identifiers and state names. From a savepoint-compatibility point of view this means an application can be evolved in three ways:

1. Updating or extending the logic of an application without changing or removing an existing state. This includes adding of stateful or stateless operators to the application.

2. Removing a state from the application.

3. Modifying the state of an existing operator by changing the state primitive or data type of the state.

In the following sections, we discuss these three cases.

Updating an Application without Modifying Existing State

If an application is updated without removing or changing existing state, it is always savepoint compatible and can be started from a savepoint of an earlier version.

If you add a new stateful operator to the application or a new state to an existing operator, the state will be initialized as empty when the application is started from a savepoint.

Changing the Input Data Type of Built-in Stateful Operators

Note that changing the input data type of built-in stateful operators, such as window aggregation, time-based joins, or asyncronous functions, often modifies the type of their internal state. Therefore, such changes are not safepoint compatible even though they look unobtrusive.

Removing State from an Application

Instead of adding new states to an application, you might also want to adjust an application by removing state—either by removing a complete stateful operator or just a state from a function. When the new version of the application is started from a savepoint of the previous version, the savepoint contains state that cannot be mapped to the restarted application. This is also the case if the unique identifier of an operator or the name of a state was changed.

By default, Flink will not start applications that do not restore all states that are contained in a savepoint to avoid losing the state in the savepoint. However, it is possible to disable this safety check as described in "Running and Managing Streaming Applications" on page 245. Hence, it is not difficult to update an application by removing stateful operators or state from an existing operator.

Modifying the State of an Operator

While adding or removing state from an application is rather easy and does not affect savepoint compatibility, modifying the state of an existing operator is more involved. There are two ways state can be modified:

- By changing the data type of a state, such as changing a `ValueState[Int]` to a `ValueState[Double]`
- By changing the type of a state primitive, as for example by changing a `Value State[List[String]]` to a `ListState[String]`

Changing the data type of a state is possible in a few specific cases. However, Flink currently does not support changing the primitive (or structure) of a state. There are some ideas to support this case by offering an offline tool to convert savepoints. However, as of Flink 1.7 no such tool exists. In the following we focus on changing the data type of a state.

In order to grasp the problem of modifying the data type of a state, we have to understand how state data is represented within a savepoint. A savepoint consists mainly of serialized state data. The serializers that convert the state JVM objects into bytes are generated and configured by Flink's type system. This conversion is based on the data type of the state. For example, if you have a `ValueState[String]`, Flink's type system generates a `StringSerializer` to convert `String` objects into bytes. The serializer is also used to convert the raw bytes back into JVM objects. Depending on whether the state backend stores the data serialized (like the `RocksDBStateBackend`) or as objects on the heap (like the `FSStateBackend`), this happens when the state is read by a function or when an application is restarted from a savepoint.

Since Flink's type system generates serializers depending on the data type of a state, the serializers are likely to change when the data type of a state changes. For example, if you changed the `ValueState[String]` to a `ValueState[Double]`, Flink would create a `DoubleSerializer` to access the state. It is not surprising that using a `DoubleSer ializer` to deserialize the binary data generated by serializing a `String` with a `StringSerializer` will fail. Hence, changing the data type of a state is only supported in very specific cases.

In Flink 1.7, changing the data type of a state is supported if the data type was defined as an Apache Avro type and if the new data type is also an Avro type that was evolved from the original type according to Avro's schema evolution rules. Flink's type system will automatically generate serializers that can read previous versions of the data type.

State evolution and migration is an important topic in the Flink community and receives a lot of attention. You can expect improved support for these scenarios in future versions of Apache Flink. Despite all these efforts, we recommend always double checking if an application can be evolved as planned before putting it into production.

Queryable State

Many stream processing applications need to share their results with other applications. A common pattern is to write results into a database or key-value store and have other applications retrieve the result from that datastore. Such an architecture implies that a separate system needs to be set up and maintained, which can be a major effort, especially if this needs to be a distributed system as well.

Apache Flink features queryable state to address use cases that usually would require an external datastore to share data. In Flink, any keyed state can be exposed to external applications as queryable state and act as a read-only key-value store. The stateful streaming application processes events as usual and stores and updates its intermediate or final results in a queryable state. External applications can request the state for a key while the streaming application is running.

Note that only key point queries are supported. It is not possible to request key ranges or even run more complex queries.

Queryable state does not address all use cases that require an external datastore. For example, the queryable state is only accessible while the application is running. It is not accessible while the application is restarted due to an error, for rescaling the application, or to migrate it to another cluster. However, it makes many applications much easier to realize, such as real-time dashboards or other monitoring applications.

In the following, we discuss the architecture of Flink's queryable state service and explain how streaming applications can expose queryable state and external applications can query it.

Architecture and Enabling Queryable State

Flink's queryable state service consists of three processes:

- The QueryableStateClient is used by an external application to submit queries and retrieve results.

- The `QueryableStateClientProxy` accepts and serves client requests. Each Task-Manager runs a client proxy. Since keyed state is distributed across all parallel instances of an operator, the proxy needs to identify the TaskManager that maintains the state for the requested key. This information is requested from the Job-Manager that manages the key group assignment, and is cached once received.[6] The client proxy retrieves the state from the state server of the respective Task-Manager and serves the result to the client.

- The `QueryableStateServer` serves the requests of a client proxy. Each TaskManager runs a state server that fetches the state of a queried key from the local state backend and returns it to the requesting client proxy.

Figure 7-1 shows the architecture of the queryable state service.

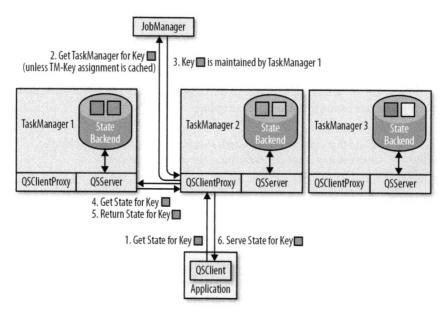

Figure 7-1. Architecture of Flink's queryable state service

In order to enable the queryable state service in a Flink setup—to start client proxy and server threads within the TaskManagers—you need to add the *flink-queryable-state-runtime* JAR file to the classpath of the TaskManager process. This is done by copying it from the *./opt* folder of your installation into the *./lib* folder. When the JAR file is in the classpath, the queryable state threads are automatically started and can

---

6 Key groups are discussed in Chapter 3.

serve requests of the queryable state client. When properly configured, you will find the following log message in the TaskManager logs:

```
Started the Queryable State Proxy Server @ …
```

The ports used by the client proxy and server and additional parameters can be configured in the *./conf/flink-conf.yaml* file.

Exposing Queryable State

Implementing a streaming application with queryable state is easy. All you have to do is define a function with keyed state and make the state queryable by calling the set Queryable(String) method on the StateDescriptor before obtaining the state handle. Example 7-14 shows how to make lastTempState queryable to illustrate the usage of the keyed state.

Example 7-14. Configuring keyed state to be queryable

```
override def open(parameters: Configuration): Unit = {

  // create state descriptor
  val lastTempDescriptor =
    new ValueStateDescriptor[Double]("lastTemp", classOf[Double])
  // enable queryable state and set its external identifier
  lastTempDescriptor.setQueryable("lastTemperature")
  // obtain the state handle
  lastTempState = getRuntimeContext
    .getState[Double](lastTempDescriptor)
}
```

The external identifier that is passed with the setQueryable() method can be freely chosen and is only used to configure the queryable state client.

In addition to the generic way of enabling queries on any type of keyed state, Flink also offers shortcuts to define stream sinks that store the events of a stream in a queryable state. Example 7-15 shows how to use a queryable state sink.

Example 7-15. Writing a DataStream into a queryable state sink

```
val tenSecsMaxTemps: DataStream[(String, Double)] = sensorData
  // project to sensor id and temperature
  .map(r => (r.id, r.temperature))
  // compute every 10 seconds the max temperature per sensor
  .keyBy(_._1)
  .timeWindow(Time.seconds(10))
  .max(1)

// store max temperature of the last 10 secs for each sensor
// in a queryable state
```

```
tenSecsMaxTemps
  // key by sensor id
  .keyBy(_._1)
  .asQueryableState("maxTemperature")
```

The `asQueryableState()` method appends a queryable state sink to the stream. The
type of the queryable state is `ValueState`, which holds values of the type of the input
stream—our example (`String, Double`). For each received record, the queryable
state sink upserts the record into `ValueState`, so that the latest event per key is always
stored.

An application with a function that has a queryable state is executed just like any
other application. You only have to ensure that the TaskManagers are configured to
start their queryable state services as discussed in the previous section.

Querying State from External Applications

Any JVM-based application can query the queryable state of a running Flink application by using `QueryableStateClient`. This class is provided by the `flink-
queryable-state-client-java` dependency, which you can add to your project as
follows:

```
<dependency>
  <groupid>org.apache.flink</groupid>
  <artifactid>flink-queryable-state-client-java_2.12</artifactid>
  <version>1.7.1</version>
</dependency>
```

The `QueryableStateClient` is initialized with the hostname of any TaskManager and
the port on which the queryable state client proxy is listening. By default, the client
proxy listens on port 9067, but the port can be configured in the *./conf/flink-
conf.yaml* file:

```
val client: QueryableStateClient =
  new QueryableStateClient(tmHostname, proxyPort)
```

Once you obtain a state client, you can query the state of an application by calling the
`getKvState()` method. The method takes several parameters, such as the `JobID` of
the running application, the state identifier, the key for which the state should be
fetched, the `TypeInformation` for the key, and the `StateDescriptor` of the queried
state. The `JobID` can be obtained via the REST API, the Web UI, or the log files. The
`getKvState()` method returns a `CompletableFuture[S]` where `S` is the type of the
state (e.g., `ValueState[_]` or `MapState[_, _]`). Hence, the client can send out multiple asynchronous queries and wait for their results. Example 7-16 shows a simple
console dashboard that queries the queryable state of the application shown in the
previous section.

Example 7-16. A simple dashboard application that queries the state of a Flink application

```scala
object TemperatureDashboard {

  // assume local setup and TM runs on same machine as client
  val proxyHost = "127.0.0.1"
  val proxyPort = 9069

  // jobId of running QueryableStateJob
  // can be looked up in logs of running job or the web UI
  val jobId = "d2447b1a5e0d952c372064c886d2220a"

  // how many sensors to query
  val numSensors = 5
  // how often to query the state
  val refreshInterval = 10000

  def main(args: Array[String]): Unit = {
    // configure client with host and port of queryable state proxy
    val client = new QueryableStateClient(proxyHost, proxyPort)

    val futures = new Array[
      CompletableFuture[ValueState[(String, Double)]]](numSensors)
    val results = new Array[Double](numSensors)

    // print header line of dashboard table
    val header =
      (for (i <- 0 until numSensors) yield "sensor_" + (i + 1))
        .mkString("\t| ")
    println(header)

    // loop forever
    while (true) {
      // send out async queries
      for (i <- 0 until numSensors) {
        futures(i) = queryState("sensor_" + (i + 1), client)
      }
      // wait for results
      for (i <- 0 until numSensors) {
        results(i) = futures(i).get().value()._2
      }
      // print result
      val line = results.map(t => f"$t%1.3f").mkString("\t| ")
      println(line)

      // wait to send out next queries
      Thread.sleep(refreshInterval)
    }
    client.shutdownAndWait()
  }
```

```
def queryState(
    key: String,
    client: QueryableStateClient)
  : CompletableFuture[ValueState[(String, Double)]] = {

  client
    .getKvState[String, ValueState[(String, Double)], (String, Double)](
      JobID.fromHexString(jobId),
      "maxTemperature",
      key,
      Types.STRING,
      new ValueStateDescriptor[(String, Double)](
        "", // state name not relevant here
        Types.TUPLE[(String, Double)]))
  }
}
```

In order to run the example, you have to start the streaming application with the queryable state first. Once it is running, look for the JobID in the log file or the web UI; set the JobID in the code of the dashboard and run it as well. The dashboard will then start querying the state of the running streaming application.

Summary

Just about every nontrivial streaming application is stateful. The DataStream API provides powerful yet easy-to-use tools to access and maintain operator state. It offers different types of state primitives and supports pluggable state backends. While developers have lots of flexibility to interact with state, Flink's runtime manages terabytes of state and ensures exactly-once semantics in case of failure. The combination of time-based computations as discussed in Chapter 6 and scalable state management empowers developers to realize sophisticated streaming applications. Queryable state is an easy-to-use feature and can save you the effort of setting up and maintaining a database or key-value store to expose the results of a streaming application to external applications.

## CHAPTER 8

Reading from and Writing to External Systems

Data can be stored in many different systems, such as filesystems, object stores, relational database systems, key-value stores, search indexes, event logs, message queues, and so on. Each class of systems has been designed for specific access patterns and excels at serving a certain purpose. Consequently, today's data infrastructures often consist of many different storage systems. Before adding a new component into the mix, a logical question to ask should be, "How well does it work with the other components in my stack?"

Adding a data processing system, such as Apache Flink, requires careful considerations because it does not include its own storage layer but relies on external storage systems to ingest and persist data. Hence, it is important for data processors like Flink to provide a well-equipped library of connectors to read data from and write data to external systems as well as an API to implement custom connectors. However, just being able to read or write data to external datastores is not sufficient for a stream processor that wants to provide meaningful consistency guarantees in the case of failure.

In this chapter, we discuss how source and sink connectors affect the consistency guarantees of Flink streaming applications and present Flink's most popular connectors to read and write data. You will learn how to implement custom source and sink connectors and how to implement functions that send asynchronous read or write requests to external datastores.

Application Consistency Guarantees

In "Checkpoints, Savepoints, and State Recovery", you learned that Flink's checkpointing and recovery mechanism periodically takes consistent checkpoints of an application's state. In case of a failure, the state of the application is restored from the latest completed checkpoint and processing continues. However, being able to reset the state of an application to a consistent point is not sufficient to achieve satisfying processing guarantees for an application. Instead, the source and sink connectors of an application need to be integrated with Flink's checkpointing and recovery mechanism and provide certain properties to be able to give meaningful guarantees.

In order to provide exactly-once state consistency for an application,[1] each source connector of the application needs to be able to set its read positions to a previously checkpointed position. When taking a checkpoint, a source operator persists its reading positions and restores these positions during recovery. Examples for source connectors that support the checkpointing of reading positions are file-based sources that store the reading offsets in the byte stream of the file or a Kafka source that stores the reading offsets in the topic partitions it consumes. If an application ingests data from a source connector that is not able to store and reset a reading position, it might suffer from data loss in the case of a failure and only provide at-most-once guarantees.

The combination of Flink's checkpointing and recovery mechanism and resettable source connectors guarantees that an application will not lose any data. However, the application might emit results twice because all results that have been emitted after the last successful checkpoint (the one to which the application falls back in the case of a recovery) will be emitted again. Therefore, resettable sources and Flink's recovery mechanism are not sufficient to provide end-to-end exactly-once guarantees even though the application state is exactly-once consistent.

An application that aims to provide end-to-end exactly-once guarantees requires special sink connectors. There are two techniques that sink connectors can apply in different situations to achieve exactly-once guarantees: *idempotent* writes and *transactional* writes.

Idempotent Writes

An idempotent operation can be performed several times but will only result in a single change. For example, repeatedly inserting the same key-value pair into a hashmap is an idempotent operation because the first insert operation adds the value for the key into the map and all following insertions will not change the map since it already

---

1 Exactly-once state consistency is a requirement for end-to-end exactly-once consistency but is not the same.

contains the key-value pair. On the other hand, an append operation is not an idempotent operation, because appending an element multiple times results in multiple appends. Idempotent write operations are interesting for streaming applications because they can be performed multiple times without changing the results. Hence, they can to some extent mitigate the effect of replayed results as caused by Flink's checkpointing mechanism.

It should be noted an application that relies on idempotent sinks to achieve exactly-once results must guarantee that it overrides previously written results while it replays. For example, an application with a sink that upserts into a key-value store must ensure that it deterministically computes the keys that are used to upsert. Moreover, applications that read from the sink system might observe unexpected results during the time when an application recovers. When the replay starts, previously emitted results might be overridden by earlier results. Hence, an application that consumes the output of the recovering application might witness a jump back in time, e.g., read a smaller count than before. Also, the overall result of the streaming application will be in an inconsistent state while the replay is in progress because some results will be overridden while others are not. Once the replay completes and the application is past the point at which it previously failed, the result will be consistent again.

Transactional Writes

The second approach to achieve end-to-end exactly-once consistency is based on transactional writes. The idea here is to only write those results to an external sink system that have been computed before the last successful checkpoint. This behavior guarantees end-to-end exactly-once because in case of a failure, the application is reset to the last checkpoint and no results have been emitted to the sink system after that checkpoint. By only writing data once a checkpoint is completed, the transactional approach does not suffer from the replay inconsistency of the idempotent writes. However, it adds latency because results only become visible when a checkpoint completes.

Flink provides two building blocks to implement transactional sink connectors—a generic *write-ahead-log (WAL)* sink and a *two-phase-commit (2PC)* sink. The WAL sink writes all result records into application state and emits them to the sink system once it receives the notification that a checkpoint was completed. Since the sink buffers records in the state backend, the WAL sink can be used with any kind of sink system. However, it cannot provide bulletproof exactly-once guarantees,[2] adds to the state size of an application, and the sink system has to deal with a spiky writing pattern.

---

2 We discuss the consistency guarantees of a WAL sink in more detail in "GenericWriteAheadSink".

In contrast, the 2PC sink requires a sink system that offers transactional support or exposes building blocks to emulate transactions. For each checkpoint, the sink starts a transaction and appends all received records to the transaction, writing them to the sink system without committing them. When it receives the notification that a checkpoint completed, it commits the transaction and materializes the written results. The mechanism relies on the ability of a sink to commit a transaction after recovering from a failure that was opened before a completed checkpoint.

The 2PC protocol piggybacks on Flink's existing checkpointing mechanism. The checkpoint barriers are notifications to start a new transaction, the notifications of all operators about the success of their individual checkpoint are their commit votes, and the messages of the JobManager that notify about the success of a checkpoint are the instructions to commit the transactions. In contrast to WAL sinks, 2PC sinks can achieve exactly-once output depending on the sink system and the sink's implementation. Moreover, a 2PC sink continuously writes records to the sink system compared to the spiky writing pattern of a WAL sink.

Table 8-1 shows the end-to-end consistency guarantees for different types of source and sink connectors that can be achieved in the *best case*; depending on the implementation of the sink, the actual consistency might be worse.

Table 8-1. End-to-end consistency guarantees for different combinations of sources and sinks

	Nonresettable source	Resettable source
Any sink	At-most-once	At-least-once
Idempotent sink	At-most-once	Exactly-once* (temporary inconsistencies during recovery)
WAL sink	At-most-once	At-least-once
2PC sink	At-most-once	Exactly-once

Provided Connectors

Apache Flink provides connectors to read data from and write data to a variety of storage systems. Message queues and event logs, such as Apache Kafka, Kinesis, or RabbitMQ, are common sources to ingest data streams. In batch processing-dominated environments, data streams are also often ingested by monitoring a file-system directory and reading files as they appear.

On the sink side, data streams are often produced into message queues to make the events available to subsequent streaming applications, written to filesystems for archiving or making the data available for offline analytics or batch applications, or inserted into key-value stores or relational database systems, like Cassandra, Elastic-Search, or MySQL, to make the data searchable and queryable, or to serve dashboard applications.

Unfortunately, there are no standard interfaces for most of these storage systems, except JDBC for relational DBMS. Instead, every system features its own connector library with a proprietary protocol. As a consequence, processing systems like Flink need to maintain several dedicated connectors to be able to read events from and write events to the most commonly used message queues, event logs, filesystems, key-value stores, and database systems.

Flink provides connectors for Apache Kafka, Kinesis, RabbitMQ, Apache Nifi, various filesystems, Cassandra, ElasticSearch, and JDBC. In addition, the Apache Bahir project provides additional Flink connectors for ActiveMQ, Akka, Flume, Netty, and Redis.

In order to use a provided connector in your application, you need to add its dependency to the build file of your project. We explained how to add connector dependencies in "Including External and Flink Dependencies" on page 107.

In the following section, we discuss the connectors for Apache Kafka, file-based sources and sinks, and Apache Cassandra. These are the most widely used connectors and they also represent important types of source and sink systems. You can find more information about the other connectors in the documentation for Apache Flink (*http://bit.ly/2UtSrGk*) or Apache Bahir (*http://bit.ly/2HOGWmE*).

Apache Kafka Source Connector

Apache Kafka is a distributed streaming platform. Its core is a distributed publish-subscribe messaging system that is widely adopted to ingest and distribute event streams. We briefly explain the main concepts of Kafka before we dive into the details of Flink's Kafka connector.

Kafka organizes event streams as so-called topics. A topic is an event log that guarantees that events are read in the same order in which they were written. In order to scale writing to and reading from a topic, it can be split into partitions that are distributed across a cluster. The ordering guarantee is limited to a partition—Kafka does not provide ordering guarantees when reading from different partitions. The reading position in a Kafka partition is called an offset.

Flink provides source connectors for all common Kafka versions. Through Kafka 0.11, the API of the client library evolved and new features were added. For instance, Kafka 0.10 added support for record timestamps. Since release 1.0, the API has remained stable. Flink provides a universal Kafka connector that works for all Kafka versions since 0.11. Flink also features version-specific connectors for the Kafka versions 0.8, 0.9, 0.10, and 0.11. For the remainder of this section, we focus on the universal connector and for the version-specific connectors, we refer you to Flink's documentation.

The dependency for the universal Flink Kafka connector is added to a Maven project as shown in the following:

```
<dependency>
    <groupId>org.apache.flink</groupId>
    <artifactId>flink-connector-kafka_2.12</artifactId>
    <version>1.7.1</version>
</dependency>
```

The Flink Kafka connector ingests event streams in parallel. Each parallel source task can read from one or more partitions. A task tracks for each partition its current reading offset and includes it into its checkpoint data. When recovering from a failure, the offsets are restored and the source instance continues reading from the checkpointed offset. The Flink Kafka connector does not rely on Kafka's own offset-tracking mechanism, which is based on so-called consumer groups. Figure 8-1 shows the assignment of partitions to source instances.

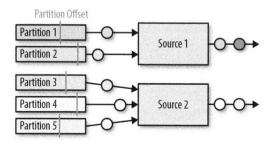

Figure 8-1. Read offsets of Kafka topic partitions

A Kafka source connector is created as shown in Example 8-1.

Example 8-1. Creating a Flink Kafka source

```
val properties = new Properties()
properties.setProperty("bootstrap.servers", "localhost:9092")
properties.setProperty("group.id", "test")

val stream: DataStream[String] = env.addSource(
  new FlinkKafkaConsumer[String](
    "topic",
    new SimpleStringSchema(),
    properties))
```

The constructor takes three arguments. The first argument defines the topics to read from. This can be a single topic, a list of topics, or a regular expression that matches all topics to read from. When reading from multiple topics, the Kafka connector treats all partitions of all topics the same and multiplexes their events into a single stream.

The second argument is a `DeserializationSchema` or `KeyedDeserialization Schema`. Kafka messages are stored as raw byte messages and need to be deserialized into Java or Scala objects. The `SimpleStringSchema`, which is used in Example 8-1, is a built-in `DeserializationSchema` that simply deserializes a byte array into a `String`. In addition, Flink provides implementations for Apache Avro and text-based JSON encodings. `DeserializationSchema` and `KeyedDeserializationSchema` are public interfaces so you can always implement custom deserialization logic.

The third parameter is a `Properties` object that configures the Kafka client that is internally used to connect to and read from Kafka. A minimum `Properties` configuration consists of two entries, `"bootstrap.servers"` and `"group.id"`. Consult the Kafka documentation for additional configuration properties.

In order to extract event-time timestamps and generate watermarks, you can provide an `AssignerWithPeriodicWatermark` or an `AssignerWithPunctuatedWatermark` to a Kafka consumer by calling a `FlinkKafkaConsumer.assignTimestampsAndWater mark()`.[3] An assigner is applied to each partition to leverage the per partition ordering guarantees, and the source instance merges the partition watermarks according to the watermark propagation protocol (see "Watermark Propagation and Event Time").

 Note that the watermarks of a source instance cannot make progress if a partition becomes inactive and does not provide messages. As a consequence, a single inactive partition causes the whole application to stall because the application's watermarks do not make progress.

As of version 0.10.0, Kafka supports message timestamps. When reading from Kafka version 0.10 or later, the consumer will automatically extract the message timestamp as an event-time timestamp if the application runs in event-time mode. In this case, you still need to generate watermarks and should apply an `AssignerWithPeriodicWa termark` or an `AssignerWithPunctuatedWatermark` that forwards the previously assigned Kafka timestamp.

There are a few more notable configuration options. You can configure the starting position from which the partitions of a topic are initially read. Valid options are:

- The last reading position known by Kafka for the consumer group that was configured via the `group.id` parameter. This is the default behavior: `FlinkKafkaConsumer.setStartFromGroupOffsets()`

---

3 See Chapter 6 for details about the timestamp assigner interfaces.

- The earliest offset of each individual partition:
  `FlinkKafkaConsumer.setStartFromEarliest()`

- The latest offset of each individual partition:
  `FlinkKafkaConsumer.setStartFromLatest()`

- All records with a timestamp greater than a given timestamp (requires Kafka 0.10.x or later):
  `FlinkKafkaConsumer.setStartFromTimestamp(long)`

- Specific reading positions for all partitions as provided by a `Map` object:
  `FlinkKafkaConsumer.setStartFromSpecificOffsets(Map)`

 Note that this configuration only affects the first reading positions. In the case of a recovery or when starting from a savepoint, an application will start reading from the offsets stored in the checkpoint or savepoint.

A Flink Kafka consumer can be configured to automatically discover new topics that match the regular expression or new partitions that were added to a topic. These features are disabled by default and can be enabled by adding the parameter `flink.partition-discovery.interval-millis` with a nonnegative value to the `Properties` object.

Apache Kafka Sink Connector

Flink provides sink connectors for all Kafka versions since 0.8. Through Kafka 0.11, the API of the client library evolved and new features were added, such as record timestamp support with Kafka 0.10 and transactional writes with Kafka 0.11. Since release 1.0, the API has remained stable. Flink provides a universal Kafka connector that works for all Kafka versions since 0.11. Flink also features version-specific connectors for Kafka versions 0.8, 0.9, 0.10, and 0.11. For the remainder of this section, we focus on the universal connector and refer you to Flink's documentation for the version-specific connectors. The dependency for Flink's universal Kafka connector is added to a Maven project as shown in the following:

```
<dependency>
    <groupId>org.apache.flink</groupId>
    <artifactId>flink-connector-kafka_2.12</artifactId>
    <version>1.7.1</version>
</dependency>
```

A Kafka sink is added to a DataStream application as shown in Example 8-2.

Example 8-2. Creating a Flink Kafka sink

```
val stream: DataStream[String] = ...

val myProducer = new FlinkKafkaProducer[String](
  "localhost:9092",        // broker list
  "topic",                 // target topic
  new SimpleStringSchema)  // serialization schema

stream.addSink(myProducer)
```

The constructor used in Example 8-2 receives three parameters. The first parameter is a comma-separated string of Kafka broker addresses. The second is the name of the topic to which the data is written, and the last is a `SerializationSchema` that converts the input types of the sink (`String` in Example 8-2) into a byte array. `SerializationSchema` is the counterpart of the `DeserializationSchema` that we discussed in the Kafka source section.

`FlinkKafkaProducer` provides more constructors with different combinations of arguments as follows:

- Similar to the Kafka source connector, you can pass a `Properties` object to provide custom options to the internal Kafka client. When using `Properties`, the list of brokers has to be provided as a `"bootstrap.servers"` property. Have a look at the Kafka documentation for a comprehensive list of parameters.

- You can specify a `FlinkKafkaPartitioner` to control how records are mapped to Kafka partitions. We will discuss this feature in more depth later in this section.

- Instead of using a `SerializationSchema` to convert records into byte arrays, you can also specify a `KeyedSerializationSchema`, which serializes a record into two byte arrays—one for the key and one for the value of a Kafka message. Moreover, `KeyedSerializationSchema` also exposes more Kafka-specific functionality, such as overriding the target topic to write to multiple topics.

At-least-once guarantees for the Kafka sink

The consistency guarantees that Flink's Kafka sink provides depend on its configuration. The Kafka sink provides at-least-once guarantees under the following conditions:

- Flink's checkpointing is enabled and all sources of the application are resettable.

- The sink connector throws an exception if a write does not succeed, causing the application to fail and recover. This is the default behavior. The internal Kafka client can be configured to retry writes before declaring them failed by setting the `retries` property to a value larger than zero (the default). You can also configure the sink to log write only failures by calling `setLogFailuresOnly(true)` on the sink object. Note that this will void any output guarantees of the application.

- The sink connector waits for Kafka to acknowledge in-flight records before completing its checkpoint. This is the default behavior. By calling `setFlushOnCheckpoint(false)` on the sink object, you can disable this waiting. However, this will also disable any output guarantees.

Exactly-once guarantees for the Kafka sink

Kafka 0.11 introduced support for transactional writes. Due to this feature, Flink's Kafka sink is also able to provide exactly-once output guarantees given that the sink and Kafka are properly configured. Again, a Flink application must enable checkpointing and consume from resettable sources. Moreover, `FlinkKafkaProducer` provides a constructor with a `Semantic` parameter that controls the consistency guarantees provided by the sink. Possible consistency values are:

- `Semantic.NONE`, which provides no guarantees—records might be lost or written multiple times.
- `Semantic.AT_LEAST_ONCE`, which guarantees that no write is lost but might be duplicated. This is the default setting.
- `Semantic.EXACTLY_ONCE`, which builds on Kafka's transactions to write each record exactly once.

There are a few things to consider when running a Flink application with a Kafka sink that operates in exactly-once mode, and it helps to roughly understand how Kafka processes transactions. In a nutshell, Kafka's transactions work by appending all messages to the log of a partition and marking messages of open transactions as uncommitted. Once a transaction is committed, the markers are changed to committed. A consumer that reads from a topic can be configured with an isolation level (via the `isolation.level` property) to declare whether it can read uncommitted messages (read_uncommitted, the default) or not (read_committed). If the consumer is configured to read_committed, it stops consuming from a partition once it encounters an uncommitted message and resumes when the message is committed. Hence, open transactions can block consumers from reading a partition and introduce significant delays. Kafka guards against this by rejecting and closing transactions after a timeout interval, which is configured with the `transaction.timeout.ms` property.

In the context of Flink's Kafka sink, this is important because transactions that time out—due to long recovery cycles, for example—lead to data loss. So, it is crucial to configure the transaction timeout property appropriately. By default, the Flink Kafka sink sets `transaction.timeout.ms` to one hour, which means you probably need to adjust the `transaction.max.timeout.ms` property of your Kafka setup, which is set to 15 minutes by default. Moreover, the visibility of committed messages depends on the checkpoint interval of a Flink application. Refer to the Flink documentation to learn about a few other corner cases when enabling exactly-once consistency.

 Check the Configuration of Your Kafka Cluster

The default configuration of a Kafka cluster can still lead to data loss, even after a write is acknowledged. You should carefully revise the configuration of your Kafka setup, paying special attention to the following parameters:

- `acks`
- `log.flush.interval.messages`
- `log.flush.interval.ms`
- `log.flush.*`

We refer you to the Kafka documentation for details about its configuration parameters and guidelines for a suitable configuration.

Custom Partitioning and Writing Message Timestamps

When writing messages to a Kafka topic, a Flink Kafka sink task can choose to which partition of the topic to write. `FlinkKafkaPartitioner` can be defined in some constructors of the Flink Kafka sink. If not specified, the default partitioner maps each sink task to a single Kafka partition—all records emitted by the same sink task are written to the same partition and a single partition may contain the records of multiple sink tasks if there are more tasks than partitions. If the number of partitions is larger than the number of subtasks, the default configuration results in empty partitions, which can cause problems for Flink applications consuming the topic in event-time mode.

By providing a custom `FlinkKafkaPartitioner`, you can control how records are routed to topic partitions. For example, you can create a partitioner based on a key attribute of the records or a round-robin partitioner for even distribution. There is also the option to delegate the partitioning to Kafka based on the message key. This requires a `KeyedSerializationSchema` in order to extract the message keys and configure the `FlinkKafkaPartitioner` parameter with `null` to disable the default partitioner.

Finally, Flink's Kafka sink can be configured to write message timestamps as supported since Kafka 0.10. Writing the event-time timestamp of a record to Kafka is enabled by calling `setWriteTimestampToKafka(true)` on the sink object.

Filesystem Source Connector

Filesystems are commonly used to store large amounts of data in a cost-efficient way. In big data architectures they often serve as data source and data sink for batch processing applications. In combination with advanced file formats, such as Apache Parquet or Apache ORC, filesystems can efficiently serve analytical query engines such as Apache Hive, Apache Impala, or Presto. Therefore, filesystems are commonly used to "connect" streaming and batch applications.

Apache Flink features a resettable source connector to ingest data in files as streams. The filesystem source is part of the `flink-streaming-java` module. Hence, you do not need to add any other dependency to use this feature. Flink supports different types of filesystems, such as local filesystems (including locally mounted NFS or SAN shares, Hadoop HDFS, Amazon S3, and OpenStack Swift FS). Refer to "Filesystem Configuration" on page 237 to learn how to configure filesystems in Flink. Example 8-3 shows how to ingest a stream by reading text files line-wise.

Example 8-3. Creating a filesystem source

```
val lineReader = new TextInputFormat(null)

val lineStream: DataStream[String] = env.readFile[String](
  lineReader,                  // The FileInputFormat
  "hdfs:///path/to/my/data",   // The path to read
  FileProcessingMode
    .PROCESS_CONTINUOUSLY,     // The processing mode
  30000L)                      // The monitoring interval in ms
```

The arguments of the `StreamExecutionEnvironment.readFile()` method are:

- A `FileInputFormat`, which is responsible for reading the content of the files. We discuss the details of this interface later in this section. The `null` parameter of `TextInputFormat` in Example 8-3 defines the path that is separately set.

- The path that should be read. If the path refers to a file, the single file is read. If it refers to a directory, `FileInputFormat` scans the directory for files to read.

- The mode in which the path should be read. The mode can either be PRO CESS_ONCE or PROCESS_CONTINUOUSLY. In PROCESS_ONCE mode, the read path is scanned once when the job is started and all matching files are read. In PRO CESS_CONTINUOUSLY, the path is periodically scanned (after an initial scan) and new and modified files are continuously read.

- The interval in milliseconds in which the path is periodically scanned. The parameter is ignored in PROCESS_ONCE mode.

FileInputFormat is a specialized InputFormat to read files from a filesystem.[4] A FileInputFormat reads files in two steps. First it scans a filesystem path and creates so-called input splits for all matching files. An input split defines a range on a file, typically via a start offset and a length. After dividing a large file into multiple splits, the splits can be distributed to multiple reader tasks to read the file in parallel. Depending on the encoding of a file, it can be necessary to only generate a single split to read the file as a whole. The second step of a FileInputFormat is to receive an input split, read the file range that is defined by the split, and return all corresponding records.

A FileInputFormat used in a DataStream application should also implement the CheckpointableInputFormat interface, which defines methods to checkpoint and reset the the current reading position of an InputFormat within a file split. The file-system source connector provides only at-least-once guarantees when checkpointing is enabled if the FileInputFormat does not implement the CheckpointableInputFormat interface because the input format will start reading from the beginning of the split that was processed when the last complete checkpoint was taken.

In version 1.7, Flink provides a few classes that extend FileInputFormat and implement CheckpointableInputFormat. TextInputFormat reads text files line-wise (split by newline characters), subclasses of CsvInputFormat read files with comma-separated values, and AvroInputFormat reads files with Avro-encoded records.

In PROCESS_CONTINUOUSLY mode, the filesystem source connector identifies new files based on their modification timestamp. This means a file is completely reprocessed if it is modified because its modification timestamp changes. This includes modifications due to appending writes. Therefore, a common technique to continuously ingest files is to write them in a temporary directory and atomically move them to the monitored directory once they are finalized. When a file is completely ingested and a checkpoint completed, it can be removed from the directory. Monitoring ingested files by tracking the modification timestamp also has implications if you read from file stores with eventually consistent list operations, such as S3. Since files might not appear in order of their modification timestamps, they may be ignored by the filesystem source connector.

Note that in PROCESS_ONCE mode, no checkpoints are taken after the filesystem path is scanned and all splits are created.

If you want to use a filesystem source connector in an event-time application, you should be aware that it can be challenging to generate watermarks since input splits are generated in a single process and round-robin distributed to all parallel readers

---

4 InputFormat is Flink's interface to define data sources in the DataSet API.

that process them in order of the modification timestamp of the file. In order to generate satisfying watermarks you need to reason about the smallest timestamp of a record that is included in a split later processed by the task.

Filesystem Sink Connector

Writing a stream into files is a common requirement, for example, to prepare data with low latency for offline ad-hoc analysis. Since most applications can only read files once they are finalized and streaming applications run for long periods of time, streaming sink connectors typically chunk their output into multiple files. Moreover, it is common to organize records into so-called buckets, so that consuming applications have more control over which data to read.

Like the filesystem source connector, Flink's `StreamingFileSink` connector is contained in the `flink-streaming-java` module. Hence, you do not need to add a dependency to your build file to use it.

`StreamingFileSink` provides end-to-end exactly-once guarantees for an application given that the application is configured with exactly-once checkpoints and all its sources are reset in the case of a failure. We will discuss the recovery mechanism in more detail later in this section. Example 8-4 shows how to create a `StreamingFile Sink` with minimal configuration and append it to a stream.

Example 8-4. Creating a StreamingFileSink in row-encoding mode

```
val input: DataStream[String] = …
val sink: StreamingFileSink[String] = StreamingFileSink
  .forRowFormat(
    new Path("/base/path"),
    new SimpleStringEncoder[String]("UTF-8"))
  .build()

input.addSink(sink)
```

When a `StreamingFileSink` receives a record, the record is assigned to a bucket. A bucket is a subdirectory of the base path that is configured with the builder of `Stream ingFileSink`—`"/base/path"` in Example 8-4.

The bucket is chosen by a `BucketAssigner`, which is a public interface and returns for every record a `BucketId` that determines the directory to which the record will be written. The `BucketAssigner` can be configured on the builder using the `withBucketAssigner()` method. If no `BucketAssigner` is explicitly specified, it uses a `DateTimeBucketAssigner` that assigns records to hourly buckets based on the processing time when they are written.

Each bucket directory contains multiple part files that are concurrently written by multiple parallel instances of the `StreamingFileSink`. Moreover, each parallel instance chunks its output into multiple part files. The path of a part file has the following format:

```
[base-path]/[bucket-path]/part-[task-idx]-[id]
```

For example, given a base path of `"/johndoe/demo"` and a part prefix of `"part"`, the path `"/johndoe/demo/2018-07-22--17/part-4-8"` points to the eight file that was written by the fifth (0-indexed) sink task to bucket `"2018-07-22--17"`—the 5 p.m. bucket of July 22, 2018.

IDs of Committed Files May Not Be Consecutive

Nonconsecutive file IDs, the last number in a committed file's name, do not indicate data loss. `StreamingFileSink` simply increments the file IDs. When discarding pending files it does not reuse their IDs.

A `RollingPolicy` determines when a task creates a new part file. You can configure the `RollingPolicy` with the `withRollingPolicy()` method on the builder. By default, `StreamingFileSink` uses a `DefaultRollingPolicy`, which is configured to roll part files when they exceed 128 MB or are older than 60 seconds. You can also configure an inactivity interval after which a part file is rolled.

`StreamingFileSink` supports two modes of writing records to part files: row encoding and bulk encoding. In row encoding mode, every record is individually encoded and appended to a part file. In bulk encoding, records are collected and written in batches. Apache Parquet, which organizes and compresses records in a columnar format, is a file format that requires bulk encoding.

Example 8-4 creates a `StreamingFileSink` with row encoding by providing an `Encoder` that writes single records to a part file. In Example 8-4, we use a `SimpleStringEncoder`, which calls the `toString()` method of the record and writes the `String` representation of the record to the file. `Encoder` is a simple interface with a single method that can be easily implemented.

A bulk-encoding `StreamingFileSink` is created as shown in Example 8-5.

Example 8-5. Creating a StreamingFileSink in bulk-encoding mode

```
val input: DataStream[String] = …
val sink: StreamingFileSink[String] = StreamingFileSink
  .forBulkFormat(
    new Path("/base/path"),
    ParquetAvroWriters.forSpecificRecord(classOf[AvroPojo]))
```

```
    .build()
```

```
input.addSink(sink)
```

A `StreamingFileSink` in bulk-encoding mode requires a `BulkWriter.Factory`. In Example 8-5 we use a Parquet writer for Avro files. Note that the Parquet writer is contained in the `flink-parquet` module, which needs to be added as a dependency. As usual, `BulkWriter.Factory` is an interface that can be implemented for custom file formats, such as Apache Orc.

> A StreamingFileSink in bulk-encoding mode cannot choose a `Roll ingPolicy`. Bulk-encoding formats can only be combined with the `OnCheckpointRollingPolicy`, which rolls in-progress part files on every checkpoint.

`StreamingFileSink` provides exactly-once output guarantees. The sink achieves this by a commit protocol that moves files through different stages, in progress, pending, and finished, and that is based on Flink's checkpointing mechanism. While a sink writes to a file, the file is in the in-progress state. When the `RollingPolicy` decides to roll a file, it is closed and moved into the pending state by renaming it. Pending files are moved into the finished state (again by renaming) when the next checkpoint completes.

Pending Files Might Never Be Committed

In some situations, a pending file is never committed. The `Stream ingFileSink` ensures this does not result in data loss. However, these files are not automatically cleaned up.

Before manually deleting a pending file, you need to check whether it is lingering or about to be committed. Once you find a committed file with the same task index and a higher ID, you can safely remove a pending file.

In the case of a failure, a sink task needs to reset its current in-progress file to its writing offset at the last successful checkpoint. This is done by closing the current in-progress file and discarding the invalid part at the file's end, for example, by using the filesystem's truncate operation.

StreamingFileSink Requires Checkpointing Be Enabled

`StreamingFileSink` will never move files from pending into finished state, if an application does not enable checkpointing.

Apache Cassandra Sink Connector

Apache Cassandra is a popular, scalable, and highly available column store database system. Cassandra models datasets as tables of rows that consist of multiple typed columns. One or more columns have to be defined as (composite) primary keys. Each row can be uniquely identified by its primary key. Among other APIs, Cassandra features the Cassandra Query Language (CQL), a SQL-like language to read and write records and create, modify, and delete database objects, such as keyspaces and tables.

Flink provides a sink connector to write data streams to Cassandra. Cassandra's data model is based on primary keys, and all writes to Cassandra happen with upsert semantics. In combination with exactly-once checkpointing, resettable sources, and deterministic application logic, upsert writes yield eventually exactly-once output consistency. The output is only eventually consistent, because results are reset to a previous version during recovery, meaning consumers might read older results than read previously. Also, the versions of values for multiple keys might be out of sync.

In order to prevent temporal inconsistencies during recovery and provide exactly-once output guarantees for applications with nondeterministic application logic, Flink's Cassandra connector can be configured to leverage a WAL. We will discuss the WAL mode in more detail later in this section. The following code shows the dependency you need to add to the build file of your application in order to use the Cassandra sink connector:

```
<dependency>
  <groupId>org.apache.flink</groupId>
  <artifactId>flink-connector-cassandra_2.12</artifactId>
  <version>1.7.1</version>
</dependency>
```

To illustrate the use of the Cassandra sink connector, we use the simple example of a Cassandra table that holds data about sensor readings and consists of two columns, sensorId and temperature. The CQL statements in Example 8-6 create a keyspace "example" and a table "sensors" in that keyspace.

Example 8-6. Defining a Cassandra example table

```
CREATE KEYSPACE IF NOT EXISTS example
  WITH replication = {'class': 'SimpleStrategy', 'replication_factor': '1'};

CREATE TABLE IF NOT EXISTS example.sensors (
  sensorId VARCHAR,
  temperature FLOAT,
  PRIMARY KEY(sensorId)
);
```

Flink provides different sink implementations to write data streams of different data types to Cassandra. Flink's Java tuples and Row type and Scala's built-in tuples and case classes are handled differently than user-defined POJO types. We discuss both cases separately. Example 8-7 shows how to create a sink that writes a DataStream of tuples, case classes, or rows into a Cassandra table. In this example, a DataStream[(String, Float)] is written into the "sensors" table.

Example 8-7. Creating a Cassandra sink for tuples

```
val readings: DataStream[(String, Float)] = ???

val sinkBuilder: CassandraSinkBuilder[(String, Float)] =
  CassandraSink.addSink(readings)
sinkBuilder
  .setHost("localhost")
  .setQuery(
    "INSERT INTO example.sensors(sensorId, temperature) VALUES (?, ?);")
  .build()
```

Cassandra sinks are created and configured using a builder that is obtained by calling the CassandraSink.addSink() method with the DataStream object that should be emitted. The method returns the right builder for the data type of the DataStream. In Example 8-7, it returns a builder for a Cassandra sink that handles Scala tuples.

The Cassandra sink builders for tuples, case classes, and rows require the specification of a CQL INSERT query.[5] The query is configured using the CassandraSink Builder.setQuery() method. During execution, the sink registers the query as a prepared statement and converts the fields of tuples, case classes, or rows into parameters for the prepared statement. The fields are mapped to the parameters based on their position; the first value is converted to the first parameter and so on.

Since POJO fields do not have a natural order, they need to be treated differently. Example 8-8 shows how to configure a Cassandra sink for a POJO of type SensorReading.

Example 8-8. Create a Cassandra sink for POJOs

```
val readings: DataStream[SensorReading] = ???

CassandraSink.addSink(readings)
  .setHost("localhost")
  .build()
```

---

5 In contrast to SQL INSERT statements, CQL INSERT statements behave like upsert queries—they override existing rows with the same primary key.

As you can see in Example 8-8, we do not specify an INSERT query. Instead, POJOs are handed to Cassandra's Object Mapper, which automatically maps POJO fields to fields of a Cassandra table. In order for this to work, the POJO class and its fields need to be annotated with Cassandra annotations and provide setters and getters for all fields as shown in Example 8-9. The default constructor is required by Flink as mentioned in "Supported Data Types" on page 98 when discussing supported data types.

Example 8-9. POJO class with Cassandra Object Mapper annotations

```
@Table(keyspace = "example", name = "sensors")
class SensorReadings(
  @Column(name = "sensorId") var id: String,
  @Column(name = "temperature") var temp: Float) {

  def this() = {
      this("", 0.0)
 }

  def setId(id: String): Unit = this.id = id
  def getId: String = id
  def setTemp(temp: Float): Unit = this.temp = temp
  def getTemp: Float = temp
}
```

In addition to the configuration options in Figures 8-7 and 8-8, a Cassandra sink builder provides a few more methods to configure the sink connector:

- setClusterBuilder(ClusterBuilder): The ClusterBuilder builds a Cassandra Cluster that manages the connection to Cassandra. Among other options, it can configure the hostnames and ports of one or more contact points; define load balancing, retry, and reconnection policies; and provide access credentials.

- setHost(String, [Int]): This method is a shortcut for a simple Cluster Builder configured with the hostname and port of a single contact point. If no port is configured, Cassandra's default port 9042 is used.

- setQuery(String): This specifies the CQL INSERT query to write tuples, case classes, or rows to Cassandra. A query must not be configured to emit POJOs.

- setMapperOptions(MapperOptions): This provides options for Cassandra's Object Mapper, such as configurations for consistency, time-to-live (TTL), and null field handling. The options are ignored if the sink emits tuples, case classes, or rows.

- enableWriteAheadLog([CheckpointCommitter]): This enables the WAL to provide exactly-once output guarantees in the case of nondeterministic application logic. CheckpointCommitter is used to store information about completed checkpoints in an external datastore. If no `CheckpointCommitter` is configured, the information is written into a specific Cassandra table.

The Cassandra sink connector with WAL is implemented based on Flink's `GenericWriteAheadSink` operator. How this operator works, including the role of the `CheckpointCommitter`, and which consistency guarantees it provides, is described in more detail in "Transactional Sink Connectors" on page 209.

Implementing a Custom Source Function

The DataStream API provides two interfaces to implement source connectors along with corresponding `RichFunction` abstract classes:

- `SourceFunction` and `RichSourceFunction` can be used to define nonparallel source connectors—sources that run with a single task.
- `ParallelSourceFunction` and `RichParallelSourceFunction` can be used to define source connectors that run with multiple parallel task instances.

With the exception of being nonparallel and parallel, both interfaces are identical. Just like the rich variants of processing functions,[6] subclasses of `RichSourceFunction` and `RichParallelSourceFunction` can override the `open()` and `close()` methods and access a `RuntimeContext` that provides the number of parallel task instances and the index of the current instance, among other things.

`SourceFunction` and `ParallelSourceFunction` define two methods:

- `void run(SourceContext<T> ctx)`
- `void cancel()`

The `run()` method is doing the actual work of reading or receiving records and ingesting them into a Flink application. Depending on the system from which the data is received, the data might be pushed or pulled. The `run()` method is called once by Flink and runs in a dedicated source thread, typically reading or receiving data and emitting records in an endless loop (infinite stream). The task can be explicitly canceled at some point in time or terminated in the case of a finite stream when the input is fully consumed.

The `cancel()` method is invoked by Flink when the application is canceled and shut down. In order to perform a graceful shutdown, the `run()` method, which runs in a separate thread, should terminate as soon as the `cancel()` method is called. Example 8-10 shows a simple source function that counts from 0 to `Long.MaxValue`.

---

6 Rich functions were discussed in Chapter 5.

Example 8-10. SourceFunction that counts to Long.MaxValue

```
class CountSource extends SourceFunction[Long] {
  var isRunning: Boolean = true

  override def run(ctx: SourceFunction.SourceContext[Long]) = {

    var cnt: Long = -1
    while (isRunning && cnt < Long.MaxValue) {
      cnt += 1
      ctx.collect(cnt)
    }
  }

  override def cancel() = isRunning = false
}
```

Resettable Source Functions

Earlier in this chapter we explained that Flink can only provide satisfying consistency guarantees for applications that use source connectors that can replay their output data. A source function can replay its output if the external system that provides the data exposes an API to retrieve and reset a reading offset. Examples of such systems are filesystems that provide the offset of a file stream and a seek method to move a file stream to a specific position or Apache Kafka, which provides offsets for each partition of a topic and can set the reading position of a partition. A counterexample is a source connector that reads data from a network socket, which immediately discards delivered the data.

A source function that supports output replay needs to be integrated with Flink's checkpointing mechanism and must persist all current reading positions when a checkpoint is taken. When the application is started from a savepoint or recovers from a failure, the reading offsets are retrieved from the latest checkpoint or savepoint. If the application is started without existing state, the reading offsets must be set to a default value. A resettable source function needs to implement the Checkpoin tedFunction interface and should store the reading offsets and all related meta information, such as file paths or partition ID, in operator list state or operator union list state depending on how the offsets should be distributed to parallel task instances in the case of a rescaled application. See "Scaling Stateful Operators" on page 56 for details on the distribution behavior of operator list state and union list state.

In addition, it is important to ensure that the SourceFunction.run() method, which runs in a separate thread, does not advance the reading offset and emit data while a checkpoint is taken; in other words, while the CheckpointedFunction.snapshot State() method is called. This is done by guarding the code in run() that advances the reading position and emits records in a block that synchronizes on a lock object, which is obtained from the SourceContext.getCheckpointLock() method. Example 8-11 makes the CountSource of Example 8-10 resettable.

Example 8-11. A resettable SourceFunction

```scala
class ResettableCountSource
    extends SourceFunction[Long] with CheckpointedFunction {

  var isRunning: Boolean = true
  var cnt: Long = _
  var offsetState: ListState[Long] = _

  override def run(ctx: SourceFunction.SourceContext[Long]) = {
    while (isRunning && cnt < Long.MaxValue) {
      // synchronize data emission and checkpoints
      ctx.getCheckpointLock.synchronized {
        cnt += 1
        ctx.collect(cnt)
      }
    }
  }

  override def cancel() = isRunning = false

  override def snapshotState(snapshotCtx: FunctionSnapshotContext): Unit = {
    // remove previous cnt
    offsetState.clear()
    // add current cnt
    offsetState.add(cnt)
  }

  override def initializeState(
      initCtx: FunctionInitializationContext): Unit = {

    val desc = new ListStateDescriptor[Long]("offset", classOf[Long])
    offsetState = initCtx.getOperatorStateStore.getListState(desc)
    // initialize cnt variable
    val it = offsetState.get()
    cnt = if (null == it || !it.iterator().hasNext) {
      -1L
    } else {
      it.iterator().next()
    }
  }
}
```

Source Functions, Timestamps, and Watermarks

Another important aspect of source functions are timestamps and watermarks. As pointed out in "Event-Time Processing" and "Assigning Timestamps and Generating

Watermarks", the DataStream API provides two options to assign timestamps and generate watermarks. Timestamps and watermarks can be assigned and generate by a dedicated `TimestampAssigner` (see "Assigning Timestamps and Generating Watermarks" for details) or be assigned and generated by a source function.

A source function assigns timestamps and emits watermarks through its `SourceContext` object. `SourceContext` provides the following methods:

- `def collectWithTimestamp(T record, long timestamp): Unit`
- `def emitWatermark(Watermark watermark): Unit`

`collectWithTimestamp()` emits a record with its associated timestamp and `emitWatermark()` emits the provided watermark.

Besides removing the need for an additional operator, assigning timestamps and generating watermarks in a source function can be beneficial if one parallel instance of a source function consumes records from multiple stream partitions, such as partitions of a Kafka topic. Typically, external systems, such as Kafka, only guarantee message order within a stream partition. Given the case of a source function operator that runs with a parallelism of two and that reads data from a Kafka topic with six partitions, each parallel instance of the source function will read records from three Kafka topic partitions. Consequently, each instance of the source function multiplexes the records of three stream partitions to emit them. Multiplexing records most likely introduces additional out-of-orderness with respect to the event-time timestamps such that a downstream timestamp assigner might produce more late records than expected.

To avoid such behavior, a source function can generate watermarks for each stream partition independently and always emit the smallest watermark of its partitions as its watermark. This way, it can ensure that the order guarantees on each partition are leveraged and no unnecessary late records are emitted.

Another problem source functions have to deal with are instances that become idle and do not emit anymore data. This can be very problematic, because it may prevent the whole application from advancing its watermarks and hence lead to a stalling application. Since watermarks should be data driven, a watermark generator (either integrated in a source function or in a timestamp assigner) will not emit new watermarks if it does not receive input records. If you look at how Flink propagates and updates watermarks (see "Watermark Propagation and Event Time"), you can see that a single operator that does not advance watermarks can grind all watermarks of an application to a halt if the application involves a shuffle operation (`keyBy()`, `rebalance()`, etc.).

Flink provides a mechanism to avoid such situations by marking source functions as temporarily idle. While being idle, Flink's watermark propagation mechanism will ignore the idle stream partition. The source is automatically set as active as soon as it starts to emit records again. A source function can decide when to mark itself as idle and does so by calling the method SourceContext.markAsTemporarilyIdle().

Implementing a Custom Sink Function

In Flink's DataStream API, any operator or function can send data to an external system or application. A DataStream does not have to eventually flow into a sink operator. For instance, you could implement a FlatMapFunction that emits each incoming record via an HTTP POST call and not via its Collector. Nonetheless, the DataStream API provides a dedicated SinkFunction interface and a corresponding RichSinkFunction abstract class.[7] The SinkFunction interface provides a single method:

```
void invoke(IN value, Context ctx)
```

The Context object of SinkFunction provides access to the current processing time, the current watermark (i.e., the current event time at the sink), and the timestamp of the record.

Example 8-12 shows a simple SinkFunction that writes sensor readings to a socket. Note that you need to start a process that listens on the socket before starting the program. Otherwise, the program fails with a ConnectException because a connection to the socket could not be opened. Run the command nc -l localhost 9191 on Linux to listen on localhost:9191.

Example 8-12. A simple SinkFunction that writes to a socket

```
val readings: DataStream[SensorReading] = ???

// write the sensor readings to a socket
readings.addSink(new SimpleSocketSink("localhost", 9191))
  // set parallelism to 1 because only one thread can write to a socket
  .setParallelism(1)

// -----

class SimpleSocketSink(val host: String, val port: Int)
    extends RichSinkFunction[SensorReading] {

  var socket: Socket = _
  var writer: PrintStream = _
```

---

7 Usually the RichSinkFunction interface is used because sink functions typically need to set up a connection to an external system in the RichFunction.open() method. See Chapter 5 for details on the RichFunction interface.

```scala
  override def open(config: Configuration): Unit = {
    // open socket and writer
    socket = new Socket(InetAddress.getByName(host), port)
    writer = new PrintStream(socket.getOutputStream)
  }

  override def invoke(
      value: SensorReading,
      ctx: SinkFunction.Context[_]): Unit = {
    // write sensor reading to socket
    writer.println(value.toString)
    writer.flush()
  }

  override def close(): Unit = {
    // close writer and socket
    writer.close()
    socket.close()
  }
}
```

As discussed, the end-to-end consistency guarantees of an application depend on the properties of its sink connectors. In order to achieve end-to-end exactly-once semantics, an application requires either idempotent or transactional sink connectors. The SinkFunction in Example 8-12 neither performs idempotent writes nor features transactional writes. Due to the append-only characteristic of a socket, it is not possible to perform idempotent writes. Since a socket does not have built-in transactional support, transactional writes can only be done using Flink's generic WAL sink. In the following sections, you will learn how to implement idempotent or transactional sink connectors.

Idempotent Sink Connectors

For many applications, the SinkFunction interface is sufficient to implement an idempotent sink connector. This is possible if the following two properties hold:

1. The result data has a deterministic (composite) key, on which idempotent updates can be performed. For an application that computes the average temperature per sensor and minute, a deterministic key could be the ID of the sensor and the timestamp for each minute. Deterministic keys are important to ensure all writes are correctly overwritten in case of a recovery.

2. The external system supports updates per key, such as a relational database system or a key-value store.

Example 8-13 illustrates how to implement and use an idempotent SinkFunction that writes to a JDBC database, in this case an embedded Apache Derby database.

Example 8-13. An idempotent SinkFunction that writes to a JDBC database

```scala
val readings: DataStream[SensorReading] = ???

// write the sensor readings to a Derby table
readings.addSink(new DerbyUpsertSink)

// -----

class DerbyUpsertSink extends RichSinkFunction[SensorReading] {
  var conn: Connection = _
  var insertStmt: PreparedStatement = _
  var updateStmt: PreparedStatement = _

  override def open(parameters: Configuration): Unit = {
    // connect to embedded in-memory Derby
    conn = DriverManager.getConnection(
      "jdbc:derby:memory:flinkExample",
      new Properties())
    // prepare insert and update statements
    insertStmt = conn.prepareStatement(
      "INSERT INTO Temperatures (sensor, temp) VALUES (?, ?)")
    updateStmt = conn.prepareStatement(
      "UPDATE Temperatures SET temp = ? WHERE sensor = ?")
  }

  override def invoke(r: SensorReading, context: Context[_]): Unit = {
    // set parameters for update statement and execute it
    updateStmt.setDouble(1, r.temperature)
    updateStmt.setString(2, r.id)
    updateStmt.execute()
    // execute insert statement if update statement did not update any row
    if (updateStmt.getUpdateCount == 0) {
      // set parameters for insert statement
      insertStmt.setString(1, r.id)
      insertStmt.setDouble(2, r.temperature)
      // execute insert statement
      insertStmt.execute()
    }
  }

  override def close(): Unit = {
    insertStmt.close()
    updateStmt.close()
    conn.close()
  }
}
```

Since Apache Derby does not provide a built-in UPSERT statement, the example sink performs UPSERT writes by first trying to update a row and inserting a new row if no row with the given key exists. The Cassandra sink connector follows the same approach when the WAL is not enabled.

Transactional Sink Connectors

Whenever an idempotent sink connector is not suitable, either the characteristics of the application's output, the properties of the required sink system, or due to stricter consistency requirements, transactional sink connectors can be an alternative. As described before, transactional sink connectors need to be integrated with Flink's checkpointing mechanism because they may only commit data to the external system when a checkpoint completes successfully.

In order to ease the implementation of transactional sinks, Flink's DataStream API provides two templates that can be extended to implement custom sink operators. Both templates implement the CheckpointListener interface to receive notifications from the JobManager about completed checkpoints (see "Receiving Notifications About Completed Checkpoints" for details about the interface):

- The GenericWriteAheadSink template collects all outgoing records per checkpoint and stores them in the operator state of the sink task. The state is checkpointed and recovered in the case of a failure. When a task receives a checkpoint completion notification, it writes the records of the completed checkpoints to the external system. The Cassandra sink connector with WAL-enabled implements this interface.

- The TwoPhaseCommitSinkFunction template leverages transactional features of the external sink system. For every checkpoint, it starts a new transaction and writes all following records to the sink system in the context of the current transaction. The sink commits a transaction when it receives the completion notification of the corresponding checkpoint.

In the following, we describe both interfaces and their consistency guarantees.

GenericWriteAheadSink

GenericWriteAheadSink eases the implementation of sink operators with improved consistency properties. The operator is integrated with Flink's checkpointing mechanism and aims to write each record exactly once to an external system. However, you should be aware that failure scenarios exist in which a write-ahead log sink emits records more than once. Hence, a GenericWriteAheadSink does not provide bullet-proof exactly-once guarantees but only at-least-once guarantees. We will discuss these scenarios in more detail later in this section.

GenericWriteAheadSink works by appending all received records to a write-ahead log that is segmented by checkpoints. Every time the sink operator receives a checkpoint barrier, it starts a new section and all the following records are appended to the new section. The WAL is stored and checkpointed as operator state. Since the log will be recovered, no records will be lost in the case of a failure.

When GenericWriteAheadSink receives a notification about a completed checkpoint, it emits all records that are stored in the WAL in the segment corresponding to the successful checkpoint. Depending on the concrete implementation of the sink operator, the records can be written to any kind of storage or message system. When all records have been successfully emitted, the corresponding checkpoint must be internally committed.

A checkpoint is committed in two steps. First, the sink persistently stores the information that the checkpoint was committed and secondly it removes the records from the WAL. It is not possible to store the commit information in Flink's application state because it is not persistent and would be reset in case of a failure. Instead, GenericWriteAheadSink relies on a pluggable component called CheckpointCommit ter to store and look up information about committed checkpoints in an external persistent storage. For example, the Cassandra sink connector by default uses a Check pointCommitter that writes to Cassandra.

Thanks to the built-in logic of GenericWriteAheadSink, it is not difficult to implement a sink that leverages a WAL. Operators that extend GenericWriteAheadSink need to provide three constructor parameters:

- A CheckpointCommitter as discussed before
- A TypeSerializer to serialize the input records
- A job ID that is passed to the CheckpointCommitter to identify commit information across application restarts

Moreover, the write-ahead operator needs to implement a single method:

```
boolean sendValues(Iterable<IN> values, long chkpntId, long timestamp)
```

GenericWriteAheadSink calls the sendValues() method to write the records of a completed checkpoint to the external storage system. The method receives an Iterable over all records of a checkpoint, the ID of the checkpoint, and the timestamp of when the checkpoint was taken. The method must return true if all writes succeeded and false if a write failed.

Example 8-14 shows the implementation of a write-ahead sink that writes to the standard output. It uses FileCheckpointCommitter, which we do not discuss here. You can look up its implementation in the repository that contains the examples of the book.

Note that GenericWriteAheadSink does not implement the Sink Function interface. So, sinks that extend GenericWriteAheadSink cannot be added using DataStream.addSink() but are attached using the DataStream.transform() method.

Example 8-14. A WAL sink that writes to the standard output

```
val readings: DataStream[SensorReading] = ???

// write the sensor readings to the standard out via a write-ahead log
readings.transform(
  "WriteAheadSink", new SocketWriteAheadSink)

// -----

class StdOutWriteAheadSink extends GenericWriteAheadSink[SensorReading](
    // CheckpointCommitter that commits checkpoints to the local filesystem
    new FileCheckpointCommitter(System.getProperty("java.io.tmpdir")),
    // Serializer for records
    createTypeInformation[SensorReading]
      .createSerializer(new ExecutionConfig),
    // Random JobID used by the CheckpointCommitter
    UUID.randomUUID.toString) {

  override def sendValues(
      readings: Iterable[SensorReading],
      checkpointId: Long,
      timestamp: Long): Boolean = {

    for (r <- readings.asScala) {
      // write record to standard out
      println(r)
    }
    true
  }
}
```

The examples repository contains an application that fails and recovers in regular intervals to demonstrate the behavior of StdOutWriteAheadSink and a regular Data Stream.print() sink in case of failures.

As mentioned earlier, GenericWriteAheadSink cannot provide bulletproof exactly-once guarantees. There are two failure cases that can result in records being emitted more than once:

1. The program fails while a task is running the sendValues() method. If the external sink system cannot atomically write multiple records—either all or none—some records might have been written and others not. Since the checkpoint was not committed yet, the sink will write all records again during recovery.

2. All records are correctly written and the `sendValues()` method returns true; however, the program fails before `CheckpointCommitter` is called or `Checkpoint Committer` fails to commit the checkpoint. During recovery, all records of not-yet-committed checkpoints will be written again.

 Note that these failure scenarios do not affect the exactly-once guarantees of the Cassandra sink connector because it performs UPSERT writes. The Cassandra sink connector benefits from the WAL because it guards from nondeterministic keys and prevents inconsistent writes to Cassandra.

TwoPhaseCommitSinkFunction

Flink provides the `TwoPhaseCommitSinkFunction` interface to ease the implementation of sink functions that provide end-to-end exactly-once guarantees. However, whether a 2PC sink function provides such guarantees or not depends on the implementation details. We start the discussion of this interface with a question: "Isn't the 2PC protocol too expensive?"

In general, 2PCs are an expensive approach to ensuring consistency in a distributed system. However, in the context of Flink, the protocol is only run once for every checkpoint. Moreover, the protocol of `TwoPhaseCommitSinkFunction` piggybacks on Flink's regular checkpointing mechanism and thus adds little overhead. The `TwoPhase CommitSinkFunction` works quite similar to the WAL sink, but it does not collect records in Flink's application state; rather, it writes them in an open transaction to an external sink system.

The `TwoPhaseCommitSinkFunction` implements the following protocol. Before a sink task emits its first record, it starts a transaction on the external sink system. All subsequently received records are written in the context of the transaction. The voting phase of the 2PC protocol starts when the JobManager initiates a checkpoint and injects barriers in the sources of the application. When an operator receives the barrier, it checkpoints it state and sends an acknowledgment message to the JobManager once it is done. When a sink task receives the barrier, it persists its state, prepares the current transaction for committing, and acknowledges the checkpoint at the JobManager. The acknowledgment messages to the JobManager are analogous to the commit vote of the textbook 2PC protocol. The sink task must not yet commit the transaction, because it is not guaranteed that all tasks of the job will complete their checkpoints. The sink task also starts a new transaction for all records that arrive before the next checkpoint barrier.

When the JobManager receives successful checkpoint notifications from all task instances, it sends the checkpoint completion notification to all interested tasks. This

---

notification corresponds to the 2PC protocol's commit command. When a sink task receives the notification, it commits all open transactions of previous checkpoints.[8] Once a sink task acknowledges its checkpoint, it must be able to commit the corresponding transaction, even in the case of a failure. If the transaction cannot be committed, the sink loses data. An iteration of the 2PC protocol succeeds when all sink tasks committed their transactions.

Let's summarize the requirements for the external sink system:

- The external sink system must provide transactional support or the sink must be able to emulate transactions on the external system. Hence, the sink should be able to write to the sink system, but the written data must not be made visible to the outside before it is committed.

- A transaction must be open and accept writes for the duration of a checkpoint interval.

- A transaction must wait to be committed until a checkpoint completion notification is received. In the case of a recovery cycle, this may take some time. If the sink system closes a transaction (e.g., with a timeout), the not committed data will be lost.

- The sink must be able to recover a transaction after a process failed. Some sink systems provide a transaction ID that can be used to commit or abort an open transaction.

- Committing a transaction must be an idempotent operation—the sink or external system should be able to notice that a transaction was already committed or a repeated commit must have no effect.

The protocol and the requirements of the sink system might be easier to understand by looking at a concrete example. Example 8-15 shows a TwoPhaseCommitSinkFunction that writes with exactly-once guarantees to a filesystem. Essentially, this is a simplified version of the BucketingFileSink discussed earlier.

Example 8-15. A transactional sink that writes to files

```
class TransactionalFileSink(val targetPath: String, val tempPath: String)
    extends TwoPhaseCommitSinkFunction[(String, Double), String, Void](
      createTypeInformation[String].createSerializer(new ExecutionConfig),
      createTypeInformation[Void].createSerializer(new ExecutionConfig)) {

  var transactionWriter: BufferedWriter = _
```

---

8 A task might need to commit multiple transactions if an acknowledgment message is lost.

```scala
/** Creates a temporary file for a transaction into which the records are
  * written.
  */
override def beginTransaction(): String = {
  // path of transaction file is built from current time and task index
  val timeNow = LocalDateTime.now(ZoneId.of("UTC"))
    .format(DateTimeFormatter.ISO_LOCAL_DATE_TIME)
  val taskIdx = this.getRuntimeContext.getIndexOfThisSubtask
  val transactionFile = s"$timeNow-$taskIdx"

  // create transaction file and writer
  val tFilePath = Paths.get(s"$tempPath/$transactionFile")
  Files.createFile(tFilePath)
  this.transactionWriter = Files.newBufferedWriter(tFilePath)
  println(s"Creating Transaction File: $tFilePath")
  // name of transaction file is returned to later identify the transaction
  transactionFile
}

/** Write record into the current transaction file. */
override def invoke(
    transaction: String,
    value: (String, Double),
    context: Context[_]): Unit = {
  transactionWriter.write(value.toString)
  transactionWriter.write('\n')
}

/** Flush and close the current transaction file. */
override def preCommit(transaction: String): Unit = {
  transactionWriter.flush()
  transactionWriter.close()
}

/** Commit a transaction by moving the precommitted transaction file
  * to the target directory.
  */
override def commit(transaction: String): Unit = {
  val tFilePath = Paths.get(s"$tempPath/$transaction")
  // check if the file exists to ensure that the commit is idempotent
  if (Files.exists(tFilePath)) {
    val cFilePath = Paths.get(s"$targetPath/$transaction")
    Files.move(tFilePath, cFilePath)
  }
}

/** Aborts a transaction by deleting the transaction file. */
override def abort(transaction: String): Unit = {
  val tFilePath = Paths.get(s"$tempPath/$transaction")
  if (Files.exists(tFilePath)) {
    Files.delete(tFilePath)
  }
```

```
    }
}
```

`TwoPhaseCommitSinkFunction[IN, TXN, CONTEXT]` has three type parameters:

- `IN` specifies the type of the input records. In Example 8-15, this is a `Tuple2` with a `String` and a `Double` field.

- `TXN` defines a transaction identifier that can be used to identify and recover a transaction after a failure. In Example 8-15, this is a string holding the name of the transaction file.

- `CONTEXT` defines an optional custom context. `TransactionalFileSink` in Example 8-15 does not need the context and hence sets the type to `Void`.

The constructor of `TwoPhaseCommitSinkFunction` requires two `TypeSerializer`—one for the `TXN` type and the other for the `CONTEXT` type.

Finally, `TwoPhaseCommitSinkFunction` defines five functions that need to be implemented:

- `beginTransaction(): TXN` starts a new transaction and returns the transaction identifier. `TransactionalFileSink` in Example 8-15 creates a new transaction file and returns its name as the identifier.

- `invoke(txn: TXN, value: IN, context: Context[_]): Unit` writes a value to the current transaction. The sink in Example 8-15 appends the value as a `String` to the transaction file.

- `preCommit(txn: TXN): Unit` precommits a transaction. A precommitted transaction may not receive further writes. Our implementation in Example 8-15 flushes and closes the transaction file.

- `commit(txn: TXN): Unit` commits a transaction. This operation must be idempotent—records must not be written twice to the output system if this method is called twice. In Example 8-15, we check if the transaction file still exists and move it to the target directory if that is the case.

- `abort(txn: TXN): Unit` aborts a transaction. This method may also be called twice for a transaction. Our `TransactionalFileSink` in Example 8-15 checks if the transaction file still exists and deletes it if that is the case.

As you can see, the implementation of the interface is not too involved. However, the complexity and consistency guarantees of an implementation depend on, among other things, the features and capabilities of the sink system. For instance, Flink's Kafka producer implements the `TwoPhaseCommitSinkFunction` interface. As mentioned before, the connector might lose data if a transaction is rolled back due to a timeout.[9] Hence, it does not offer definitive exactly-once guarantees even though it implements the `TwoPhaseCommitSinkFunction` interface.

Asynchronously Accessing External Systems

Besides ingesting or emitting data streams, enriching a data stream by looking up information in a remote database is another common use case that requires interacting with an external storage system. An example is the well-known Yahoo! stream processing benchmark, which is based on a stream of advertisement clicks that need to be enriched with details about their corresponding campaign that are stored in a key-value store.

The straightforward approach for such use cases is to implement a `MapFunction` that queries the datastore for every processed record, waits for the query to return a result, enriches the record, and emits the result. While this approach is easy to implement, it suffers from a major issue: each request to the external datastore adds significant latency (a request/response involves two network messages) and the `MapFunction` spends most of its time waiting for query results.

Apache Flink provides the `AsyncFunction` to mitigate the latency of remote I/O calls. `AsyncFunction` concurrently sends multiple queries and processes their results asynchronously. It can be configured to preserve the order of records (requests might return in a different order than the order in which they were sent out) or return the results in the order of the query results to further reduce the latency. The function is also properly integrated with Flink's checkpointing mechanism—input records that are currently waiting for a response are checkpointed and queries are repeated in the case of a recovery. Moreover, `AsyncFunction` properly works with event-time processing because it ensures watermarks are not overtaken by records even if out-of-order results are enabled.

In order to take advantage of `AsyncFunction`, the external system should provide a client that supports asynchronous calls, which is the case for many systems. If a system only provides a synchronous client, you can spawn threads to send requests and handle them. The interface of `AsyncFunction` is shown in the following:

```
trait AsyncFunction[IN, OUT] extends Function {
  def asyncInvoke(input: IN, resultFuture: ResultFuture[OUT]): Unit
}
```

The type parameters of the function define its input and output types. The `asyncInvoke()` method is called for each input record with two parameters. The first parameter is the input record and the second parameter is a callback object to return

---

9 See details in "Apache Kafka Sink Connector".

the result of the function or an exception. In Example 8-16, we show how to apply
`AsyncFunction` on a `DataStream`.

Example 8-16. Applying AsyncFunction on a DataStream

```
val readings: DataStream[SensorReading] = ???

val sensorLocations: DataStream[(String, String)] = AsyncDataStream
  .orderedWait(
    readings,
    new DerbyAsyncFunction,
    5, TimeUnit.SECONDS,    // timeout requests after 5 seconds
    100)                    // at most 100 concurrent requests
```

The asynchronous operator that applies an `AsyncFunction` is configured with the
`AsyncDataStream` object,[10] which provides two static methods: `orderedWait()` and
`unorderedWait()`. Both methods are overloaded for different combinations of
parameters. `orderedWait()` applies an asynchronous operator that emits results in
the order of the input records, while the operator of `unorderWait()` only ensures
watermarks and checkpoint barriers remain aligned. Additional parameters specify
when to time out the asynchronous call for a record and how many concurrent
requests to start. Example 8-17 shows `DerbyAsyncFunction`, which queries an
embedded Derby database via its JDBC interface.

Example 8-17. AsyncFunction that queries a JDBC database

```
class DerbyAsyncFunction
    extends AsyncFunction[SensorReading, (String, String)] {

  // caching execution context used to handle the query threads
  private lazy val cachingPoolExecCtx =
    ExecutionContext.fromExecutor(Executors.newCachedThreadPool())
  // direct execution context to forward result future to callback object
  private lazy val directExecCtx =
    ExecutionContext.fromExecutor(
      org.apache.flink.runtime.concurrent.Executors.directExecutor())

  /**
    * Executes JDBC query in a thread and handles the resulting Future
    * with an asynchronous callback.
    */
  override def asyncInvoke(
      reading: SensorReading,
      resultFuture: ResultFuture[(String, String)]): Unit = {
```

---

10 The Java API provides an `AsyncDataStream` class with the respective static methods.

```scala
      val sensor = reading.id
      // get room from Derby table as Future
      val room: Future[String] = Future {
        // Creating a new connection and statement for each record.
        // Note: This is NOT best practice!
        // Connections and prepared statements should be cached.
        val conn = DriverManager
          .getConnection(
            "jdbc:derby:memory:flinkExample",
            new Properties())
        val query = conn.createStatement()

        // submit query and wait for result; this is a synchronous call
        val result = query.executeQuery(
          s"SELECT room FROM SensorLocations WHERE sensor = '$sensor'")

        // get room if there is one
        val room = if (result.next()) {
          result.getString(1)
        } else {
          "UNKNOWN ROOM"
        }

        // close resultset, statement, and connection
        result.close()
        query.close()
        conn.close()
        // return room
        room
      }(cachingPoolExecCtx)

      // apply result handling callback on the room future
      room.onComplete {
        case Success(r) => resultFuture.complete(Seq((sensor, r)))
        case Failure(e) => resultFuture.completeExceptionally(e)
      }(directExecCtx)
    }
}
```

The `asyncInvoke()` method of `DerbyAsyncFunction` in Example 8-17 wraps the blocking JDBC query in a `Future`, which is executed via `CachedThreadPool`. To keep the example concise, we create a new JDBC connection for each record, which is, of course, quite inefficient and should be avoided. `Future[String]` holds the result of the JDBC query.

Finally, we apply an `onComplete()` callback on `Future` and pass the result (or a possible exception) to the `ResultFuture` handler. In contrast to the JDBC query `Future`, the `onComplete()` callback is processed by `DirectExecutor` because passing the result to `ResultFuture` is a lightweight operation that does not require a dedicated thread. Note that all operations are done in a nonblocking fashion.

It is important to point out that an `AsyncFunction` instance is sequentially called for each of its input records—a function instance is not called in a multithreaded fashion. Therefore, the `asyncInvoke()` method should quickly return by starting an asynchronous request and handling the result with a callback that forwards the result to `ResultFuture`. Common antipatterns that must be avoided include:

- Sending a request that blocks the `asyncInvoke()` method
- Sending an asynchronous request but waiting inside the `asyncInvoke()` method for the request to complete

Summary

In this chapter you learned how Flink DataStream applications can read data from and write data to external systems and the requirements for an application to achieve different end-to-end consistency guarantees. We presented Flink's most commonly used built-in source and sink connectors, which also serve as representatives for different types of storage systems, such as message queues, filesystems, and key-value stores.

Subsequently, we showed you how to implement custom source and sink connectors, including WAL and 2PC sink connectors, providing detailed examples. Finally, you learned about Flink's `AsyncFunction`, which can significantly improve the performance of interacting with external systems by performing and handling requests asynchronously.

## CHAPTER 9

Setting Up Flink for Streaming Applications

Today's data infrastructures are diverse. Distributed data processing frameworks like Apache Flink need to be set up to interact with several components such as resource managers, filesystems, and services for distributed coordination.

In this chapter, we discuss the different ways to deploy Flink clusters and how to configure them securely and make them highly available. We explain Flink setups for different Hadoop versions and filesystems and discuss the most important configuration parameters of Flink's master and worker processes. After reading this chapter, you will know how to set up and configure a Flink cluster.

Deployment Modes

Flink can be deployed in different environments, such as a local machine, a bare-metal cluster, a Hadoop YARN cluster, or a Kubernetes cluster. In "Components of a Flink Setup", we introduced the different components of a Flink setup: the JobManager, TaskManager, ResourceManager, and Dispatcher. In this section, we explain how to configure and start Flink in different environments—including standalone clusters, Docker, Apache Hadoop YARN, and Kubernetes—and how Flink's components are assembled in each setup.

Standalone Cluster

A standalone Flink cluster consists of at least one master process and at least one TaskManager process that run on one or more machines. All processes run as regular Java JVM processes. Figure 9-1 shows a standalone Flink setup.

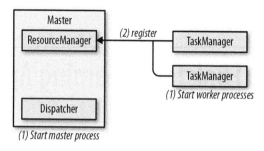

Figure 9-1. Starting a standalone Flink cluster

The master process runs a Dispatcher and a ResourceManager in separate threads. Once they start running, the TaskManagers register themselves at the ResourceManager. Figure 9-2 shows how a job is submitted to a standalone cluster.

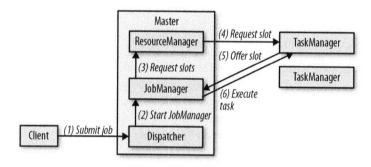

Figure 9-2. Submitting an application to a Flink standalone cluster

A client submits a job to the Dispatcher, which internally starts a JobManager thread and provides the JobGraph for execution. The JobManager requests the necessary processing slots from the ResourceManager and deploys the job for execution once the requested slots have been received.

In a standalone deployment, the master and workers are not automatically restarted in the case of a failure. A job can recover from a worker failure if a sufficient number of processing slots is available. This can be ensured by running one or more standby workers. Job recovery from a master failure requires a highly available setup as discussed later in this chapter.

In order to set up a standalone Flink cluster, download a binary distribution from the Apache Flink website and extract the tar archive with the command:

```
tar xfz ./flink-1.7.1-bin-scala_2.12.tgz
```

The extracted directory includes a *./bin* folder with bash scripts[1] to start and stop Flink processes. The *./bin/start-cluster.sh* script starts a master process on the local machine and one or more TaskManagers on the local or remote machines.

Flink is preconfigured to run a local setup and start a single master and a single Task-Manager on the local machine. The start scripts must be able to start a Java process. If the java binary is not on the PATH, the base folder of a Java installation can be specified by exporting the JAVA_HOME environment variable or setting the env.java.home parameter in *./conf/flink-conf.yaml*. A local Flink cluster is started by calling ./bin/start-cluster.sh. You can visit Flink's Web UI at *http://localhost:8081* and check the number of connected TaskManagers and available slots.

In order to start a distributed Flink cluster that runs on multiple machines, you need to adjust the default configuration and complete a few more steps.

- The hostnames (or IP addresses) of all machines that should run TaskManagers need to be listed in the *./conf/slaves* file.

- The *start-cluster.sh* script requires a passwordless SSH configuration on all machines to be able to start the TaskManager processes.

- The Flink distribution folder must be located on all machines at the same path. A common approach is to mount a network-shared directory with the Flink distribution on each machine.

- The hostname (or IP address) of the machine that runs the master process needs to be configured in the *./conf/flink-conf.yaml* file with the config key jobman ager.rpc.address.

Once everything has been set up, you can start the Flink cluster by calling ./bin/start-cluster.sh. The script will start a local JobManager and start one TaskManager for each entry in the *slaves* file. You can check if the master process was started and all TaskManager were successfully registered by accessing the Web UI on the machine that runs the master process. A local or distributed standalone cluster is stopped by calling ./bin/stop-cluster.sh.

Docker

Docker is a popular platform used to package and run applications in containers. Docker containers are run by the operating system kernel of the host system and are therefore more lightweight than virtual machines. Moreover, they are isolated and

---

1 In order to run Flink on Windows, you can use a provided bat script or you can use the regular bash scripts on the Windows Subsystem for Linux (WSL) or Cygwin. All scripts only work for local setups.

communicate only through well-defined channels. A container is started from an image that defines the software in the container.

Members of the Flink community configure and build Docker images for Apache Flink and upload them to Docker Hub, a public repository for Docker images.[2] The repository hosts Docker images for the most recent Flink versions.

Running Flink in Docker is an easy way to set up a Flink cluster on your local machine. For a local Docker setup you have to start two types of containers, a master container that runs the Dispatcher and ResourceManager, and one or more worker containers that run the TaskManagers. The containers work together like a stand-alone deployment (see "Standalone Cluster"). After starting, a TaskManager registers itself at the ResourceManager. When a job is submitted to the Dispatcher, it spawns a JobManager thread, which requests processing slots from the ResourceManager. The ResourceManager assigns TaskManagers to the JobManager, which deploys the job once all required resources are available.

Master and worker containers are started from the same Docker image with different parameters as shown in Example 9-1.

Example 9-1. Starting a master and a worker container in Docker

```
// start master process
docker run -d --name flink-jobmanager \
  -e JOB_MANAGER_RPC_ADDRESS=jobmanager \
  -p 8081:8081 flink:1.7 jobmanager

// start worker process (adjust the name to start more than one TM)
docker run -d --name flink-taskmanager-1 \
  --link flink-jobmanager:jobmanager \
  -e JOB_MANAGER_RPC_ADDRESS=jobmanager flink:1.7 taskmanager
```

Docker will download the requested image and its dependencies from Docker Hub and start the containers running Flink. The Docker internal hostname of the Job-Manager is passed to the containers via the `JOB_MANAGER_RPC_ADDRESS` variable, which is used in the entry point of the container to adjust Flink's configuration.

The `-p 8081:8081` parameter of the first command maps port 8081 of the master container to port 8081 of the host machine to make the Web UI accessible from the host. You can access the Web UI by opening *http://localhost:8081* in your browser. The Web UI can be used to upload application JAR files and run the application. The port also exposes Flink's REST API. Hence, you can also submit applications using

---

2 Flink Docker images are not part of the official Apache Flink release.

Flink's CLI client at *./bin/flink*, manage running applications, or request information about the cluster or running applications.

 Note that it is currently not possible to pass a custom configuration into the Flink Docker images. You need to build your own Docker image if you want to adjust some of the parameters. The build scripts of the available Docker Flink images are a good starting point for customized images.

Instead of manually starting two (or more) containers, you can also create a Docker Compose configuration script, which automatically starts and configures a Flink cluster running in Docker containers and possibly other services such as ZooKeeper and Kafka. We will not go into the details of this mode, but among other things, a Docker Compose configuration needs to specify the network configuration so that Flink processes that run in isolated containers can communicate with each other. We refer you to Apache Flink's documentation for details.

Apache Hadoop YARN

YARN is the resource manager component of Apache Hadoop. It manages compute resources of a cluster environment—CPU and memory of the cluster's machines—and provides them to applications that request resources. YARN grants resources as containers[3] that are distributed in the cluster and in which applications run their processes. Due to its origin in the Hadoop ecosystem, YARN is typically used by data processing frameworks.

Flink can run on YARN in two modes: the job mode and the session mode. In job mode, a Flink cluster is started to run a single job. Once the job terminates, the Flink cluster is stopped and all resources are returned. Figure 9-3 shows how a Flink job is submitted to a YARN cluster.

---

3 Note that the concept of a container in YARN is different from a container in Docker.

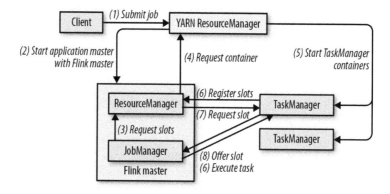

Figure 9-3. Starting a Flink cluster on YARN in job mode

When the client submits a job for execution, it connects to the YARN ResourceMan-ager to start a new YARN application master process that consists of a JobManager thread and a ResourceManager. The JobManager requests the required slots from the ResourceManager to run the Flink job. Subsequently, Flink's ResourceManager requests containers from YARN's ResourceManager and starts TaskManager pro-cesses. Once started, the TaskManagers register their slots at Flink's ResourceMan-ager, which provides them to the JobManager. Finally, the JobManager submits the job's tasks to the TaskManagers for execution.

The session mode starts a long-running Flink cluster that can run multiple jobs and needs to be manually stopped. If started in session mode, Flink connects to YARN's ResourceManager to start an application master that runs a Dispatcher thread and a Flink ResourceManager thread. Figure 9-4 shows an idle Flink YARN session setup.

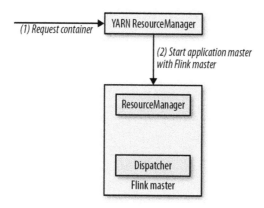

Figure 9-4. Starting a Flink cluster on YARN in session mode

When a job is submitted for execution, the Dispatcher starts a JobManager thread, which requests slots from Flink's ResourceManager. If not enough slots are available, Flink's ResourceManager requests additional containers from the YARN Resource-Manager to start TaskManager processes, which register themselves at the Flink ResourceManager. Once enough slots are available, Flink's ResourceManager assigns them to the JobManager and the job execution starts. Figure 9-5 shows how a job is executed in Flink's YARN session mode.

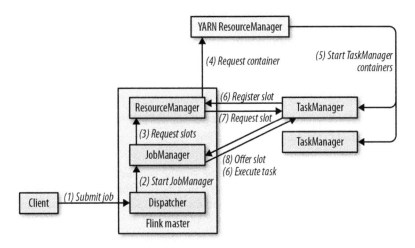

Figure 9-5. Submitting a job to a Flink YARN session cluster

For both setups—job and session mode—failed TaskManagers will be automatically restarted by Flink's ResourceManager. There are a few parameters in the *./conf/flink-conf.yaml* configuration file you can use to control Flink's recovery behavior on YARN. For example, you can configure the maximum number of failed containers until an application is terminated. In order to recover from master failures, a highly available setup needs to be configured as described in a later section.

Regardless of whether you run Flink in job or session mode on YARN, it needs to have access to Hadoop dependencies in the correct version and the path to the Hadoop configuration. "Integration with Hadoop Components" on page 236 describes the required configuration in detail.

Given a working and well-configured YARN and HDFS setup, a Flink job can be submitted to be executed on YARN using Flink's command-line client with the following command:

```
./bin/flink run -m yarn-cluster ./path/to/job.jar
```

The parameter -m defines the host to which the job is submitted. If set to the keyword yarn-cluster, the client submits the job to the YARN cluster as identified by the

Hadoop configuration. Flink's CLI client supports many more parameters, such as the ability to control the memory of TaskManager containers. Refer to the documentation for a reference of available parameters. The Web UI of the started Flink cluster is served by the master process running on some node in the YARN cluster. You can access it via YARN's Web UI, which provides a link on the Application Overview page under "Tracking URL: ApplicationMaster."

A Flink YARN session is started with the `./bin/yarn-session.sh` script, which also uses various parameters to control the size of containers, the name of the YARN application, or provide dynamic properties. By default, the script prints the connection information of the session cluster and does not return. The session is stopped and all resources are freed when the script is terminated. It is also possible to start a YARN session in detached mode using the `-d` flag. A detached Flink session can be terminated using YARN's application utilities.

Once a Flink YARN session is running, you can submit jobs to the session with the command `./bin/flink run ./path/to/job.jar`.

 Note that you do not need to provide connection information, as Flink memorized the connection details of the Flink session running on YARN. Similar to job mode, Flink's Web UI is linked from the Application Overview of YARN's Web UI.

Kubernetes

Kubernetes is an open source platform that enables users to deploy and scale containerized applications in a distributed environment. Given a Kubernetes cluster and an application that is packaged into a container image, you can create a deployment of the application that tells Kubernetes how many instances of the application to start. Kubernetes will run the requested number of containers anywhere on its resources and restart them in the case of a failure. Kubernetes can also take care of opening network ports for internal and external communication and can provide services for process discovery and load balancing. Kubernetes runs on-premise, in cloud environments, or on hybrid infrastructure.

Deploying data processing frameworks and applications on Kubernetes has become very popular. Apache Flink can be deployed on Kubernetes as well. Before diving into the details of how to set up Flink on Kubernetes, we need to briefly explain a few Kubernetes terms:

- A *pod* is a container that is started and managed by Kubernetes.[4]

---

4 Kubernetes also supports pods consisting of multiple tightly linked containers.

- A *deployment* defines a specific number of pods, or containers, to run. Kubernetes ensures the requested number of pods is continuously running, and automatically restarts failed pods. Deployments can be scaled up or down.

- Kubernetes may run a pod anywhere on its cluster. When a pod is restarted after a failure or when deployments are scaled up or down, the IP address can change. This is obviously a problem if pods need to communicate with each other. Kubernetes provides services to overcome the issue. A *service* defines a policy for how a certain group of pods can be accessed. It takes care of updating the routing when a pod is started on a different node in the cluster.

 Running Kubernetes on a Local Machine

Kubernetes is designed for cluster operations. However, the Kubernetes project provides Minikube, an environment to run a single-node Kubernetes cluster locally on a single machine for testing or daily development. We recommend setting up Minikube if you would like to try to run Flink on Kubernetes and do not have a Kubernetes cluster at hand.

In order to successfully run applications on a Flink cluster that is deployed on Minikube, you need to run the following command before deploying Flink: `minikube ssh 'sudo ip link set docker0 promisc on'`.

A Flink setup for Kubernetes is defined with two deployments—one for the pod running the master process and the other for the worker process pods. There is also a service that exposes the ports of the master pod to the worker pods. The two types of pods—master and worker—behave just like the processes of a standalone or Docker deployment we described before. The master deployment configuration is shown in Example 9-2.

Example 9-2. A Kubernetes deployment for a Flink master

```
apiVersion: extensions/v1beta1
kind: Deployment
metadata:
  name: flink-master
spec:
  replicas: 1
  template:
    metadata:
      labels:
        app: flink
        component: master
    spec:
```

```
        containers:
        - name: master
          image: flink:1.7
          args:
          - jobmanager
          ports:
          - containerPort: 6123
            name: rpc
          - containerPort: 6124
            name: blob
          - containerPort: 6125
            name: query
          - containerPort: 8081
            name: ui
          env:
          - name: JOB_MANAGER_RPC_ADDRESS
            value: flink-master
```

This deployment specifies that a single master container should be run (`replicas:`
`1`). The master container is started from the Flink 1.7 Docker image (`image: flink:`
`1.7`) with an argument that starts the master process (`args: - jobmanager`). Moreover, the deployment configures which ports of the container to open for RPC communication, the blob manager (to exchange large files), the queryable state server,
and the Web UI and REST interface. Example 9-3 shows the deployment for worker
pods.

Example 9-3. A Kubernetes deployment for two Flink workers

```
apiVersion: extensions/v1beta1
kind: Deployment
metadata:
  name: flink-worker
spec:
  replicas: 2
  template:
    metadata:
      labels:
        app: flink
        component: worker
    spec:
      containers:
      - name: worker
        image: flink:1.7
        args:
        - taskmanager
        ports:
        - containerPort: 6121
          name: data
        - containerPort: 6122
          name: rpc
```

```
    - containerPort: 6125
      name: query
  env:
  - name: JOB_MANAGER_RPC_ADDRESS
    value: flink-master
```

The worker deployment looks almost identical to the master deployment with a few differences. First of all, the worker deployment specifies two replicas, which means that two worker containers are started. The worker containers are based on the same Flink Docker image but started with a different argument (`args: -taskmanager`). Moreover, the deployment also opens a few ports and passes the service name of the Flink master deployment so that the workers can access the master. The service definition that exposes the master process and makes it accessible to the worker containers is shown in Example 9-4.

Example 9-4. A Kubernetes service for the Flink master

```
apiVersion: v1
kind: Service
metadata:
  name: flink-master
spec:
  ports:
  - name: rpc
    port: 6123
  - name: blob
    port: 6124
  - name: query
    port: 6125
  - name: ui
    port: 8081
  selector:
    app: flink
    component: master
```

You can create a Flink deployment for Kubernetes by storing each definition in a separate file, such as *master-deployment.yaml*, *worker-deployment.yaml*, or *master-service.yaml*. The files are also provided in our repository. Once you have the definition files, you can register them to Kubernetes using the `kubectl` command:

```
kubectl create -f master-deployment.yaml
kubectl create -f worker-deployment.yaml
kubectl create -f master-service.yaml
```

When running these commands, Kubernetes starts to deploy the requested containers. You can show the status of all deployments by running the following command:

```
kubectl get deployments
```

When you create the deployments for the first time, it will take a while until the Flink container image is downloaded. Once all pods are up, you will have a Flink cluster running on Kubernetes. However, with the given configuration, Kubernetes does not export any port to external environments. Hence, you cannot access the master container to submit an application or access the Web UI. You first need to tell Kubernetes to create a port forwarding from the master container to your local machine. This is done by running the following command:

```
kubectl port-forward deployment/flink-master 8081:8081
```

When port forwarding is running, you can access the Web UI at *http://localhost:8081*.

Now you can upload and submit jobs to the Flink cluster running on Kubernetes. Moreover, you can submit applications using the Flink CLI client (*./bin/flink*) and access the REST interface to request information about the Flink cluster or manage running applications.

When a worker pod fails, Kubernetes will automatically restart the failed pod and the application will be recovered (given that checkpointing was activated and properly configured). In order to recover from a master pod failure, you need to configure a highly available setup.

You can shut down a Flink cluster running on Kubernetes by running the following commands:

```
kubectl delete -f master-deployment.yaml
kubectl delete -f worker-deployment.yaml
kubectl delete -f master-service.yaml
```

It is not possible to customize the configuration of the Flink deployment with the Flink Docker images we used in this section. You would need to build custom Docker images with an adjusted configuration. The build script for the provided image is a good starting point for a custom image.

Highly Available Setups

Most streaming applications are ideally executed continuously with as little downtime as possible. Therefore, many applications must be able to automatically recover from failure of any process involved in the execution. While worker failures are handled by the ResourceManager, failures of the JobManager component require the configuration of a highly available (HA) setup.

Flink's JobManager holds metadata about an application and its execution, such as the application JAR file, the JobGraph, and pointers to completed checkpoints. This information needs to be recovered in case of a master failure. Flink's HA mode relies on Apache ZooKeeper, a service for distributed coordination and consistent storage, and a persistent remote storage, such as HDFS, NFS, or S3. The JobManager stores all relevant data in the persistent storage and writes a pointer to the information—the storage path—to ZooKeeper. In case of a failure, a new JobManager looks up the pointer from ZooKeeper and loads the metadata from the persistent storage. We presented the mode of operation and internals of Flink's HA setup in more detail in "Highly Available Setup" on page 42. In this section, we will configure this mode for different deployment options.

A Flink HA setup requires a running Apache ZooKeeper cluster and a persistent remote storage, such as HDFS, NFS, or S3. To help users start a ZooKeeper cluster quickly for testing purposes, Flink provides a helper script for bootstrapping. First, you need to configure the hosts and ports of all ZooKeeper processes involved in the cluster by adjusting the *./conf/zoo.cfg* file. Once that is done, you can call `./bin/start-zookeeper-quorum.sh` to start a ZooKeeper process on each configured node.

Do Not Use start-zookeeper-quorum.sh for Production Setups

You should not use Flink's ZooKeeper script for production environments but instead carefully configure and deploy a Zoo-Keeper cluster yourself.

The Flink HA mode is configured in the *./conf/flink-conf.yaml* file by setting the parameters as shown in Example 9-5.

Example 9-5. Configuration of a HA Flink cluster

```
# REQUIRED: enable HA mode via ZooKeeper
high-availability: zookeeper

# REQUIRED: provide a list of all ZooKeeper servers of the quorum
high-availability.zookeeper.quorum: address1:2181[,...],addressX:2181

# REQUIRED: set storage location for job metadata in remote storage
high-availability.storageDir: hdfs:///flink/recovery

# RECOMMENDED: set the base path for all Flink clusters in ZooKeeper.
# Isolates Flink from other frameworks using the ZooKeeper cluster.
high-availability.zookeeper.path.root: /flink
```

HA Standalone Setup

A Flink standalone deployment does not rely on a resource provider, such as YARN or Kubernetes. All processes are manually started, and there is no component that monitors these processes and restarts them in case of a failure. Therefore, a standalone Flink cluster requires standby Dispatcher and TaskManager processes that can take over the work of failed processes.

Besides starting standby TaskManagers, a standalone deployment does not need additional configuration to be able to recover from TaskManager failures. All started TaskManager processes register themselves at the active ResourceManager. An application can recover from a TaskManager failure as long as enough processing slots are on standby to compensate for the lost TaskManager. The ResourceManager hands out the previously idling processing slots and the application restarts.

If configured for HA, all Dispatchers of a standalone setup register at ZooKeeper. ZooKeeper elects a leader Dispatcher responsible for executing applications. When an application is submitted, the responsible Dispatcher starts a JobManager thread that stores its metadata in the configured persistent storage and a pointer in ZooKeeper as discussed before. If the master process that runs the active Dispatcher and JobManager fails, ZooKeeper elects a new Dispatcher as the leader. The leading Dispatcher recovers the failed application by starting a new JobManager thread that looks up the metadata pointer in ZooKeeper and loads the metadata from the persistent storage.

In addition to the previously discussed configuration, an HA standalone deployment requires the following configuration changes. In *./conf/flink-conf.yaml* you need to set a cluster identifier for each running cluster. This is required if multiple Flink clusters rely on the same ZooKeeper instance for failure recovery:

```
# RECOMMENDED: set the path for the Flink cluster in ZooKeeper.
# Isolates multiple Flink clusters from each other.
# The cluster id is required to look up the metadata of a failed cluster.
high-availability.cluster-id: /cluster-1
```

If you have a ZooKeeper quorum running and Flink properly configured, you can use the regular *./bin/start-cluster.sh* script to start a HA standalone cluster by adding additional hostnames and ports to the *./conf/masters* file.

HA YARN Setup

YARN is a cluster resource and container manager. By default, it automatically restarts failed master and TaskManager containers. Hence, you do not need to run standby processes in a YARN setup to achieve HA.

Flink's master process is started as a YARN ApplicationMaster.[5] YARN automatically restarts a failed ApplicationMaster but tracks and limits the number of restarts to prevent infinite recovery cycles. You need to configure the number of maximum ApplicationManager restarts in the YARN configuration file *yarn-site.xml* as shown:

```
<property>
  <name>yarn.resourcemanager.am.max-attempts</name>
```

---

5 ApplicationMaster is YARN's master process of an application.

```
        <value>4</value>
        <description>
          The maximum number of application master execution attempts.
          Default value is 2, i.e., an application is restarted at most once.
        </description>
      </property>
```

Moreover, you need to adjust Flink's configuration file *./conf/flink-conf.yaml* and configure the number of application restart attempts:

```
# Restart an application at most 3 times (+ the initial start).
# Must be less or equal to the configured maximum number of attempts.
yarn.application-attempts: 4
```

YARN only counts the number of restarts due to application failures—restarts due to preemption, hardware failures, or reboots are not taken into account for the number of application attempts. If you run Hadoop YARN version 2.6 or later, Flink automatically configures an attempt failure's validity interval. This parameter specifies that an application is only completely canceled if it exceeds its restart attempts within the validity interval, meaning attempts that predate the interval are not taken into account. Flink configures the interval to the same value as the `akka.ask.timeout` parameter in *./conf/flink-conf.yaml* with a default value of 10 seconds.

Given a running ZooKeeper cluster and properly configured YARN and Flink setups, you can start a Flink cluster in job mode or session mode as if HA were not enabled—by using `./bin/flink run -m yarn-cluster` and `./bin/yarn-session.sh`.

> Note that you must configure different cluster IDs for all Flink session clusters that connect to the same ZooKeeper cluster. When starting a Flink cluster in job mode, the cluster ID is automatically set to the ID of the started application and is therefore unique.

HA Kubernetes Setup

When running Flink on Kubernetes with a master deployment and a worker deployment as described in "Kubernetes" on page 228, Kubernetes will automatically restart failed containers to ensure the right number of pods is up and running. This is sufficient to recover from worker failures, which are handled by the ResourceManager. However, recovering from master failures requires additional configuration as discussed before.

In order to enable Flink's HA mode, you need to adjust Flink's configuration and provide information such as the hostnames of the ZooKeeper quorum nodes, a path to a persistent storage, and a cluster ID for Flink. All of these parameters need to be added to Flink's configuration file (*./conf/flink-conf.yaml*).

Custom Configuration in Flink Images

Unfortunately, the Flink Docker image we used in the Docker and Kubernetes examples before does not support setting custom configuration parameters. Hence, the image cannot be used to set up a HA Flink cluster on Kubernetes. Instead, you need to build a custom image that either "hardcodes" the required parameters or is flexible enough to adjust the configuration dynamically through parameters or environment variables. The standard Flink Docker images are a good starting point to customize your own Flink images.

Integration with Hadoop Components

Apache Flink can be easily integrated with Hadoop YARN and HDFS and other components of the Hadoop ecosystem, such as HBase. In all of these cases, Flink requires Hadoop dependencies on its classpath.

There are three ways to provide Flink with Hadoop dependencies:

1. Use a binary distribution of Flink that was built for a particular Hadoop version. Flink provides builds for the most commonly used vanilla Hadoop versions.

2. Build Flink for a specific Hadoop version. This is useful if none of Flink's binary distributions works with the Hadoop version deployed in your environment; for example, if you run a patched Hadoop version or a Hadoop version of a distributor, such as Cloudera, Hortonworks, or MapR.

   In order to build Flink for a specific Hadoop version, you need Flink's source code, which can be obtained by downloading the source distribution from the website or cloning a stable release branch from the project's Git repository, a Java JDK of at least version 8, and Apache Maven 3.2. Enter the base folder of Flink's source code and run one of the commands in the following:

   ```
   // build Flink for a specific official Hadoop version
   mvn clean install -DskipTests -Dhadoop.version=2.6.1

   // build Flink for a Hadoop version of a distributor
   mvn clean install -DskipTests -Pvendor-repos \
   -Dhadoop.version=2.6.1-cdh5.0.0
   ```

   The completed build is located in the *./build-target* folder.

3. Use the Hadoop-free distribution of Flink and manually configure the classpath for Hadoop's dependencies. This approach is useful if none of the provided builds work for your setup. The classpath of the Hadoop dependencies must be declared in the HADOOP_CLASSPATH environment variable. If the variable is not configured,

you can automatically set it with the following command if the `hadoop` command is accessible: `export HADOOP_CLASSPATH=`hadoop classpath``.

The `classpath` option of the `hadoop` command prints its configured classpath.

In addition to configuring the Hadoop dependencies, you need to provide the location of Hadoop's configuration directory. This should be done by exporting either the `HADOOP_CONF_DIR` (preferred) or `HADOOP_CONF_PATH` environment variable. Once Flink knows about Hadoop's configuration, it can connect to YARN's ResourceManager and HDFS.

Filesystem Configuration

Apache Flink uses filesystems for various tasks. Applications can read their input from and write their results to files (see "Filesystem Source Connector"), application checkpoints and metadata are persisted in remote filesystems for recovery (see "Checkpoints, Savepoints, and State Recovery"), and some internal components leverage filesystems to distribute data to tasks, such as application JAR files.

Flink supports a wide variety of filesystems. Since Flink is a distributed system and runs processes on cluster or cloud environments, filesystems typically need to be globally accessible. Hence, Hadoop HDFS, S3, and NFS are commonly used filesystems.

Similar to other data processing systems, Flink looks at the URI scheme of a path to identify the filesystem the path refers to. For example, *file:///home/user/data.txt* points to a file in the local filesystem and *hdfs:///namenode:50010/home/user/data.txt* to a file in the specified HDFS cluster.

A filesystem is represented in Flink by an implementation of the `org.apache.flink.core.fs.FileSystem` class. A `FileSystem` class implements filesystem operations, such as reading from and writing to files, creating directories or files, and listing the contents of a directory. A Flink process (JobManager or TaskManager) instantiates one `FileSystem` object for each configured filesystem and shares it across all local tasks to guarantee that configured constraints such as limits on the number of open connections are enforced.

Flink provides implementations for the most commonly used filesystems as follows:

Local filesystem
   Flink has built-in support for local filesystems, including locally mounted network filesystems, such as NFS or SAN, and does not require additional configuration. Local filesystems are referenced by the *file://* URI scheme.

Hadoop HDFS

Flink's connector for HDFS is always in the classpath of Flink. However, it requires Hadoop dependencies on the classpath in order to work. "Integration with Hadoop Components" on page 236 explains how to ensure Hadoop dependencies are loaded. HDFS paths are prefixed with the *hdfs://* scheme.

Amazon S3

Flink provides two alternative filesystem connectors to connect to S3, which are based on Apache Hadoop and Presto. Both connectors are fully self-contained and do not expose any dependencies. To install either of both connectors, move the respective JAR file from the *./opt* folder into the *./lib* folder. The Flink documentation provides more details on the configuration of S3 filesystems. S3 paths are specified with the *s3://* scheme.

OpenStack Swift FS

Flink provides a connector to Swift FS, which is based on Apache Hadoop. The connector is fully self-contained and does not expose any dependencies. It is installed by moving the swift-connector JAR file from the *./opt* to the *./lib* folder. Swift FS paths are identified by the *swift://* scheme.

For filesystems for which Flink does not provide a dedicated connector, Flink can delegate to the Hadoop filesystem connector if it is correctly configured. This is why Flink is able to support all HCFSs.

Flink provides a few configuration options in *./conf/flink-conf.yaml* to specify a default filesystem and limit the number of filesystem connections. You can specify a default filesystem scheme (*fs.default-scheme*) that is automatically added as a prefix if a path does not provide a scheme. If you, for example, specify *fs.default-scheme: hdfs://nnode1:9000*, the path */result* will be extended to *hdfs://nnode1:9000/result*.

You can limit the number of connections that read from (input) and write to (output) a filesystem. The configuration can be defined per URI scheme. The relevant configuration keys are:

```
fs.<scheme>.limit.total: (number, 0/-1 mean no limit)
fs.<scheme>.limit.input: (number, 0/-1 mean no limit)
fs.<scheme>.limit.output: (number, 0/-1 mean no limit)
fs.<scheme>.limit.timeout: (milliseconds, 0 means infinite)
fs.<scheme>.limit.stream-timeout: (milliseconds, 0 means infinite)
```

The number of connections are tracked per TaskManager process and path authority —*hdfs://nnode1:50010* and *hdfs://nnode2:50010* are separately tracked. The connection limits can be configured either separately for input and output connections or as the total number of connections. When the filesystem reaches its connection limit and tries to open a new connection, it will block and wait for another connection to close. The timeout parameters define how long to wait until a connection request fails (fs.<scheme>.limit.timeout) and how long to wait until an idle connection is closed (fs.<scheme>.limit.stream-timeout).

You can also provide a custom filesystem connector. Take a look at the Flink documentation (*http://bit.ly/2HxINvi*) to learn how to implement and register a custom filesystem.

System Configuration

Apache Flink offers many parameters to configure its behavior and tweak its performance. All parameters can be defined in the *./conf/flink-conf.yaml* file, which is organized as a flat YAML file of key-value pairs. The configuration file is read by different components, such as the start scripts, the master and worker JVM processes, and the CLI client. For example, the start scripts, such as *./bin/start-cluster.sh*, parse the configuration file to extract JVM parameters and heap size settings, and the CLI client (*./bin/flink*) extracts the connection information to access the master process. Changes in the configuration file are not effective until Flink is restarted.

To improve the out-of-the-box experience, Flink is preconfigured for a local setup. You need to adjust the configuration to successfully run Flink in distributed environments. In this section, we discuss different aspects that typically need to be configured when setting up a Flink cluster. We refer you to the official documentation (*http://bit.ly/2O4T7fv*) for a comprehensive list and detailed descriptions of all parameters.

Java and Classloading

By default, Flink starts JVM processes using the Java executable linked by the PATH environment variable. If Java is not on the PATH or if you want to use a different Java version you can specify the root folder of a Java installation via the JAVA_HOME environment variable or the env.java.home key in the configuration file. Flink's JVM processes can be started with custom Java options—for example, to fine-tune the garbage collector or to enable remote debugging, with the keys env.java.opts, env.java.opts.jobmanager, and env.java.opts.taskmanager.

Classloading issues are not uncommon when running jobs with external dependencies. In order to execute a Flink application, all classes in the application's JAR file must be loaded by a classloader. Flink registers the classes of every job into a separate user-code classloader to ensure the dependencies of the job do not infer with Flink's runtime dependencies or the dependencies of other jobs. User-code class loaders are disposed of when the corresponding job terminates. Flink's system class loader loads all JAR files in the *./lib* folder and the user-code classloaders are derived from the system classloader.

By default, Flink looks up user-code classes first in the child (user-code) classloader and then in parent (system) classloader to prevent version clashes in case a job uses the same dependency as Flink. However, you can also invert the lookup order with the `classloader.resolve-order` configuration key.

 Note that some classes are always resolved first in the parent classloader (`classloader.parent-first-patterns.default`). You can extend the list by providing a whitelist of classname patterns that are first resolved from the parent classloader (`classloader.parent-first-patterns.additional`).

CPU

Flink does not actively limit the amount of CPU resources it consumes. However, it uses processing slots (see "Task Execution" on page 40 for a detailed discussion) to control the number of tasks that can be assigned to a worker process (TaskManager). A TaskManager provides a certain number of slots that are registered at and governed by the ResourceManager. A JobManager requests one or more slots to execute an application. Each slot can process one slice of an application, one parallel task of every operator of the application. Hence, the JobManager needs to acquire at least as many slots as the application's maximum operator parallelism.[6] Tasks are executed as threads within the worker (TaskManager) process and take as much CPU resources as they need.

The number of slots a TaskManager offers is controlled with the `taskmanager.num berOfTaskSlots` key in the configuration file. The default is one slot per TaskManager. The number of slots usually only needs to be configured for standalone setups as running Flink on a cluster resource manager (YARN, Kubernetes, Mesos) makes it easy to spin up multiple TaskManagers (each with one slot) per compute node.

Main Memory and Network Buffers

Flink's master and worker processes have different memory requirements. A master process mainly manages compute resources (ResourceManager) and coordinates the execution of applications (JobManager), while a worker process takes care of the heavy lifting and processes potentially large amounts of data.

Usually, the master process has moderate memory requirements. By default, it is started with 1 GB JVM heap memory. If the master process needs to manage several applications or an application with many operators, you might need to increase the JVM heap size with the `jobmanager.heap.size` configuration key.

---

6 It is possible to assign operators to different slot-sharing groups and thus assign their tasks to distinct slots.

Configuring the memory of a worker process is a bit more involved because there are multiple components that allocate different types of memory. The most important parameter is the size of the JVM heap memory, which is set with the key `taskmanager.heap.size`. The heap memory is used for all objects, including the TaskManager runtime, operators and functions of the application, and in-flight data. The state of an application that uses the in-memory or filesystem state backend is also stored on the JVM. Note that a single task can potentially consume the whole heap memory of the JVM that it is running on. Flink does not guarantee or grant heap memory per task or slot. Configurations with a single slot per TaskManager have better resource isolation and can prevent a misbehaving application from interfering with unrelated applications. If you run applications with many dependencies, the JVM's nonheap memory can also grow significantly because it stores all TaskManager and user-code classes.

In addition to the JVM, there are two other major memory consumers, Flink's network stack and RocksDB, when it is used as a state backend. Flink's network stack is based on the Netty library, which allocates network buffers from native (off-heap) memory. Flink requires a sufficient number of network buffers to be able to ship records from one worker process to the other. The number of buffers depends on the total number of network connections between operator tasks. For two operators connected by a partitioning or broadcasting connection the number of network buffers depends on the product of the sending and receiving operator parallelism. For applications with several partitioning steps, this quadratic dependency can quickly sum up to a significant amount of memory that is required for network transfer.

Flink's default configuration is only suitable for a smaller scale distributed setup and needs to be adjusted for more serious scale. If the number of buffers is not appropriately configured, a job submission will fail with a `java.io.IOException: Insufficient number of network buffers`. In this case, you should provide more memory to the network stack.

The amount of memory assigned for network buffers is configured with the `taskmanager.network.memory.fraction` key, which determines the fraction of the JVM size allocated for network buffers. By default, 10% of the JVM heap size is used. Since the buffers are allocated as off-heap memory, the JVM heap is reduced by that amount. The configuration key `taskmanager.memory.segment-size` determines the size of a network buffer, which is 32 KB by default. Reducing the size of a network buffer increases the number of buffers but can reduce the efficiency of the network stack. You can also specify a minimum (`taskmanager.network.memory.min`) and a maximum (`taskmanager.network.memory.max`) amount of memory that is used for network buffers (by default 64 MB and 1 GB, respectively) to set absolute limits for the relative configuration value.

RocksDB is another memory consumer that needs to be taken into consideration when configuring the memory of a worker process. Unfortunately, figuring out the memory consumption of RocksDB is not straightforward because it depends on the number of keyed states in an application. Flink creates a separate (embedded) RocksDB instance for each task of a keyed operator. Within each instance, every distinct state of the operator is stored in a separate column family (or table). With the default configuration, each column family requires about 200 MB to 240 MB of off-heap memory. You can adjust RocksDB's configuration and tweak its performance with many parameters.

When configuring the memory setting of a TaskManager, you should size the JVM heap memory so there is enough memory left for the JVM nonheap memory (classes and metadata) and RocksDB if it is configured as a state backend. Network memory is automatically subtracted from the configured JVM heap size. Keep in mind that some resource managers, such as YARN, will immediately kill a container if it exceeds its memory budget.

Disk Storage

A Flink worker process stores data on the local filesystem for multiple reasons, including receiving application JAR files, writing log files, and maintaining application state if the RocksDB state backend is configured. With the io.tmp.dirs configuration key, you can specify one or more directories (separated by colons) that are used to store data in the local filesystem. By default, data is written to the default temporary directory as determined by the Java system property java.io.tmpdir, or /tmp on Linux and MacOS. The io.tmp.dirs parameter is used as the default value for the local storage path of most components of Flink. However, these paths can also be individually configured.

Ensure Temporary Directories Are Not Automatically Cleaned

Some Linux distribution periodically clean the temporary directory /tmp. Make sure to disable this behavior or configure a different directory if you plan to run continuous Flink applications. Otherwise job recovery might miss metadata that was stored in the temporary directory and fail.

The blob.storage.directory key configures the local storage directory of the blob server, which is used to exchange larger files such as the application JAR files. The env.log.dir key configures the directory into which a TaskManager writes its log files (by default, the ./log directory in the Flink setup). Finally, the RocksDB state backend maintains application state in the local filesystem. The directory is configured using the `state.backend.rocksdb.localdir` key. If the storage directory is not explicitly configured, RocksDB uses the value of the `io.tmp.dirs` parameter.

Checkpointing and State Backends

Flink offers a few options to configure how state backends checkpoint their state. All parameters can be explicitly specified within the code of an application as described in "Tuning Checkpointing and Recovery". However, you can also provide default settings for a Flink cluster through Flink's configuration file, which are applied if job-specific options are not declared.

An important choice that affects the performance of an application is the state backend that maintains its state. You can define the default state backend of a cluster with the `state.backend` key. Moreover, you can enable asynchronous checkpointing (`state.backend.async`) and incremental checkpointing (`state.backend.incremental`). Some backends do not support all options and might ignore them. You can also configure the root directories at the remote storage to which checkpoints (`state.checkpoints.dir`) and savepoints (`state.savepoints.dir`) are written.

Some checkpointing options are backend specific. For the RocksDB state backend you can define one or more paths at which RocksDB stores its local files (`state.backend.rocksdb.localdir`) and whether timer state is stored on the heap (default) or in RocksDB (`state.backend.rocksdb.timer-service.factory`).

Finally, you can enable and configure local recovery for a Flink cluster by default.[7] To enable local recovery, set the parameter `state.backend.local-recovery` to true. The storage location of the local state copy can be specified as well (`taskmanager.state.local.root-dirs`).

Security

Data processing frameworks are sensitive components of a company's IT infrastructure and need to be secured against unauthorized use and access to data. Apache Flink supports Kerberos authentication and can be configured to encrypt all network communication with SSL.

Flink features Kerberos integration with Hadoop and its components (YARN, HDFS, HBase), ZooKeeper, and Kafka. You can enable and configure the Kerberos support for each service separately. Flink supports two authentication modes—keytabs and Hadoop delegation tokens. Keytabs are the preferred approach because tokens expire after some time, which can cause problems for long-running stream processing applications. Note that the credentials are tied to a Flink cluster and not to a running job;

---

7 See "Configuring Recovery" for details on this feature.

all applications that run on the same cluster use the same authentication token. If you need to work with different credentials, you should start a new cluster. Consult the Flink documentation (*http://bit.ly/2Fc4i3e*) for detailed instructions on enabling and configuring Kerberos authentication.

Flink supports mutual authentication of communication partners and encryption of network communication with SSL for internal and external communication. For internal communication (RPC calls, data transfer, and blob service communication to distribute libraries or other artifacts) all Flink processes (Dispatcher, ResourceManager, JobManager, and TaskManager) perform mutual authentication— senders and receivers validate each other via an SSL certificate. The certificate acts as a shared secret and can be embedded into containers or attached to a YARN setup.

All external communication with Flink services—submitting and controlling applications and accessing the REST interface—happens over REST/HTTP endpoints.[8] You can enable SSL encryption for these connections as well. Mutual authentication can also be enabled. However, the recommended approach is setting up and configuring a dedicated proxy service that controls access to the REST endpoint. The reason is that proxy services offer more authentication and configuration options than Flink. Encryption and authentication for communication to queryable state is not supported yet.

By default, SSL authentication and encryption is not enabled. Since the setup requires several steps, such as generating certificates, setting up TrustStores and KeyStores, and configuring cipher suites, we refer you to the official Flink documentation (*http://bit.ly/2Fc4i3e*). The documentation also includes how-tos and tips for different environments, such as standalone clusters, Kubernetes, and YARN.

Summary

In this chapter we discussed how Flink is set up in different environments and how to configure HA setups. We explained how to enable support for various filesystems and how to integrate them with Hadoop and its components. Finally, we discussed the most important configuration options. We did not provide a comprehensive configuration guide; instead, we refer you to the official documentation of Apache Flink (*http://bit.ly/2O5ikGP*) for a complete list and detailed descriptions of all configuration options.

---

8 Chapter 10 discusses job submission and the REST interface.

CHAPTER 10
Operating Flink and Streaming Applications

Streaming applications are long-running and their workloads are often unpredictable. It is not uncommon for a streaming job to be continuously running for months, so its operational needs are quite different than those of short-lived batch jobs. Consider a scenario where you detect a bug in your deployed application. If your application is a batch job, you can easily fix the bug offline and then redeploy the new application code once the current job instance finishes. But what if your job is a long-running streaming job? How do you apply a reconfiguration with low effort while guaranteeing correctness?

If you are using Flink, you have nothing to worry about. Flink will do all the hard work so you can easily monitor, operate, and reconfigure your jobs with minimal effort while preserving exactly-once state semantics. In this chapter, we present the tools Flink offers for operating and maintaining continuously running streaming applications. We will show you how to collect metrics and monitor your applications and how to preserve result consistency when you want to update application code or adjust the resources of your application.

Running and Managing Streaming Applications

As you might expect, maintaining streaming applications is more challenging than maintaining batch applications. While streaming applications are stateful and continuously running, batch applications are periodically executed. Reconfiguring, scaling, or updating a batch application can be done between executions, which is a lot easier than upgrading an application that is continuously ingesting, processing, and emitting data.

However, Apache Flink has many features to significantly ease the maintenance of streaming applications. Most of these features are based on savepoints.[1] Flink exposes the following interfaces to monitor and control its master and worker processes, and applications:

1. The command-line client is a tool used to submit and control applications.

2. The REST API is the underlying interface that is used by the command-line client and Web UI. It can be accessed by users and scripts and provides access to all system and application metrics as well as endpoints to submit and manage applications.

3. The Web UI is a web interface that provides details and metrics about a Flink cluster and running applications. It also offers basic functionality to submit and manage applications. The Web UI is described in "Flink Web UI".

In this section, we explain the practical aspects of savepoints and discuss how to start, stop, pause and resume, scale, and upgrade stateful streaming applications using Flink's command-line client and Flink's REST API.

Savepoints

A savepoint is basically identical to a checkpoint—it is a consistent and complete snapshot of an application's state. However, the lifecycles of checkpoints and savepoints differ. Checkpoints are automatically created, loaded in case of a failure, and automatically removed by Flink (depending on the configuration of the application). Moreover, checkpoints are automatically deleted when an application is canceled, unless the application explicitly enabled checkpoint retention. In contrast, savepoints must be manually triggered by a user or an external service and are never automatically removed by Flink.

A savepoint is a directory in a persistent data storage. It consists of a subdirectory that holds the data files containing the states of all tasks and a binary metadata file that includes absolute paths to all data files. Because the paths in the metadata file are absolute, moving a savepoint to a different path will render it unusable. Here is the structure of a savepoint:

```
# Savepoint root path
/savepoints/

# Path of a particular savepoint
/savepoints/savepoint-:shortjobid-:savepointid/

# Binary metadata file of a savepoint
```

---

[1] See Chapter 3 to learn about savepoints and what you can do with them.

```
/savepoints/savepoint-:shortjobid-:savepointid/_metadata

# Checkpointed operator states
/savepoints/savepoint-:shortjobid-:savepointid/:xxx
```

Managing Applications with the Command-Line Client

Flink's command-line client provides the functionality to start, stop, and manage Flink applications. It reads its configuration from the *./conf/flink-conf.yaml* file (see "System Configuration"). You can call it from the root directory of a Flink setup with the command `./bin/flink`.

When run without additional parameters, the client prints a help message.

Command-Line Client on Windows

The command-line client is based on a bash script. Therefore, it does not work with the Windows command line. The *./bin/flink.bat* script for the Windows command line provides only very limited functionality. If you are a Windows user, we recommend using the regular command-line client and running it on WSL or Cygwin.

Starting an application

You can start an application with the `run` command of the command-line client:

```
./bin/flink run ~/myApp.jar
```

The above command starts the application from the `main()` method of the class that is referenced in the `program-class` property of the JAR file's *META-INF/MANIFEST.MF* file without passing any arguments to the application. The client submits the JAR file to the master process, which distributes it to the worker nodes.

You can pass arguments to the `main()` method of an application by appending them at the end of the command:

```
./bin/flink run ~/myApp.jar my-arg1 my-arg2 my-arg3
```

By default, the client does not return after submitting the application but waits for it to terminate. You can submit an application in detached mode with the `-d` flag as shown here:

```
./bin/flink run -d ~/myApp.jar
```

Instead of waiting for the application to terminate, the client returns and prints the JobID of the submitted job. The JobID is used to specify the job when taking a savepoint, canceling, or rescaling an application. You can specify the default parallelism of an application with the `-p` flag:

```
./bin/flink run -p 16 ~/myApp.jar
```

The above command sets the default parallelism of the execution environment to 16. The default parallelism of an execution environment is overwritten by all settings explicitly specified by the source code of the application—the parallelism that is defined by calling `setParallelism()` on `StreamExecutionEnvironment` or on an operator has precedence over the default value.

If the manifest file of your application JAR file does not specify an entry class, you can specify the class using the `-c` parameter:

```
./bin/flink run -c my.app.MainClass ~/myApp.jar
```

The client will try to start the static `main()` method of the `my.app.MainClass` class.

By default, the client submits an application to the Flink master specified by the *./conf/flink-conf.yaml* file (see the configuration for different setups in "System Configuration"). You can submit an application to a specific master process using the `-m` flag:

```
./bin/flink run -m myMasterHost:9876 ~/myApp.jar
```

This command submits the application to the master that runs on host `myMasterHost` at port `9876`.

> Note that the state of an application will be empty if you start it for the first time or do not provide a savepoint or checkpoint to initialize the state. In this case, some stateful operators run special logic to initialize their state. For example, a Kafka source needs to choose the partition offsets from which it consumes a topic if no restored read positions are available.

Listing running applications

For all actions you want to apply to a running job, you need to provide a JobID that identifies the application. The ID of a job can be obtained from the Web UI, the REST API, or using the command-line client. The client prints a list of all running jobs, including their JobIDs, when you run the following command:

```
./bin/flink list -r
Waiting for response...
------------------ Running/Restarting Jobs ------------------
17.10.2018 21:13:14 : bc0b2ad61ecd4a615d92ce25390f61ad :
Socket Window WordCount (RUNNING)
--------------------------------------------------------------
```

In this example, the JobID is `bc0b2ad61ecd4a615d92ce25390f61ad`.

Taking and disposing of a savepoint

A savepoint can be taken for a running application with the command-line client as follows:

```
./bin/flink savepoint <jobId> [savepointPath]
```

The command triggers a savepoint for the job with the provided JobID. If you explicitly specify a savepoint path, it is stored in the provided directory. Otherwise, the default savepoint directory as configured in the *flink-conf.yaml* file is used.

To trigger a savepoint for the job bc0b2ad61ecd4a615d92ce25390f61ad and store it in the directory *hdfs:///xxx:50070/savepoints*, we call the command-line client:

```
./bin/flink savepoint bc0b2ad61ecd4a615d92ce25390f61ad \
hdfs:///xxx:50070/savepoints
Triggering savepoint for job bc0b2ad61ecd4a615d92ce25390f61ad.
Waiting for response...
Savepoint completed.
Path: hdfs:///xxx:50070/savepoints/savepoint-bc0b2a-63cf5d5ccef8
You can resume your program from this savepoint with the run command.
```

Savepoints can occupy a significant amount of space and are not automatically deleted by Flink. You need to manually remove them to free the consumed storage. A savepoint is removed with the command:

```
./bin/flink savepoint -d <savepointPath>
```

In order to remove the savepoint we triggered before, call the command:

```
./bin/flink savepoint -d \
hdfs:///xxx:50070/savepoints/savepoint-bc0b2a-63cf5d5ccef8
Disposing savepoint 'hdfs:///xxx:50070/savepoints/savepoint-bc0b2a-63cf5d5ccef8'.
Waiting for response...
Savepoint 'hdfs:///xxx:50070/savepoints/savepoint-bc0b2a-63cf5d5ccef8' disposed.
```

Deleting a Savepoint

You must not delete a savepoint before another checkpoint or savepoint is completed. Since savepoints are handled by the system similarly to regular checkpoints, operators also receive checkpoint completion notifications for completed savepoints and act on them. For example, transactional sinks commit changes to external systems when a savepoint completes. To guarantee exactly-once output, Flink must recover from the latest completed checkpoint or savepoint. A failure recovery would fail if Flink attempted to recover from a savepoint that was removed. Once another checkpoint (or savepoint) completes, you can safely remove a savepoint.

Canceling an application

An application can be canceled in two ways: with or without a savepoint. To cancel a running application without taking a savepoint run the following command:

```
./bin/flink cancel <jobId>
```

In order to take a savepoint before canceling a running application add the -s flag to the cancel command:

```
./bin/flink cancel -s [savepointPath] <jobId>
```

If you do not specify a savepointPath, the default savepoint directory as configured in the *./conf/flink-conf.yaml* file is used (see "System Configuration"). The command fails if the savepoint folder is neither explicitly specified in the command nor available from the configuration. To cancel the application with the JobID bc0b2ad61ecd4a615d92ce25390f61ad and store the savepoint at *hdfs:///xxx:50070/savepoints*, run the command:

```
./bin/flink cancel -s \
hdfs:///xxx:50070/savepoints d5fdaff43022954f5f02fcd8f25ef855
Cancelling job bc0b2ad61ecd4a615d92ce25390f61ad
with savepoint to hdfs:///xxx:50070/savepoints.
Cancelled job bc0b2ad61ecd4a615d92ce25390f61ad.
Savepoint stored in hdfs:///xxx:50070/savepoints/savepoint-bc0b2a-d08de07fbb10.
```

Canceling an Application Might Fail

Note that the job will continue to run if taking the savepoint fails. You will need to make another attempt at canceling the job.

Starting an application from a savepoint

Starting an application from a savepoint is fairly simple. All you have to do is start an application with the run command and additionally provide a path to a savepoint with the -s option:

```
./bin/flink run -s <savepointPath> [options] <jobJar> [arguments]
```

When the job is started, Flink matches the individual state snapshots of the savepoint to all states of the started application. This matching is done in two steps. First, Flink compares the unique operator identifiers of the savepoint and application's operators. Second, it matches for each operator the state identifiers (see "Savepoints" for details) of the savepoint and the application.

You Should Define Unique Operator IDs

If you do not assign unique IDs to your operators with the `uid()` method, Flink assigns default identifiers, which are hash values that depend on the type of the operator and all previous operators. Since it is not possible to change the identifiers in a savepoint, you will have fewer options to update and evolve your application if you do not manually assign operator identifiers using `uid()`.

As mentioned, an application can only be started from a savepoint if it is compatible with the savepoint. An unmodified application can always be restarted from its savepoint. However, if the restarted application is not identical to the application from which the savepoint was taken, there are three cases to consider:

- If you *added a new state* to the application or changed the unique identifier of a stateful operator, Flink will not find a corresponding state snapshot in the savepoint. In this case, the new state is initialized as empty.

- If you *removed a state* from the application or changed the unique identifier of a stateful operator, there is state in the savepoint that cannot be matched to the application. In this case, Flink does not start the application to avoid losing the state in the savepoint. You can disable this safety check by adding the `-n` option to the run command.

- If you *changed a state* in the application—changed the state primitive or modified the data type of the state—the application fails to start. This means that you cannot easily evolve the data type of a state in your application, unless you designed your application with state evolution in mind from the start. The Flink community is currently working on improving the support for state evolution. (See "Modifying the State of an Operator".)

Scaling an Application In and Out

Decreasing or increasing the parallelism of an application is not difficult. You need to take a savepoint, cancel the application, and restart it with an adjusted parallelism from the savepoint. The state of the application is automatically redistributed to the larger or smaller number of parallel operator tasks. See "Scaling Stateful Operators" on page 56 for details on how the different types of operator state and keyed state are scaled. However, there are a few things to consider.

If you require exactly-once results, you should take the savepoint and stop the application with the integrated savepoint-and-cancel command. This prevents another checkpoint from completing after the savepoint, which would trigger exactly-once sinks to emit data after the savepoint.

As discussed in "Setting the Parallelism" on page 96, the parallelism of an application and its operators can be specified in different ways. By default, operators run with the default parallelism of their associated `StreamExecutionEnvironment`. The default parallelism can be specified when starting an application (e.g., using the `-p` parameter in the CLI client). If you implement the application such that the parallelism of its operators depends on the default environment parallelism, you can simply scale an application by starting it from the same JAR file and specifying a new parallelism. However, if you hardcoded the parallelism on the `StreamExecutionEnvironment` or on some of the operators, you might need to adjust the source code and recompile and repackage your application before submitting it for execution.

If the parallelism of your application depends on the environment's default parallelism, Flink provides an atomic rescale command that takes a savepoint, cancels the application, and restarts it with a new default parallelism:

```
./bin/flink modify <jobId> -p <newParallelism>
```

To rescale the application with the jobId `bc0b2ad61ecd4a615d92ce25390f61ad` to a parallelism of 16, run the command:

```
./bin/flink modify bc0b2ad61ecd4a615d92ce25390f61ad -p 16
Modify job bc0b2ad61ecd4a615d92ce25390f61ad.
Rescaled job bc0b2ad61ecd4a615d92ce25390f61ad. Its new parallelism is 16.
```

As described in "Scaling Stateful Operators" on page 56, Flink distributes keyed state on the granularity of so-called key groups. Consequently, the number of key groups of a stateful operator determines its maximum parallelism. The number of key groups is configured per operator using the `setMaxParallelism()` method. (See "Defining the Maximum Parallelism of Keyed State Operators".)

Managing Applications with the REST API

The REST API can be directly accessed by users or scripts and exposes information about the Flink cluster and its applications, including metrics as well as endpoints to submit and control applications. Flink serves the REST API and the Web UI from the same web server, which runs as part of the Dispatcher process. By default, both are exposed on port 8081. You can configure a different port at the *./conf/flink-conf.yaml* file with the configuration key `rest.port`. A value of -1 disables the REST API and Web UI.

A common command-line tool to interact with REST API is `curl`. A typical `curl` REST command looks like:

```
curl -X <HTTP-Method> [-d <parameters>] http://hostname:port/v1/<REST-point>
```

The `v1` indicates the version of the REST API. Flink 1.7 exposes the first version (`v1`) of the API. Assuming you are running a local Flink setup that exposes its REST API

on port 8081, the following `curl` command submits a `GET` request to the `/overview`
REST point:

```
curl -X GET http://localhost:8081/v1/overview
```

The command returns some basic information about the cluster, such as the Flink
version, the number of TaskManagers, slots, and jobs that are running, finished, cancelled, or failed:

```
{
  "taskmanagers":2,
  "slots-total":8,
  "slots-available":6,
  "jobs-running":1,
  "jobs-finished":2,
  "jobs-cancelled":1,
  "jobs-failed":0,
  "flink-version":"1.7.1",
  "flink-commit":"89eafb4"
}
```

In the following, we list and briefly describe the most important REST calls. Refer to
the official documentation (*http://bit.ly/2TAPy6N*) of Apache Flink for a complete list
of supported calls. "Managing Applications with the Command-Line Client" on page
247 provides more details about some of the operations, such as upgrading or scaling
an application.

Managing and monitoring a Flink cluster

The REST API exposes endpoints to query information about a running cluster and
to shut it down. Tables 10-1, 10-2, and 10-3 show the REST requests to obtain information about a Flink cluster, such as the number of task slots, running and finished
jobs, the configuration of the JobManager, or a list of all connected TaskManagers.

Table 10-1. REST request to get basic cluster information

Request	GET /overview
Response	Basic information about the cluster as shown above

Table 10-2. REST request to get the JobManager configuration

Request	GET /jobmanager/config
Response	Returns the configuration of the JobManager as defined in *./conf/flink-conf.yaml*

Table 10-3. REST request to list all connected TaskManagers

Request	GET /taskmanagers
Response	Returns a list of all TaskManagers including their IDs and basic information, such as memory statistics and connection ports

Table 10-4 shows the REST request to list all metrics that are collected for the Job-Manager.

Table 10-4. REST request to list available JobManager metrics

Request	`GET /jobmanager/metrics`
Response	Returns a list of metrics that are available for the JobManager

In order to retrieve one or more JobManager metrics, add the `get` query parameter with all the requested metrics to the request:

```
curl -X GET http://hostname:port/v1/jobmanager/metrics?get=metric1,metric2
```

Table 10-5 shows the REST request to list all metrics that are collected for the Task-Managers.

Table 10-5. REST request to list available TaskManager metrics

Request	`GET /taskmanagers/<tmId>/metrics`
Parameters	tmId: The ID of a connected TaskManager
Response	Returns a list of metrics available for the chosen TaskManager

To retrieve one or more metrics for a TaskManager, add the `get` query parameter with all the requested metrics to the request:

```
curl -X GET http://hostname:port/v1/taskmanagers/<tmId>/metrics?get=metric1
```

You can also shutdown a cluster using the REST call that is shown in Table 10-6.

Table 10-6. REST request to shutdown the cluster

Request	`DELETE /cluster`
Action	Shuts down the Flink cluster. Note that in standalone mode, only the master process will be terminated and the worker processes will continue to run.

Managing and montioring Flink applications

The REST API can also be used to manage and monitor Flink applications. To start an application, you first need to upload the application's JAR file to the cluster. Tables 10-7, 10-8, and 10-9 show the REST endpoints to manage these JAR files.

Table 10-7. REST request to upload a JAR file

Request	`POST /jars/upload`
Parameters	The file must be sent as multipart data
Action	Uploads a JAR file to the cluster
Response	The storage location of the uploaded JAR file

The curl command to upload a JAR file:

```
curl -X POST -H "Expect:" -F "jarfile=@path/to/flink-job.jar" \
  http://hostname:port/v1/jars/upload
```

Table 10-8. REST request to list all uploaded JAR files

Request	GET /jars
Response	A list of all uploaded JAR files. The list includes the internal ID of a JAR file, its original name, and the time when it was uploaded.

Table 10-9. REST request to delete a JAR file

Request	DELETE /jars/<jarId>
Parameters	jarId: The ID of the JAR file as provided by the list JAR file command
Action	Deletes the JAR file referenced by the provided ID

An application is started from an uploaded JAR file using the REST call that is shown in Table 10-10 .

Table 10-10. REST request to start an application

Request	POST /jars/<jarId>/run
Parameters	jarId: The ID of the JAR file from which the application is started. You can pass additional parameters such as the job arguments, the entry class, the default parallelism, a savepoint path, and the allow-nonrestored-state flag as a JSON object.
Action	Starts the application defined by the JAR file (and entry-class) with the provided parameters. If a savepoint path is provided, the application state is initialized from the savepoint.
Response	The job ID of the started application

The curl command to start an application with a default parallelism of 4 is:

```
curl -d '{"parallelism":"4"}' -X POST \
  http://localhost:8081/v1/jars/43e844ef-382f-45c3-aa2f-00549acd961e_App.jar/run
```

Tables 10-11, 10-12, and 10-13 show how to manage running applications using the REST API.

Table 10-11. REST request to list all applications

Request	GET /jobs
Response	Lists the job IDs of all running applications and the job IDs of the most recently failed, canceled, and finished applications.

Table 10-12. REST request to show details of an application

Request	GET /jobs/<jobId>
Parameters	jobId: The ID of a job as provided by the list application command

Response	Basic statistics such as the name of the application, the start time (and end time), and information about the executed tasks including the number of ingested and emitted records and bytes

The REST API also provides more detailed information about the following aspects of an application:

- The operator plan of the application
- The configuration of the application
- Collected metrics of an application at various levels of detail
- Checkpointing metrics
- Backpressure metrics
- The exception that caused an application to fail

Take a look at the official documentation (*http://bit.ly/2TAPy6N*) for details about how to access this information.

Table 10-13. REST request to cancel an application

Request	`PATCH /jobs/<jobId>`
Parameters	`jobId`: The ID of a job as provided by the list application command
Action	Cancels the application

You can also take a savepoint of a running application via the REST call that is shown in Table 10-14 .

Table 10-14. REST request to take a savepoint of an application

Request	`POST /jobs/<jobId>/savepoints`
Parameters	The ID of a job as provided by the list application command. In addition, you need to provide a JSON object with the path to the savepoint folder and a flag telling whether or not to terminate the application with the savepoint.
Action	Takes a savepoint of the application
Response	A request ID to check whether the savepoint trigger action completed successfully

The `curl` command to trigger a savepoint without canceling is:

```
curl -d '{"target-directory":"file:///savepoints", "cancel-job":"false"}'\
-X POST http://localhost:8081/v1/jobs/e99cdb41b422631c8ee2218caa6af1cc/savepoints
{"request-id":"ebde90836b8b9dc2da90e9e7655f4179"}
```

Canceling an Application with a Savepoint Might Fail

A request to cancel the application will only succeed if the savepoint was successfully taken. The application will continue running if the savepoint command failed.

To check if the request with the ID ebde90836b8b9dc2da90e9e7655f4179 was successful and to retrieve the path of the savepoint run:

```
curl -X GET http://localhost:8081/v1/jobs/e99cdb41b422631c8ee2218caa6af1cc/\
savepoints/ebde90836b8b9dc2da90e9e7655f4179
{"status":{"id":"COMPLETED"}
"operation":{"location":"file:///savepoints/savepoint-e99cdb-34410597dec0"}}
```

To dispose a savepoint use the REST call that is shown in Table 10-15 .

Table 10-15. REST request to dispose a savepoint

Request	POST /savepoint-disposal
Parameters	The path of the savepoint to dispose needs to be provided as a parameter in a JSON object
Action	Disposes of a savepoint
Response	A request ID to check whether the savepoint was successfully disposed or not

To dispose a savepoint with `curl`, run:

```
curl -d '{"savepoint-path":"file:///savepoints/savepoint-e99cdb-34410597"}'\
-X POST http://localhost:8081/v1/savepoint-disposal
{"request-id":"217a4ffe935ceac2c281bdded76729d6"}
```

Table 10-16 shows the REST call to rescale an application.

Table 10-16. REST request to rescale an application

Request	PATCH /jobs/<jobID>/rescaling
Parameters	jobID: The ID of a job as provided by the list application command. In addition, you need to provide the new parallelism of the application as an URL parameter.
Action	Takes a savepoint, cancels the application, and restarts it with the new default parallelism from the savepoint
Response	A request ID to check whether the rescaling request was successful or not

To rescale an application with `curl` to a new default parallelism of 16 run:

```
curl -X PATCH
http://localhost:8081/v1/jobs/129ced9aacf1618ebca0ba81a4b222c6/rescaling\
?parallelism=16
{"request-id":"39584c2f742c3594776653f27833e3eb"}
```

The Application Might Not Rescale

The application will continue to run with the original parallelism if the triggered savepoint failed. You can check the status of the rescale request using the request ID.

Bundling and Deploying Applications in Containers

So far we have explained how to start an application on a running Flink cluster. This is what we call the framework style of deploying applications. In "Application Deployment" on page 39, we briefly explained an alternative—the library mode that does not require a running Flink cluster to submit a job.

In library mode, the application is bundled into a Docker image that also includes the required Flink binaries. The image can be started in two ways—as a JobMaster container or a TaskManager container. When the image is deployed as a JobMaster, the container starts a Flink master process that immediately picks up the bundled application to start it. A TaskManager container registers itself at the JobMaster and offers its processing slots. As soon as enough slots become available, the JobMaster container deploys the application for execution.

The library style of running Flink applications resembles the deployment of microservices in a containerized environment. When being deployed on a container orchestration framework, such as Kubernetes, the framework restarts failed containers. In this section, we describe how to build a job-specific Docker image and how to deploy a library-style bundled application on Kubernetes.

Building a job-specific Flink Docker image

Apache Flink provides a script to build job-specific Flink Docker images. The script is included in the source distribution and Flink's Git repository. It is not part of Flink's binary distributions.

You can either download and extract a source distribution of Flink or clone the Git repository. Starting from the base folder of the distribution, the script is located at ./flink-container/docker/build.sh.

The build script creates and registers a new Docker image that is based on a Java Alpine image, a minimal base image that provides Java. The script requires the following parameters:

- A path to a Flink archive
- A path to an application JAR file
- The name for the new image

To build an image with Flink 1.7.1 that contains the example applications of this book, execute the script as follows:

```
cd ./flink-container/docker
./build.sh \
    --from-archive <path-to-Flink-1.7.1-archive> \
    --job-jar <path-to-example-apps-JAR-file> \
    --image-name flink-book-apps
```

If you run the `docker images` command after the build script finishes, you should see a new Docker image called `flink-book-apps`.

The *./flink-container/docker* directory also contains a *docker-compose.yml* file to deploy a Flink application with `docker-compose`.

If you run the following command, the example application from "A Quick Look at Flink" on page 12 is deployed on one master and three worker containers to Docker:

```
FLINK_DOCKER_IMAGE_NAME=flink-book-jobs \
    FLINK_JOB=io.github.streamingwithflink.chapter1.AverageSensorReadings \
    DEFAULT_PARALLELISM=3 \
    docker-compose up -d
```

You can monitor and control the application by accessing the Web UI running a *http://localhost:8081*.

Running a job-specific Docker image on Kubernetes

Running a job-specific Docker image on Kubernetes is very similar to starting a Flink cluster on Kubernetes as described in "Kubernetes" on page 228. In principle, you only need to adjust the YAML files that describe your deployments to use an image that contains the job code and configure it to automatically start the job when the container is started.

Flink provides templates for the YAML files provided in the source distribution or found in the project's Git repository. Starting from the base directory, the templates are located in:

```
./flink-container/kubernetes
```

The directory contains two template files:

- *job-cluster-job.yaml.template* configures the master container as a Kubernetes job.
- *task-manager-deployment.yaml.template* configures the worker container as a Kubernetes deployment.

Both template files contain placeholders that need to be replaced with actual values:

- `${FLINK_IMAGE_NAME}`: The name of the job-specific image.
- `${FLINK_JOB}`: The main class of the job to start.

- ${FLINK_JOB_PARALLELISM}: The degree of parallelism for the job. This parameter also determines the number of started worker containers.

As you can see, these are the same parameters we used when deploying the job-specific image with docker-compose. The directory also contains a YAML file *job-cluster-service.yaml* that defines a Kubernetes service. Once you have copied the template files and configured required values, you can deploy the application to Kubernetes as before with kubectl:

```
kubectl create -f job-cluster-service.yaml
kubectl create -f job-cluster-job.yaml
kubectl create -f task-manager-deployment.yaml
```

Running Job-Specific Images on Minikube

Running a job-specific image on a Minikube cluster requires a few more steps than those discussed in "Kubernetes" on page 228. The problem is that Minikube tries to fetch the custom image from a public Docker image registry instead of the local Docker registry of your machine.

However, you can configure Docker to deploy its images to Minikube's own registry by running the following command:

```
eval $(minikube docker-env)
```

All images you build afterwards in this shell are deployed to Minikube's image registry. Minikube needs to be running.

Moreover, you need to set the ImagePullPolicy in the YAML files to Never to ensure Minikube fetches the image from its own registry.

Once the job-specific containers are running, you can treat the cluster as a regular Flink cluster as described in "Kubernetes" on page 228.

Controlling Task Scheduling

Flink applications are executed in parallel by parallelizing operators into tasks and distributing these tasks across the worker processes in a cluster. Just like in many other distributed systems, the performance of a Flink application depends a lot on how the tasks are scheduled. The worker process to which a task is assigned, the tasks that are colocated with a task, and the number of tasks that are assigned to a worker process can have a significant impact on an application's performance.

In "Task Execution", we described how Flink assigns tasks to slots and how it leverages task chaining to reduce the cost of local data exchange. In this section, we discuss how you can tweak the default behavior and control task chaining and the assignment of tasks to slots to improve the performance of your applications.

Controlling Task Chaining

Task chaining fuses the parallel tasks of two or more operators into a single task that is executed by a single thread. The fused tasks exchange records by method calls and thus with basically no communication costs. Since task chaining improves the performance of most applications, it is enabled by default in Flink.

However, certain applications might not benefit from task chaining. One reason is to break a chain of expensive functions in order to execute them on different processing slots. You can completely disable task chaining for an application via the StreamExecutionEnvironment:

```
StreamExecutionEnvironment.disableOperatorChaining()
```

In addition to disabling chaining for the whole application, you can also control the chaining behavior of individual operators. To disable chaining for a specific operator, you can call its disableChaining() method. This will prevent the tasks of the operator from being chained to preceding and succeeding tasks (Example 10-1).

Example 10-1. Disable task chaining for an operator

```
val input: DataStream[X] = ...
val result: DataStream[Y] = input
  .filter(new Filter1())
  .map(new Map1())
  // disable chaining for Map2
  .map(new Map2()).disableChaining()
  .filter(new Filter2())
```

The code in Example 10-1 results in three tasks—a chained task for Filter1 and Map1, an individual task for Map2, and a task for Filter2, which is not allowed to be chained to Map2.

It is also possible to start a new chain with an operator by calling its startNewChain() method (Example 10-2). The tasks of the operator will not be chained to preceding tasks but will be chained to succeeding tasks if the requirements for chaining are met.

Example 10-2. Start a new task chain with an operator

```
val input: DataStream[X] = ...
val result: DataStream[Y] = input
  .filter(new Filter1())
  .map(new Map1())
  // start a new chain for Map2 and Filter2
```

```
.map(new Map2()).startNewChain()
.filter(new Filter2())
```

In Example 10-2 two chained tasks are created: one task for Filter1 and Map1 and another task for Map2 and Filter2. Note that the new chained task starts with the operator on which the startNewChain() method is called—Map2 in our example.

Defining Slot-Sharing Groups

Flink's default task scheduling strategy assigns a complete slice of a program—up to one task of each operator of an application to a single processing slot.[2] Depending on the complexity of the application and the computational costs of the operators, this default strategy can overload a processing slot. Flink's mechanism to manually control the assignment of tasks to slots is slot-sharing groups.

Each operator is a member of a slot-sharing group. All tasks of operators that are members of the same slot-sharing group are processed by the same slots. Within a slot-sharing group, the tasks are assigned to slots as described in "Task Execution" on page 40—each slot processes up to one task of each operator that is a member. Hence, a slot-sharing group requires as many processing slots as the maximum parallelism of its operators. Tasks of operators that are in different slot-sharing groups are not executed by the same slots.

By default, each operator is in the "default" slot-sharing group. For each operator, you can explicitly specify its slot-sharing group with the slotSharingGroup(String) method. An operator inherits the slot-sharing group of its input operators if they are all members of the same group. If the input operators are in different groups, the operator is in the "default" group. Example 10-3 shows how to specify slot-sharing groups in a Flink DataStream application.

Example 10-3. Controlling task scheduling with slot-sharing groups

```
// slot-sharing group "green"
val a: DataStream[A] = env.createInput(...)
  .slotSharingGroup("green")
  .setParallelism(4)
val b: DataStream[B] = a.map(...)
  // slot-sharing group "green" is inherited from a
  .setParallelism(4)

// slot-sharing group "yellow"
val c: DataStream[C] = env.createInput(...)
  .slotSharingGroup("yellow")
```

---

2 The default scheduling behavior was explained in Chapter 3.

```
  .setParallelism(2)

// slot-sharing group "blue"
val d: DataStream[D] = b.connect(c.broadcast(...)).process(...)
  .slotSharingGroup("blue")
  .setParallelism(4)
val e = d.addSink()
  // slot-sharing group "blue" is inherited from d
  .setParallelism(2)
```

The application in Example 10-3 consists of five operators, two sources, two inter-mediate operators, and a sink operator. The operators are assigned to three slot-sharing groups: green, yellow, and blue. Figure 10-1 shows the JobGraph of the application and how its tasks are mapped to processing slots.

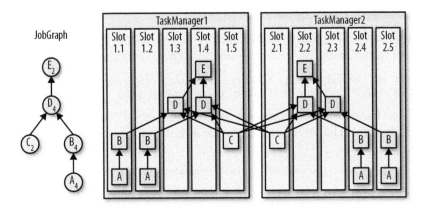

Figure 10-1. Controlling task scheduling with slot-sharing groups

The application requires 10 processing slots. The blue and green slot-sharing groups require four slots each due to the maximum parallelism of their assigned operators. The yellow slot-sharing group requires two slots.

Tuning Checkpointing and Recovery

A Flink application that runs with fault tolerance enabled periodically takes a check-point of its state. Checkpointing can be an expensive operation since the amount of data that needs to be copied to a persistent storage can be quite large. Increasing the checkpointing interval reduces the overhead of fault tolerance during regular pro-cessing. However, it also increases the amount of data a job needs to reprocess after recovering from a failure before it catches up to the tail of the stream.

Flink provides a couple of parameters to tune checkpointing and state backends. Configuring these options is important to ensure reliable and smooth operation of streaming applications in production. For instance, reducing the overhead of each checkpoint can facilitate a higher checkpointing frequency, leading to faster recovery cycles. In this section, we describe the parameters used to control checkpointing and recovery of applications.

Configuring Checkpointing

When you enable checkpointing for an application, you have to specify the checkpointing interval—the interval in which the JobManager will initiate checkpoints at the sources of the application.

Checkpoints are enabled on the `StreamExecutionEnvironment`:

```
val env: StreamExecutionEnvironment = ???

// enable checkpointing with an interval of 10 seconds.
env.enableCheckpointing(10000);
```

Further options to configure the checkpointing behavior are provided by the `Check pointConfig`, which can be obtained from the `StreamExecutionEnvironment`:

```
// get the CheckpointConfig from the StreamExecutionEnvironment
val cpConfig: CheckpointConfig = env.getCheckpointConfig
```

By default, Flink creates checkpoints to guarantee exactly-once state consistency. However, it can also be configured to provide at-least-once guarantees:

```
// set mode to at-least-once
cpConfig.setCheckpointingMode(CheckpointingMode.AT_LEAST_ONCE);
```

Depending on the characteristics of an application, the size of its state, and the state backend and its configuration, a checkpoint can take up to a few minutes. Moreover, the size of the state can grow and shrink over time, perhaps due to long-running windows. Hence, it is not uncommon for a checkpoint to take more time than the configured checkpointing interval. By default, Flink allows only one checkpoint to be in progress at a time to avoid checkpointing takeing away too many resources needed for regular processing. If—according to the configured checkpointing interval—a checkpoint needs to be started, but there is another checkpoint in progress, the second checkpoint will be put on hold until the first checkpoint completes.

If many or all checkpoints take longer than the checkpointing interval, this behavior might not be optimal for two reasons. First, it means that the regular data processing of the application will always compete for resources with the concurrent checkpointing. Hence, its processing slows down and it might not be able to make enough progress to keep up with the incoming data. Second, a checkpoint may be delayed because we need to wait for another checkpoint to complete results in a lower checkpointing interval, leading to longer catch-up processing during recovery. Flink provides parameters to address these situations.

To ensure an application can make enough progress, you can configure a minimum pause between checkpoints. If you configure the minimum pause to be 30 seconds, then no new checkpoint will be started within the first 30 seconds after a checkpoint completed. This also means the effective checkpointing interval is at least 30 seconds and there is at most one checkpoint happening at the same time.

```
// make sure we process at least 30s without checkpointing
cpConfig.setMinPauseBetweenCheckpoints(30000);
```

In certain situations you might want to ensure that checkpoints are taken in the configured checkpointing interval even though a checkpoint takes longer than the interval. One example would be when checkpoints take a long time but do not consume much resources; for example, due to operations with high-latency calls to external systems. In this case you can configure the maximum number of concurrent checkpoints.

```
// allow three checkpoint to be in progress at the same time
cpConfig.setMaxConcurrentCheckpoints(3);
```

> Savepoints are taken concurrently with checkpoints. Flink does not delay explicitly triggered savepoints due to checkpointing operations. A savepoint will always be started regardless of how many checkpoints are in progress.

To avoid long-running checkpoints, you can configure a timeout interval after which a checkpoint is canceled. By default, checkpoints are canceled after 10 minutes.

```
// checkpoints have to complete within five minutes, or are discarded
cpConfig.setCheckpointTimeout(300000);
```

Finally, you might also want to configure what happens if a checkpoint fails. By default, a failing checkpoint causes an exception that results in an application restart. You can disable this behavior and let the application continue after a checkpointing error.

```
// do not fail the job on a checkpointing error
cpConfig.setFailOnCheckpointingErrors(false);
```

Enabling checkpoint compression

Flink supports compressed checkpoints and savepoints. Until Flink 1.7, the only supported compression algorithm is Snappy. You can enable compressed checkpoints and savepoints as follows:

```
val env: StreamExecutionEnvironment = ???

// enable checkpoint compression
env.getConfig.setUseSnapshotCompression(true)
```

Note that checkpoint compression is not supported for incremental RocksDB checkpoints.

Retaining checkpoints after an application has stopped

The purpose of checkpoints is to recover an application after a failure. Hence, they clean up when a job stops running, either due to a failure or explicit cancellation. However, you can also enable a feature called externalized checkpoints to retain checkpoints after the application has stopped.

```
// Enable externalized checkpoints
cpConfig.enableExternalizedCheckpoints(
   ExternalizedCheckpointCleanup.RETAIN_ON_CANCELLATION)
```

There are two options for externalized checkpoints:

- `RETAIN_ON_CANCELLATION` retains the checkpoint after the application completely fails and when it is explicitly canceled.

- `DELETE_ON_CANCELLATION` retains the checkpoint only after the application completely fails. If the application is explicitly canceled, the checkpoint is deleted.

Externalized checkpoints do not replace savepoints. They use a state backend–specific storage format and do not support rescaling. Hence, they are sufficient to restart an application after it failed but provide less flexibility than savepoints. Once the application is running again, you can take a savepoint.

Configuring State Backends

The state backend of an application is responsible for maintaining the local state, performing checkpoints and savepoints, and recovering the application state after a failure. Hence, the choice and configuration of the application's state backend has a large impact on the performance of the checkpoints. The individual state backends are described in more detail in "Choosing a State Backend" on page 169.

The default state backend of an application is `MemoryStateBackend`. Since it holds all state in memory and checkpoints are completely stored in the volatile and JVM-size limited JobManager heap storage, it is not recommended for production environments. However, it serves well for locally developing Flink applications. "Checkpointing and State Backends" on page 243 describes how you can configure a default state backend of a Flink cluster.

You can also explicitly choose the state backend of an application:

```
val env: StreamExecutionEnvironment = ???

// create and configure state backend of your choice
val stateBackend: StateBackend = ???
// set state backend
env.setStateBackend(stateBackend)
```

The different state backends can be created with minimum settings as shown in the following. MemoryStateBackend does not require any parameters. However, there are constructors that take parameters to enable or disable asynchronous checkpointing (enabled by default) and limit the size of state (5 MB by default):

```
// create a MemoryStateBackend
val memBackend = new MemoryStateBackend()
```

FsStateBackend only requires a path to define the storage location for checkpoints. There are also constructor variants to enable or disable asynchronous checkpointing (enabled by default):

```
// create a FsStateBackend that checkpoints to the /tmp/ckp folder
val fsBackend = new FsStateBackend("file:///tmp/ckp", true)
```

RocksDBStateBackend only requires a path to define the storage location for checkpoints and takes an optional parameter to enable incremental checkpoints (disabled by default). RocksDBStateBackend is always writing checkpoints asynchronously:

```
// create a RocksDBStateBackend that writes incremental checkpoints
// to the /tmp/ckp folder
val rocksBackend = new RocksDBStateBackend("file:///tmp/ckp", true)
```

In "Checkpointing and State Backends" on page 243, we discussed the configuration options for state backends. You can, of course, also configure the state backend in your application, overriding the default values or cluster-wide configuration. For that you have to create a new backend object by passing a Configuration object to your state backend. See "Checkpointing and State Backends" on page 243 for a description of the available configuration options:

```
// all of Flink's built-in backends are configurable
val backend: ConfigurableStateBackend = ???

// create configuration and set options
val sbConfig = new Configuration()
sbConfig.setBoolean("state.backend.async", true)
sbConfig.setString("state.savepoints.dir", "file:///tmp/svp")

// create a configured copy of the backend
val configuredBackend = backend.configure(sbConfig)
```

Since RocksDB is an external component, it brings its own set of tuning parameters that can also be tweaked for your application. By default, RocksDB is optimized for SSD storage and does not provide great performance if state is stored on spinning disks. Flink provides a few predefined settings to improve the performance for common hardware setups. See the documentation (*http://bit.ly/2CQu8bg*) to learn more about the available settings. You can apply predefined options to RocksDBStateBack end as follows:

```
val backend: RocksDBStateBackend = ???

// set predefined options for spinning disk storage
backend.setPredefinedOptions(PredefinedOptions.SPINNING_DISK_OPTIMIZED)
```

Configuring Recovery

When a checkpointed application fails, it will be restarted by bringing up its tasks, recovering their states, including the reading offsets of the source tasks, and continuing the processing. Right after the application was restarted it is in a catch-up phase. Since the application's source tasks were reset to an earlier input position, it processes data that it processed before the failure and data that accumulated while the application was down.

To be able to catch up with the stream—reach its tail—the application must process the accumulated data at a higher rate than new data is arriving. While the application is catching up, the processing latency—the time at which input is available until it is actually processed—increases.

Consequently, an application needs enough spare resources for the catch-up phase after the application was restarted to successfully resume its regular processing. This means an application should not run close to 100% resource consumption during regular processing. The more resources available for recovery, the faster the catch-up phase completes and the faster processing latencies go back to normal.

Besides resource considerations for the recovery, there are two other recovery-related topics we will discuss: restart strategies and local recovery.

Restart strategies

Depending on the failure that caused an application to crash, the application could be killed by the same failure again. A common example is invalid or corrupt input data the application is not able to handle. In such a situation, an application would end up in an infinite recovery cycle consuming lots of resources without a chance of ever getting back into regular processing. Flink features three restart strategies to address this problem:

- The *fixed-delay restart strategy* restarts an application a fixed number of times and waits a configured time before a restart attempt.

- The *failure-rate restart strategy* restarts an application as long as a configurable failure rate is not exceeded. The failure rate is specified as the maximum number of failures within a time interval. For example, you can configure that an application be restarted as long as it did not fail more than three times in the last ten minutes.

- The *no-restart strategy* does not restart an application, but fails it immediately.

The restart strategy of an application is configured via `StreamExecutionEnvironment` as shown in Example 10-4.

Example 10-4. Configuring the restart strategy of an application

```
val env = StreamExecutionEnvironment.getExecutionEnvironment

env.setRestartStrategy(
  RestartStrategies.fixedDelayRestart(
    5,                             // number of restart attempts
    Time.of(30, TimeUnit.SECONDS) // delay between attempts
))
```

The default restart strategy used if no restart strategy is explicitly defined is a fixed-delay restart strategy with `Integer.MAX_VALUE` restart attempts and a 10-second delay.

Local recovery

Flink's state backends (except for `MemoryStateBackend`) store checkpoints in a remote filesystem. This ensures first that the state is saved and persistent and second that it can be redistributed if a worker node is lost or the application is rescaled. However, reading state from remote storage during recovery is not very efficient. Moreover, on recovery, it might be possible to restart an application on the same workers it was running before the failure.

Flink supports a feature called local recovery to significantly speed up recovery if the application can be restarted on the same machines. When enabled, state backends also store a copy of the checkpoint data on the local disk of their worker node in addition to writing the data to the remote storage system. When the application is restarted, Flink tries to schedule the same tasks to the same worker nodes. If that succeeds, the tasks first try to load the checkpoint data from the local disk. In case of any problem, they fall back to the remote storage.

Local recovery is implemented so that the state copy in the remote system is the source of truth. A task only acknowledges a checkpoint if the remote write succeeded.

Also, a checkpoint will not fail because a local state copy failed. Since the checkpoint data is written twice, local recovery adds overhead to checkpointing.

Local recovery can be enabled and configured for a cluster in the *flink-conf.yaml* file or per application by including the following in the state backend configuration:

- `state.backend.local-recovery`: This flag enables or disables local recovery. By default, local recovery is deactivated.

- `taskmanager.state.local.root-dirs`: This parameter specifies one or more local paths at which the local state copies are stored.

 Local recovery only affects keyed state, which is always partitioned and usually accounts for most of the state size. Operator state will not be stored locally and needs to be retrieved from the remote storage system. However, it is typically much smaller than keyed state. Moreover, local recovery is not supported by the `MemorySta teBackend`, which does not support large state anyway.

Monitoring Flink Clusters and Applications

Monitoring your streaming job is essential to ensure its healthy operation and to detect potential symptoms of misconfigurations, underprovisioning, or unexpected behavior early. Especially when a streaming job is part of a larger data processing pipeline or event-driven service in a user-facing application, you probably want to monitor its performance as precisely as possible and make sure it meets certain targets for latency, throughput, resource utilization, etc.

Flink gathers a set of predefined metrics during runtime and also provides a framework that allows you to define and track your own metrics.

Flink Web UI

The simplest way to get an overview of your Flink cluster as well as a glimpse of what your jobs are doing internally is to use Flink's Web UI. You can access the dashboard by visiting `http://<jobmanager-hostname>:8081`.

On the home screen, you will see an overview of your cluster configuration including the number of TaskManagers, number of configured and available task slots, and running and completed jobs. Figure 10-2 shows an instance of the dashboard home screen. The menu on the left links to more detailed information on jobs and configuration parameters and also allows job submission by uploading a JAR.

Figure 10-2. Apache Flink Web UI home screen

If you click on a running job, you can get a quick glimpse of running statistics per task or subtask as shown in Figure 10-3. You can inspect the duration, bytes, and records exchanged, and aggregate those per TaskManager if you prefer.

Figure 10-3. Statistics for a running job

If you click on the Task Metrics tab, you can select more metrics from a dropdown menu, as shown in Figure 10-4. These include more fine-grained statistics about your tasks, such as buffer usage, watermarks, and input/output rates.

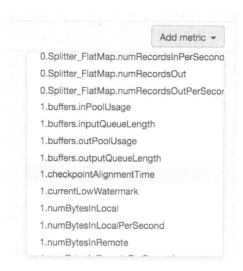

Figure 10-4. Selecting metrics to plot

Figure 10-5 shows how selected metrics are shown as continuously updated charts.

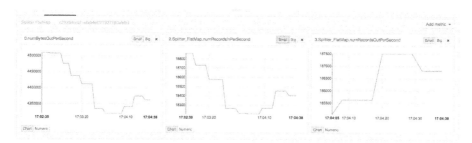

Figure 10-5. Real-time metric plots

The *Checkpoints* tab (Figure 10-3) displays statistics about previous and current checkpoints. Under *Overview* you can see how many checkpoints have been triggered, are in progress, have completed successfully, or have failed. If you click on the *History* view, you can retrieve more fine-grained information, such as the status, trigger time, state size, and how many bytes were buffered during the checkpoint's alignment phase. The *Summary* view aggregates checkpoint statistics and provides minimum, maximum, and average values over all completed checkpoints. Finally, under *Configuration*, you can inspect the configuration properties of checkpoints, such as the interval and the timeout values set.

Similarly, the *Back Pressure* tab displays back-pressure statistics per operator and subtask. If you click on a row, you trigger back-pressure sampling and you will see the message *Sampling in progress...* for about five seconds. Once sampling is complete, you will see the back-pressure status in the second column. Back-pressured tasks will display a *HIGH* sign; otherwise you should see a nice green *OK* message displayed.

Metric System

When running a data processing system such as Flink in production, it is essential to monitor its behavior to be able to discover and diagnose the cause of performance degradations. Flink collects several system and application metrics by default. Metrics are gathered per operator, TaskManager, or JobManager. Here we describe some of the most commonly used metrics and refer you to Flink's documentation for a full list of available metrics.

Categories include CPU utilization, memory used, number of active threads, garbage collection statistics, network metrics such as the number of queued input/output buffers, cluster-wide metrics such as the number or running jobs and available resources, job metrics including runtime, the number of retries and checkpointing information, I/O statistics including the number of record exchanges locally and remotely, watermark information, connector-specific metrics, etc.

Registering and using metrics

To register metrics you have to retrieve a `MetricGroup` by calling the `getMetrics()` method on the `RuntimeContext`, as shown in Example 10-5.

Example 10-5. Registering and using metrics in a FilterFunction

```
class PositiveFilter extends RichFilterFunction[Int] {

  @transient private var counter: Counter = _

  override def open(parameters: Configuration): Unit = {
    counter = getRuntimeContext
      .getMetricGroup
      .counter("droppedElements")
  }

  override def filter(value: Int): Boolean = {
    if (value > 0) {
      true
    }
    else {
      counter.inc()
      false
    }
  }
}
```

Metric groups

Flink metrics are registered and accessed through the MetricGroup interface. The Met ricGroup provides ways to create nested, named metrics hierarchies and provides methods to register the following metric types:

Counter

An org.apache.flink.metrics.Counter metric measures a count and provides methods for increment and decrement. You can register a counter metric using the counter(String name, Counter counter) method on MetricGroup.

Gauge

A Gauge metric calculates a value of any type at a point in time. To use a Gauge you implement the org.apache.flink.metrics.Gauge interface and register it using the gauge(String name, Gauge gauge) method on MetricGroup. The code in Example 10-6 shows the implementation of the WatermarkGauge metric, which exposes the current watermark.

Example 10-6. Implementation of a WatermarkGauge metric that exposes the current watermark

```
public class WatermarkGauge implements Gauge<Long> {
  private long currentWatermark = Long.MIN_VALUE;

  public void setCurrentWatermark(long watermark) {
    this.currentWatermark = watermark;
    }

  @Override
  public Long getValue() {
    return currentWatermark;
    }
}
```

Metrics Reported as Strings

Metric reporters will turn the Gauge value into a String, so make sure you provide a meaningful toString() implementation if it is not provided by the type you use.

Histogram

You can use a histogram to represent the distribution of numerical data. Flink's histogram is especially implemented for reporting metrics on long values. The org.apache.flink.metrics.Histogram interface allows you to collect values, get the current count of collected values, and create statistics, such as min, max, standard deviation, and mean, for the values seen so far.

Apart from creating your own histogram implementation, Flink also allows you to use a DropWizard (*https://github.com/dropwizard/metrics*) histogram by adding the dependency in the following:

```
<dependency>
  <groupId>org.apache.flink</groupId>
  <artifactId>flink-metrics-dropwizard</artifactId>
  <version>flink-version</version>
</dependency>
```

You can then register a >DropWizard histogram in your Flink program using the `DropwizardHistogramWrapper` class as shown in Example 10-7.

Example 10-7. Using the DropwizardHistogramWrapper

```
// create and register histogram
DropwizardHistogramWrapper histogramWrapper =
  new DropwizardHistogramWrapper(
    new com.codahale.metrics.Histogram(new SlidingWindowReservoir(500)))
metricGroup.histogram("myHistogram", histogramWrapper)

// update histogram
histogramWrapper.update(value)
```

Meter

You can use a `Meter` metric to measure the rate (in events per second) at which certain events happen. The `org.apache.flink.metrics.Meter` interface provides methods to mark the occurrence of one or more events, get the current rate of events per second, and get the current number of events marked on the meter.

As with histograms, you can use DropWizard meters by adding the `flink-metrics-dropwizard` dependency in your `pom.xml` and wrapping the meter in a `DropwizardMeterWrapper` class.

Scoping and formatting metrics

Flink metrics belong to a scope, which can be either the system scope, for system-provided metrics, or the user scope for custom, user-defined metrics. Metrics are referenced by a unique identifier that contains up to three parts:

1. The name that the user specifies when registering the metric
2. An optional user scope
3. A system scope

For instance, the name "myCounter," the user scope "MyMetrics," and the system scope "localhost.taskmanager.512" would result into the identifier "localhost.task-manager.512.MyMetrics.myCounter." You can change the default "." delimiter by setting the `metrics.scope.delimiter` configuration option.

The system scope declares what component of the system the metric refers to and what context information it should include. Metrics can be scoped to the JobManager, a TaskManager, a job, an operator, or a task. You can configure which context information the metric should contain by setting the corresponding metric options in the *flink-conf.yaml* file. We list some of these configuration options and their default values in Table 10-17.

Table 10-17. System scope configuration options and their default values

Scope	Configuration key	Default value
JobManager	metrics.scope.jm	\<host>.jobmanager
JobManager and job	metrics.scope.jm.job	\<host>.jobmanager.\<job_name>
TaskManager	metrics.scope.tm	\<host>.taskmanager.\<tm_id>
TaskManager and job	metrics.scope.tm.job	\<host>.taskmanager.\<tm_id>.\<job_name>
Task	metrics.scope.task	\<host>.taskmanager.\<tm_id>.\<job_name>.\<task_name>.\<subtask_index>
Operator	metrics.scope.operator	\<host>.taskmanager.\<tm_id>.\<job_name>.\<operator_name>.\<subtask_index>

The configuration keys contain constant strings, such as "taskmanager," and variables shown in angle brackets. The latter will be replaced at runtime with actual values. For instance, the default scope for `TaskManager` metrics might create the scope "localhost.taskmanager.512" where "localhost" and "512" are parameter values. Table 10-18 shows all variables that are available to configure metrics scopes.

Table 10-18. Available variables to configure the formatting of metrics scopes

Scope	Available Variables
JobManager:	\<host>
TaskManager:	\<host>, \<tm_id>
Job:	\<job_id>, \<job_name>
Task:	\<task_id>, \<task_name>, \<task_attempt_id>, \<task_attempt_num>, \<subtask_index>
Operator:	\<operator_id>, \<operator_name>, \<subtask_index>

Scope Identifiers per Job Must Be Unique

If multiple copies of the same job are run concurrently, metrics might become inaccurate, due to string conflicts. To avoid such risk, you should make sure that scope identifiers per job are unique. This can be easily handled by including the <job_id>.

You can also define a user scope for metrics by calling the addGroup() method of the MetricGroup, as shown in Example 10-8.

Example 10-8. Defining the user scope "MyMetrics"

```
counter = getRuntimeContext
  .getMetricGroup
  .addGroup("MyMetrics")
  .counter("myCounter")
```

Exposing metrics

Now that you have learned how to register, define, and group metrics, you might be wondering how to access them from external systems. After all, you probably gather metrics because you want to create a real-time dashboard or feed the measurements to another application. You can expose metrics to external backends through *reporters* and Flink provides implementation for several of them (see Table 10-19).

Table 10-19. List of available metrics reporters

Reporter	Implementation
JMX	org.apache.flink.metrics.jmx.JMXReporter
Graphite	org.apache.flink.metrics.graphite.GraphiteReporter
Prometheus	org.apache.flink.metrics.prometheus.PrometheusReporter
PrometheusPushGateway	org.apache.flink.metrics.prometheus.PrometheusPushGatewayReporter
StatsD	org.apache.flink.metrics.statsd.StatsDReporter
Datadog	org.apache.flink.metrics.datadog.DatadogHttpReporter
Slf4j	org.apache.flink.metrics.slf4j.Slf4jReporter

If you want to use a metrics backend that is not included in the above list, you can also define your own reporter by implementing the *org.apache.flink.metrics.reporter.MetricReporter* interface.

Reporters need to be configured in flink-conf.yaml. Adding the following lines to your configuration will define a JMX reporter "my_reporter" that listens to ports 9020-9040:

```
metrics.reporters: my_reporter
Metrics.reporter.my_jmx_reporter.class: org.apache.flink.metrics.jmx.JMXReporter
metrics.reporter.my_jmx_reporter.port: 9020-9040
```

Consult the Flink documentation (*http://bit.ly/2FcdlBe*) for a full list of configuration options per supported reporter.

Monitoring Latency

Latency is probably one of the first metrics you want to monitor to assess the performance characteristics of your streaming job. At the same time, it is also one of the trickiest metrics to define in a distributed streaming engine with rich semantics such as Flink. In "Latency" on page 20, we defined latency broadly as *the time it takes to process an event*. You can imagine how a precise implementation of this definition can get problematic in practice if we try to track the latency per event in a high-rate streaming job with a complex dataflow. Considering window operators complicate latency tracking even further, if an event contributes to several windows, do we need to report the latency of the first invocation or do we need to wait until we evaluate all windows an event might belong to? And what if a window triggers multiple times?

Flink follows a simple and low-overhead approach to provide useful latency metric measurements. Instead of trying to strictly measure latency for each and every event, it approximates latency by periodically emitting a special record at the sources and allowing users to track how long it takes for this record to arrive at the sinks. This special record is called a *latency marker*, and it bears a timestamp indicating when it was emitted.

To enable latency tracking, you need to configure how often latency markers are emitted from the sources. You can do this by setting the latencyTrackingInterval in the ExecutionConfig as shown here:

```
env.getConfig.setLatencyTrackingInterval(500L)
```

The interval is specified in milliseconds. Upon receiving a latency marker, all operators except sinks forward it downstream. Latency markers use the same dataflow channels and queues as normal stream records, thus their tracked latency reflects the time records wait to be processed. However, they do not measure the time it takes for records to be processed or the time that records wait in state until they are processed.

Operators keep latency statistics in a latency gauge that contains min, max, and mean values, as well as 50, 95, and 99 percentile values. Sink operators keep statistics on latency markers received per parallel source instance, thus checking the latency marker at sinks can be used to approximate how long it takes for records to traverse the dataflow. If you would like to customize the handling the latency marker at operators, you can override the processLatencyMarker() method and retrieve the relevant information using the LatencyMarker's methods getMarkedTime(), getVertexId(), and getSubTaskIndex().

Beware of Clock Skew

If you are not using an automatic clock synchronization service such as NTP, your machines' clocks might suffer from clock skew. In this case, latency-tracking estimation will not be reliable, as its current implementation assumes synchronized clocks.

Configuring the Logging Behavior

Logging is another essential tool for debugging and understanding the behavior of your applications. By default, Flink uses the SLF4J logging abstraction (*https:// www.slf4j.org/*) together with the log4j logging framework.

Example 10-9 shows a MapFunction that logs every input record conversion.

Example 10-9. Using logging in a MapFunction

```
import org.apache.flink.api.common.functions.MapFunction
import org.slf4j.LoggerFactory
import org.slf4j.Logger

class MyMapFunction extends MapFunction[Int, String] {

  Logger LOG = LoggerFactory.getLogger(MyMapFunction.class)

  override def map(value: Int): String = {
    LOG.info("Converting value {} to string.", value)
    value.toString
  }
}
```

To change the properties of log4j loggers, modify the *log4j.properties* file in the *conf/* folder. For instance, the following line sets the root logging level to "warning":

```
log4j.rootLogger=WARN
```

To set a custom filename and location of this file, pass the -Dlog4j.configuration= parameter to the JVM. Flink also provides the *log4j-cli.properties* file used by the command-line client and the *log4j-yarn-session.properties* file used by the command-line client when starting a YARN session.

An alternative to log4j is logback and Flink provides default configuration files for this backend as well. To use logback instead of log4j, you will need to remove log4j from the *lib/* folder. We refer you to Flink's documentation (*http://bit.ly/2JgrAZJ*) and the logback manual (*http://bit.ly/2FPJbUH*) for details on how to set up and configure the backend.

Summary

In this chapter, we discussed how to run, manage, and monitor Flink applications in production. We explained the Flink component that collects and exposes system and application metrics, how to configure a logging system, and how to start, stop, resume, and rescale applications with the command-line client and the REST API.

## CHAPTER 11

Where to Go from Here?

It has been a long journey and you have made it to the end of this book! But your Flink journey has just started, and this chapter points to the possible paths you can take from here. We will provide you with a brief tour of the additional Flink functionality not included in this book and give you some pointers to further Flink resources. There exists a vibrant community around Flink and we encourage you to connect with other users, start contributing, or find out what companies are building with Flink to help inspire your own work.

The Rest of the Flink Ecosystem

While this book is particularly focused on stream processing, Flink is in fact a general-purpose distributed data processing framework and can be used for other types of data analysis as well. Further, Flink offers domain-specific libraries and APIs for relational queries, complex event processing (CEP), and graph processing.

The DataSet API for Batch Processing

Flink is a full-fledged batch processor and can be used to implement use cases requiring one-off or periodic queries on bounded input data. DataSet programs are specified as a series of transformations just like DataStream programs with the difference that a DataSet is a bounded data collection. The DataSet API provides operators to perform filtering, mapping, selection, joins, and groupings, as well as connectors to read and write datasets from and to external systems, such as filesystems and databases. Using the DataSet API you can also define iterative Flink programs that execute a loop function for a fixed number of steps or until a convergence criterion is met.

Batch jobs are internally represented as dataflow programs and run on the same underlying execution runtime as streaming jobs. Currently, the two APIs use separate execution environments and cannot be mixed. However, the Flink community is already working on unifying the two, and providing a single API for analysis of bounded and unbounded data streams in the same program is a priority in Flink's future roadmap.

Table API and SQL for Relational Analysis

Even though the underlying DataStream and DataSet APIs are separate, you can implement unified stream and batch analytics in Flink using its higher-level relational APIs: Table API and SQL.

The Table API is a language-integrated query (LINQ) API for Scala and Java. Queries can be executed for batch or streaming analysis without modification. It offers common operators to write relational queries including selection, projection, aggregations, and joins and further has IDE support for autocompletion and syntax validation.

Flink SQL follows the ANSI SQL standard and leverages Apache Calcite (*https:// calcite.apache.org/*) for query parsing and optimization. Flink provides unified syntax and semantics for batch and streaming queries. Due to extensive support for user-defined functions, a wide variety of use cases can be covered by SQL. You can embed SQL queries into regular Flink DataSet and DataStream programs or directly submit SQL queries to a Flink cluster using the SQL CLI client. The CLI client lets you retrieve and visualize query results in the command line, which makes it a great tool to try out and debug Flink SQL queries or run exploratory queries on streaming or batch data. In addition, you can use the CLI client to submit detached queries that directly write their results into external storage systems.

FlinkCEP for Complex Event Processing and Pattern Matching

FlinkCEP is a high-level API and library for complex event pattern detection. It is implemented on top of the DataStream API and lets you specify patterns you want to detect in your stream. Common CEP use cases include financial applications, fraud detection, monitoring and alerting in complex systems, and detecting network intrusion or suspicious user behavior.

Gelly for Graph Processing

Gelly is Flink's graph processing API and library. It builds on top of the DataSet API and Flink's support for efficient batch iterations. Gelly provides high-level programming abstractions in both Java and Scala to perform graph transformations, aggregations, and iterative processing such as vertex-centric and gather-sum-apply. It also includes a set of common graph algorithms ready to use.

Flink's high-level APIs and interfaces are well integrated with each other and with the DataStream and DataSet APIs so that you can easily mix them and switch between libraries and APIs in the same program. For instance, you could extract patterns from a DataStream using the CEP library and later use SQL to analyze extracted patterns or you could use the Table API to filter and project tables into graphs before analyzing them with a graph algorithm from the Gelly library.

A Welcoming Community

Apache Flink has a growing and welcoming community with contributors and users all around the world. Here are a few resources you can use to ask questions, attend Flink-related events, and learn what people use Flink for:

Mailing lists

- *user@flink.apache.org* : user support and questions
- *dev@flink.apache.org* : development, release, and community discussions
- *community@flink.apache.org* : community news and meetups

Blogs

- *https://flink.apache.org/blog*
- *https://www.ververica.com/blog*

Meetups and conferences

- *https://flink-forward.org*
- *https://www.meetup.com/topics/apache-flink*

Again, we hope you walk away from this book with a better understanding of the capabilities and possibilities of Apache Flink. We encourage you to become an active part of its community.

Index

ExecutionGraphs, 41
external dependencies, 107, 187, 236
external systems
    application consistency guarantees, 184-186
    asynchronously accessing, 216-219
    custom sink functions, 206-216
    custom source functions, 202-206
    provided connectors, 186-202
extract–transform–load (ETL), 3

F

failed processes
    automatic recovery from, 232
    enabling failure recovery, 166
    restarting, 42, 268
    restoring application state, 59
failure-rate restart strategy, 269
fast forwarding, 30
fields, referencing, 102
filesystems
    filesystem configuration, 237-239
    sink connector, 196-198
    source connector, 194-196
filter transformation, 85
fixed-delay restart strategy, 269
flatMap transformation, 86
FlinkCEP, 282
flow control, credit-based, 45
forward data exchange strategy, 19
framework deployment style, 39
FsStateBackend, 169, 267
full window functions, 127
functions (see also under DataStream API)
    applying functions on windows, 127-133
    function classes, 105
    implementing stateful functions, 154-166
    lambda functions, 106
    process functions, 116
    rich functions, 106, 116
fundamentals
    dataflow programming, 17-19
    processing streams in parallel, 20-27
    state and consistency models, 32-35
    time semantics, 27-32

G

Gelly, 282
GenericWriteAheadSink, 209
global partitioning strategy, 96

global windows, 26
GlobalWindows assigner, 139
graph processing, 281

H

Hadoop distributed filesystem (HDFS), 4, 236, 238
HBase, 236
Hello, Flink! example
    applying transformations, 82
    data type, 79
    emitting results, 82
    executing applications, 83
    execution environment set up, 81
    reading input streams, 81
    typical application structure, 80
highly available (HA) setups
    configuring HA Flink clusters, 232
    HA Kubernetes setup, 235
    HA standalone setup, 233
    HA YARN setup, 234
    restarting failed processes, 42

I

idempotent operations, 184
idempotent sink connectors, 207
importing a project into an IDE, 72
incremental aggregation functions, 127
incremental checkpointing, 66, 118, 170, 243, 267
IngestionTime characteristic, 110
installation, 71, 221
interval join, 145

J

JAR file, 14, 38, 39, 77, 81, 83, 108, 254, 258
Java Virtual Machine (JVM), 12, 38, 75, 221, 239
job parallelism, 40, 96, 247, 251, 257
JobGraph, 41
JobManager, 38, 42, 221-235
joining streams on time, 145-148

K

Kerberos authentication, 243
key groups, 56, 168, 252
key-based data exchange strategy, 19
keyBy transformation, 87

keyed state, 54, 154
KeyedStream transformations, 87
keys, defining, 102
Kryo serialization framework, 98
Kubernetes, 228-232, 259

L

lambda architecture, 10
lambda functions, 84, 88, 106
late elements
    definition of term, 49, 148
    dropping, 148
    redirecting, 148
    updating results by including, 150
latency
    average, maximum, and percentile, 20
    definition of term, 20
    effect of watermarks on, 115
    importance of low latency, 21
    monitoring, 278
    processing-time windows, 31
    versus throughput, 22
leaking state, 171
library deployment style, 40
ListCheckpointed interface, 158
ListState, 54, 55, 154, 158
load rebalancing, 95
local filesystems, 237
local recovery, 269
logging, 279

M

maintainability, ensuring
    defining maximum parallelism of keyed
        state operators, 168
    specifying unique operator identifiers, 168,
        251
    stateful applications, 167-169
map transformation, 84
MapState, 55, 154
Maven projects
    bootstrapping Flink Maven projects, 76
    importing, 72
memory
    configuring, 241
    JVM heap memory, 242
    major consumers of, 241
    requirements, 240
MemoryStateBackend, 169, 266

MergingWindowAssigner interface, 139, 142
metrics system, 273-278
microbatching, 44
microservices design pattern, 2, 6
Minikube, 260
monitoring
    applications using REST API, 254
    clusters using REST API, 253
    Flink Web UI, 270
    latency, 278
    metrics system, 273-278
multistream transformations
    combining events of two streams, 90-93
    filtering and replicating events, 93
    merging DataStreams, 90

N

no-restart strategy, 269

O

OnTimerContext object, 117
open source stream processing, 9
OpenStack Swift FS, 238
operation
    configuring logging behavior, 279
    controlling task scheduling, 260-263
    monitoring clusters and applications,
        270-279
    running and managing applications,
        245-260
    tuning checkpoints and recovery, 263-270
operator state, 54, 154, 158, 164
operators
    built-in, 22
    defining windows operators, 122
    definition of term, 17
    input and output streams, 23
    time-based, 51
out-of-order records, 29-30, 48, 204

P

parallel windows, 26
parallelism
    defining maximum of keyed state operators,
        168
    scaling applications in and out, 251, 257
    setting, 96
partition watermarks, 50

About the Authors

Fabian Hueske is a committer to and PMC member of the Apache Flink project and has been contributing to Flink since its earliest days. Fabian is cofounder and software engineer at Ververica (formerly data Artisans), a Berlin-based startup that fosters Flink and its community. He holds a PhD in computer science from TU Berlin.

Vasiliki Kalavri is a postdoctoral fellow in the Systems Group at ETH Zurich, where she uses Apache Flink extensively for streaming systems research and teaching. Vasia is a PMC member of the Apache Flink project. An early contributor to Flink, she has worked on its graph processing library, Gelly, and on early versions of the Table API and streaming SQL.

Colophon

The animal on the cover of *Stream Processing with Apache Flink* is a Eurasian red squirrel (*Sciurus vulgaris*). Most arboreal squirrels in temperate Asia, Europe, and the Americas are of the genus *sciurus*. *Vulgaris* means "common" in Latin, and the Eurasian red squirrels are a regular sight throughout Europe and northern Asia.

Eurasian red squirrels have a white ring around their eyes, a bushy tail, and a tuft of fur over their ears. Their coloring ranges from light red to black on their heads and backs. The fur on their bellies is cream-colored or white. In the winter, the squirrel's fur grows a little taller and longer above their ears and around their paws to protect them from the cold. They spend much of the winter curled up in nests, called *dreys*.

Unless they are mating or raising young, a Eurasian red squirrel's dreys are meant to house one animal. Although they live alone, their ranges often overlap because they are so populous. On average, females give birth to five young per litter twice per year. Young squirrels leave the mother's nest after about two months. Eurasian red squirrels face many predators, including birds, snakes, and mammals, so only one quarter of the young reach one year of age.

Eurasian red squirrels sustain themselves on seeds, acorns, and nuts. They have also been caught licking tree sap, but they don't often experiment with new foods. These squirrels can grow about 9 to 10 inches long from head to hind, with a tail of about the same length. They weigh 8 to 12 ounces and can live up to 12 years. In the wild their lifespan is expected to be only 4–7 years.

What allows these tree-dwellers to scale trunks, descend headfirst, and leap across overhanging branches is a combination of their sharp, curved claws and long, fluffy tails. Eurasian red squirrels have excellent agility and balance.

Many of the animals on O'Reilly's covers are endangered; all of them are important to the world. To learn more about how you can help, go to *animals.oreilly.com*.

The cover illustration is by Karen Montgomery, based on a black and white engraving from Wood's *Animate Creation*. The cover fonts are Gilroy Semibold and Guardian Sans. The text font is Adobe Minion Pro; the heading font is Adobe Myriad Condensed; and the code font is Dalton Maag's Ubuntu Mono.

O'REILLY®

There's much more where this came from.

Experience books, videos, live online training courses, and more from O'Reilly and our 200+ partners—all in one place.

Learn more at oreilly.com/online-learning